DOGMA
for THE LAYMAN

THOMAS J. HIGGINS, S.J.
LOYOLA COLLEGE
BALTIMORE, MARYLAND

THE BRUCE PUBLISHING COMPANY
MILWAUKEE

69723

IMPRIMI POTEST:

JOHN M. DALEY, S.J.
Provincial, Maryland Province

NIHIL OBSTAT:

JOHN A. SCHULIEN, S.T.D.
Censor librorum

IMPRIMATUR:

✠ WILLIAM E. COUSINS
Archbishop of Milwaukee

August 3, 1961

Library of Congress Catalog Card Number: 61–17437

© 1961 THE BRUCE PUBLISHING COMPANY
MADE IN THE UNITED STATES OF AMERICA

FOREWORD

As THE title indicates, this book is not addressed to the experts in theology but to the lay reader with a taste for serious books. While this is not the day of summaries in theology but of intensive development of particular topics, yet the Bruce Publishing Company has asked the author to prepare a brief summary of dogmatic theology. The publishers think that the word of God is its own attraction and justification; hence if it is presented in clear readable form, it makes its own inimitable impact. Moreover, since an Ecumenical Council, which will receive wide coverage in the secular press, is about to open, one may expect from educated readers, both Catholic and non-Catholic, renewed interest in the doctrines of the Church. So it will be handy to have her dogmatic teachings summarized within the covers of one small volume.

What the sacred magistery, or official teaching body of the Church, teaches with authority, the Catholic theologians construct into the science of dogmatic theology which aims at doing these things: (1) educe the dogmas of faith from their source in Scripture and Tradition; (2) compose a rational synthesis of these dogmas and their subordinate truths; (3) endeavor to penetrate the meaning of the dogmas by the aid of sound philosophy. To do all this is clearly beyond the scope of a small book. What the author offers is a current report, that is, a summary of the theological synthesis together with simple explanations of the meanings of the dogmas and some indication of the sources from which they derive. This is a book of exposition, not of argument. In the space at our disposal we could not reproduce theological arguments. At a time when theology is seeking for its particular dogmas as wide a basis in Scripture as possible, we have no intention of pyramiding whole dogmas upon isolated texts of Scripture. The pinpoint of a single text might not sustain the weight of the superstructure imposed. Hence our citations from Scripture should be regarded, not so much as strict proofs of dogmas, but rather as illustrations in inspired language of the pronouncements of the Church.

We do not intend to engage in apologetic or dogmatic controversy but to offer a readable, informative book about the essentials of Catholic belief. It is addressed primarily to the understanding but also indirectly to the heart. For we intend it as a kind of spiritual reading in the sense that an intelligent grasp of the articles of faith is a powerful motive for living the faith.

A conscious effort has been made to make the whole book, including the citations and footnotes, of service to the general reader. Hence this explanation of the abbreviations and symbols used in the footnotes. The symbol *AAS* stands for the official publication of the Holy See, the *Acta Apostolicae Sedis*. When important excerpts from it, such as Encyclical Letters, have been translated into English, we refer to some available translation. The symbol *Den.* stands for a theological tool which students of theology revere next after the Sacred Scriptures. This book is the *Enchiridion Symbolorum* by Denzinger-Bannwart-Umbert-Rahner. It is commonly known as "Denzinger." The author has taken his selections from the thirty-first (1957) edition. A translation of most of the twenty-ninth edition and a reordering of its contents has been published under the title *The Church Teaches* (Herder, 1957). The symbol *TCT* stands for *The Church Teaches*. The author has given his own translation of Denzinger, and after each footnote reference to a number in Denzinger, he gives, whenever possible, the corresponding number in *The Church Teaches*. Unfortunately the whole of Denzinger is not reproduced in *The Church Teaches*. For citations from the *Summa Theologica* of St. Thomas, which are taken from the Latin text, the reader is referred to the English translation by the Dominican Fathers (Benziger, 1947). The symbol *PG* stands for Migne's edition of the Greek Fathers of the Church. The symbol *PL* stands for Migne's edition of the Latin Fathers. For citations from the Old Testament the Douay-Challoner version has been used; for the New Testament, the 1941 translation by the Confraternity of Christian Doctrine.

The author expresses his sincere thanks to Rev. George S. Glanzman, S.J., and Rev. John J. Heenan who read the text and offered valuable suggestions; and to Rev. Joseph d'Invilliers, S.J., who read the proofs.   THOMAS J. HIGGINS, S.J.

CONTENTS

CHAPTER ONE

GOD THE REVEALER

"I believe"

To HAVE peace of mind and a reasonable life plan to follow, thinking men want satisfying answers to the great questions: What is the world for? What is the destiny of men? What am I to do to fulfill my destiny? The right answers are available and, since they are found only among the invisible things of God, they are to be sought for in the teachings of the true religion.

Religion is man's effort to be right with God. To be effectual, it must express the correct relationship between God and man. This is the complete dependence of man upon God, and it imposes consequences of knowledge and action, which it is the business of religion to make clear. Hence religion must explain where a man stands and how he should act with regard to God. "A religion," then, is a body of beliefs and practices, purporting to supply this knowledge and indicate the right pattern of conduct. The true religion is the one which supplies this information correctly and offers mankind the right solution to its basic problems. That there be a true religion, accessible to people, is demanded by the dignity of God and the need of man.

What a religion teaches may be called a theology, for theology is knowledge about God and religious teachings are primarily about God. The name *theology,* however, is usually not used until the teachings have been systematized and reduced to some kind of unity. In a developed theology one often distinguishes between principles of knowledge — dogmas — and principles of action — morals. The distinction is not absolutely clear-cut because among dogmas there are both speculative and practical truths. But the distinction is

1

serviceable. Thus Catholics speak of faith and morals, meaning by faith dogmatic theology, and by morals moral theology.

In these pages we offer the general reader a summary of Catholic dogmatic theology. Without wishing to slight the role of morals in the attainment of destiny, we treat of faith alone, first, because dogmas are the basis of a religion — of its liturgy, morals, asceticism, and mysticism. Furthermore, although salvation finally depends, as far as the adult is concerned, on his actions, yet his actions depend on his beliefs. Full penetrating knowledge of the faith is not merely a laudable accomplishment for an educated Catholic; it furnishes the overwhelming motive for upright conduct. While Plato was not quite right in saying that all that is required for upright conduct is knowledge of the good, yet his exaggerated expression points up the close connection between possession of the truth and the leading of a good life. Our obligations of welldoing are summed up: "Thou shalt love the Lord thy God with thy whole heart."[1] Love of God cannot help but well forth where there are deep springs of faith. The truth is so influential that it is practically impossible for a person of good will to know by faith who God is and what He does for us, and yet fail to love Him.

God the supreme teacher

Theology begins with God. What can we know about Him? Without any special help from Him, we can know God as Maker and Lord of the universe to whom obedience and worship are due. By dint of hard reasoning, we can know Him as the First Cause of all things and as infinitely perfect, but we cannot know Him *as He is*. God must tell us. Furthermore, since God has plans for us which no one could suspect, God must be the principal teacher of religious truth. He teaches in two ways. First, He *publicly* reveals to the whole race what He deems it should know — the truths which are necessary for attainment of destiny. Second, He *privately* illumines individuals through the action of the Holy Spirit upon the soul. Sometimes God directly imparts knowledge, but more often the instruction is indirect; that is, divine light enables one to accept

---

[1] Mt. 22:37.

as the word of God something he has read or heard from another man. For faith comes by hearing. In either way is fulfilled what St. John says of the children of God: "And they shall all be taught of God."[2] The sole concern of theology, however, is the public revelation, the word of God.

God first revealed Himself to our first parents before the fall. No record exists of the content of that revelation but, since God had shaped man for a destiny he could not have discovered of himself, He had to tell him all that was necessary for its realization. After the fall man became so corrupt as to lose in great part the primitive revelation, but in time God began the reinstruction of man through a slowly progressing revelation. He raised up messengers of divine truth to prepare men for the most momentous event in history — the coming of the Redeemer who would repair the fall. These prophets spoke about God, man's relation to God, and, above all, the Redeemer. By solemn covenant God chose as His special people Israel, from whom the Redeemer would come, and to whom the word of God was entrusted. The religion given to Moses on Mt. Sinai was then the true religion. The final work of instructing the human race, however, was done by the Son of God. For "God, who at sundry times and in divers manners spoke in times past to the prophets, last of all in these days has spoken to us by his Son."[3] The Son then is the prophet *par excellence* of the human race foretold by Moses: "The Lord thy God will raise up to thee a prophet . . . him thou shalt hear."[4]

Jesus prophet of the human race

The Son of God is, as we shall see, the Redeemer. He entered history at the time of Caesar Augustus and was known as Jesus of Nazareth. His life and works are described in the four Gospels, which have come down to us substantially intact. Their historical value is demonstrated by Christian apologetics. In the eyes of the modern apologist, however, the Gospels are not a mere historical recital of the facts of Jesus' life. They are a picture of the faith of the Apostolic age, which believed Jesus to be divine and the One in whom the

---

[2] Jn. 6:45.   [3] Hebr. 1:1.   [4] Deut. 18:15.

messianic types and prophecies of the Hebrews are fulfilled.

The Gospels show that the first undertaking of Jesus was teaching, and acceptance of His doctrine on faith was His first demand upon men. He makes faith in His doctrine an absolute condition for the attainment of destiny. "Amen, amen, I say to you, he who hears my word, and believes him who sent me, has everlasting life, and does not come to judgment, but has passed from death to life."[5] He heals the sick and casts out devils in order to stir up faith. It is typical of Jesus' procedure that when Jairus hears that his daughter is dead, He says: "Do not be afraid, only have faith."[6]

Faith is the encounter of man with God *as He is*. It happens through man's reception of the word of God. Faith then is something intellectual, the adherence of the created mind to the First Truth. St. Paul says it is "the substance of things to be hoped for, the evidence of things that are not seen."[7] By this he means that our hope of complete happiness is founded on divine promises, and the reason we know the promises are trustworthy and the unseen things real is simply that God has told us about them. In the natural world we accept as true only the things for which we have evidence; about God's invisible world we have no evidence but only faith. Yet it is most reasonable to believe God. For "since man totally depends on God as his Creator and Lord and created reason is wholly subject to uncreated Truth, we are obliged to accord by faith full submission of intellect and will to God when He reveals. So the Catholic Church professes that this faith . . . is a supernatural power whereby, with the inspiration and aid of divine grace, we believe His revelation to be true, not because the intrinsic truth of the things revealed is beheld by the light of natural reason, but on account of the authority of God revealing, who can neither deceive nor be deceived."[8] We are to believe all that God revealed, not merely what appeals to our reason. For the motive of belief — the word of God — is present in every revealed truth; hence if we reject it in one case, we reject it for all cases. By divine faith we can believe only what God has revealed. If we think we are making an act of faith in something that God has

---

[5] Jn. 5:24.   [7] Hebr. 11:1.
[6] Mk. 5:36.   [8] Vatican Council, Denzinger, ed. 31, No. 1789 (*TCT,* 63).

not revealed, we are deluded. Hence the extreme care of theology to distinguish the word of God from all natural truths. Faith is always an assent to the truth because he who rests on God's word cannot err. Therefore, the assent of faith is more firm and sure than any natural assent. This firmness does not depend on the strength of the natural reasoning, which shows that God has spoken, or which explains God's revelation; it is measured solely by God's word.

Faith also involves submission of the will. In divine faith there is always an obscurity because we assent to what is not clear in itself. Now the mind is naturally incapable of assenting without evidence, but the will, moved by the utter fittingness of believing God, commands the mind to disregard the obscurity and take God's word in place of evidence. We freely choose to believe God. Indeed, since we have a moral obligation to believe, we must be physically free to place the act of faith or to withhold it. Moreover, since the word of God speaks also to the heart, faith is a humble sentiment of trust in God. As the child has faith in its mother or a pupil in his teacher, so the believer has confidence in God and in the witnesses of revelation.

Finally, on account of the message it conveys, faith means the involvement of the whole man. Our faith would be like the faith of the demons, if we did not apply the content of revelation to ourselves. Hence faith, as a genuine religious experience, is a personal commitment to the supernatural way of life, acceptance of Jesus by both mind and heart, the surrender of a man to the designs of God. We believe so that we may *do* the truth and thus attain destiny. But the power to believe is a pure gift from God which no one can put to use unless God alerts and sustains him.

To arouse faith Jesus wrought signs and wonders. "Since [these miracles and prophecies] clearly manifest the omnipotence and infinite knowledge of God, they are most certain signs of divine revelation and are accommodated to the intelligence of all."[9] They are the credentials of Jesus, the official seal put upon His work and doctrine to show they are from God. "If I do not perform the works of my Father, do not believe me. But if I perform them, and if you

[9] Vatican Council, *Den.* 1790 (*TCT,* 64).

are willing to believe me, believe the works."[10] Outstanding among all His works, and the one upon which He openly staked the success of His undertaking and the credibility of His doctrine, is His resurrection from the dead. Men are to believe in Him as God's ambassador, or reject Him as a fraud, accordingly as He did or did not rise from the dead. The Christian apologist has established this fact as securely as any fact of history is attested. This fact is basic to our faith, the intellectual cornerstone of Christianity. But belief in the doctrine of Jesus does not depend on the proofs for the Resurrection. These merely give assurance that the rational basis of faith is sound.

Since modern theology is no longer so involved in answering rationalistic critics who deny the existence of God and the possibility of divine revelation, many theologians think it an adequate apologetic to show that the faith of the apostolic age and the faith of the Catholic Church today are the same. As it was reasonable for a contemporary of the Apostles to see the word of God in the teaching of the Apostles and to take it on faith, so it is equally reasonable for a modern man to take on faith the teachings of the Catholic Church. How then does one identify the teachings of Jesus and the doctrines of the Church?

Jesus makes a group of men His official teaching body

Besides teaching, Jesus founded the Christian religion, the new Israel, which we shall describe later. He founded His Church upon twelve men whom He chose for the office of *Apostle*. An Apostle is *one who is sent* to mankind as a witness of the Resurrection, a bearer of the good news that God has made a new covenant with mankind and called all men to share in its benefits. He is a ruler in the new Israel and sometimes a mouthpiece of revelation. God's public revelation is complete with the death of the last Apostle.

How was this revelation to be preserved and conveyed to succeeding generations of men? Jesus might have enshrined it in sacred books and made them the sole source of revelation. Instead, He gave His revelation to His Church in which He made The Twelve an authoritative teaching body. In the person of lawful successors,

---

[10] Jn. 10:37–38.

they are to teach His doctrine until the end of time and be a *living*
source of instruction from whom all men may learn the authentic
word of God.

The grant to The Twelve of authority to teach is unmistakable.
Before His Resurrection Jesus said to them: "He who hears you,
hears me; and he who rejects you, rejects me; and he who rejects me,
rejects him who sent me."[11] Just before His Ascension He told
them: "All power in heaven and on earth has been given to me. Go,
therefore, and make disciples of all nations, baptizing them in the
name of the Father, and of the Son, and of the Holy Spirit, teaching
them to observe all that I have commanded you; and behold I am
with you all days even to the consummation of the world."[12] Before leaving the world, the Son, sent by the Father upon a mission
of instruction, redemption, and salvation, turned over the remainder
of His task to The Twelve and "willed that in His Church there be
pastors and teachers even to the end of the world."[13]

The Twelve and their successors will, through the Holy Spirit assisting them, act for Jesus until He comes the second time. The
authority to teach cannot be for the lifetime of twelve men; it has
to be for all time. For the religious needs of men are substantially the
same from age to age, and Jesus came for the sake of all men. Since
He promised to be with His Apostles to the end of the world, for
so long a time is the teaching commission to last. Though the Twelve
die, the mandate to teach abides and the Christian community is ever
conscious of it. It was only natural then that the Apostles should
appoint successors with power to rule and teach. Paul set Timothy
over the Church of Cyprus and Titus over Crete. The heads of the
primitive churches pointed to some Apostle as the source of their
authority: Jerusalem to James the Less; Ephesus and Asia Minor to
John; Rome to Peter; Alexandria to Mark, the disciple of Peter.
The apostolic office of teaching does not die. In every age, like a
city set upon a mountaintop, there will exist a living authority com-
posed of the Bishops of the Church, the legitimate successors of the

---

[11] Lk. 10:16.
[12] Mt. 28:18–20.
[13] Vatican Council, *Den.* 1821 (*TCT*, 201).

Apostles. They are the depositary and custodian of the doctrine of Jesus.

The teaching body infallible

Christ's teaching body must teach without error, for He set a terrible penalty upon lack of belief: "He who does not believe shall be condemned."[14] If one must either accept the doctrine of Christ or suffer damnation, that doctrine, unpolluted by false interpretation, must always be available. But if the authentic custodian of this doctrine should fall into error from time to time, men could never be sure they were receiving the real doctrine they are so heavily charged to believe. Furthermore, since revelation contains mysteries, which elude the understanding, and imposes precepts of conduct hard on human nature, the danger of doctrinal corruption is ever present. Modern philosophy, asserting that "truths" are only the changing expression of the aspirations of a given age, sees no problem here. But Christ says without compromise: "Heaven and earth will pass away, but my words will not pass away."[15] Foreseeing the danger to the purity of His doctrine, He forestalled it by promising that the Teaching Church would be safe from error. This infallibility does not mean that the Church will never make mistakes of policy or that individual bishops will never teach false doctrine, but that the sacred magistery cannot err when it acts in its official capacity as expounder of Christ's doctrine.

The infallibility of the Church is clear from many sources: (a) from the identification Christ makes between Himself and the Apostles — "He who hears you hears me"; (b) from the assurance He gave them of success in their teaching — "I am with you all days, even to the consummation of the world"; (c) from His promise to send them the Holy Spirit — "I will ask the Father and he will give you another Advocate to dwell with you forever, the Spirit of truth."[16] Because the Church is free from error, St. Paul calls it "the Church of the living God, the pillar and mainstay of the truth."[17] In summary, "the doctrine of faith, which God has revealed,

---

[14] Mk. 16:16.   [16] Jn. 14:16–17.
[15] Mk. 13:31.   [17] 1 Tim. 3:15.

has not been proposed to the human intelligence to be perfected like a philosophic system, but as a divine deposit has been entrusted to the Spouse of Christ to be faithfully guarded and infallibly set forth."[18]

Peter infallible head of the Church

The Apostles were not a committee of equals acting under the chairmanship of one of their number; Simon Peter had full authority over them. For Christ promised him the headship of the Church upon one occasion and gave it to him upon another.

At Caesarea Philippi Jesus asked His disciples: "Who do men say the Son of Man is?" They told Him that some thought He was John the Baptist, others Elias, still others Jeremias or one of the prophets. "But who do you say that I am?" Before anyone else could answer Simon spoke up: "Thou art the Christ, the Son of the living God." Jesus acquiesced and said: "Blessed art thou Simon Bar-Jona, for flesh and blood has not revealed it to thee, but my Father in heaven. And I say to thee, thou art Peter, and upon this rock I will build my Church, and the gates of hell will not prevail against it. And I will give thee the keys of the kingdom of heaven; and whatsoever thou shalt bind on earth shall be bound in heaven, and whatever thou shalt loose on earth shall be loosed in heaven."[19]

The change of Simon's name is significant. As God changed the names of Abram and Jacob when He was about to confer a new office on them, so Christ changed the name of Simon to Peter — the Rock — because on him the new Israel was to be built. Since the sustaining power of a society lies in its authority, Simon Peter is promised supreme authority in the Church that he may sustain it against all attacks. He is to be master of the household to whom the keys are entrusted. While metaphors like "rock" and "keys" are used, there is no mistaking their meaning, namely, that Peter will rule in the Church and, like God, will bind the consciences of men.

After the resurrection Christ fulfilled this promise. Upon the shore of Lake Genesareth Jesus called Peter apart from the group of dis-

---

[18] Vatican Council, *Den.* 1800 (*TCT*, 80).
[19] Mt. 16:13 ff.

ciples and in their sight and hearing He said to Simon Peter, "Simon, son of John, dost thou love me more than these do? He said to him, Yes, Lord, thou knowest that I love thee. He said to him, Feed my lambs. He said to him a second time, Simon, son of John, dost thou love me? He said to him, Yes, Lord, thou knowest that I love thee. He said to him, Feed my lambs. A third time he said to him, Simon, son of John, dost thou love me? Peter was grieved because he said to him for the third time, Dost thou love me? And he said to him, Lord, thou knowest all things, thou knowest that I love thee. He said to him, Feed my sheep."[20] It was then that Jesus gave His entire flock to Peter as supreme pastor. How significant that the other Apostles, who are shown in the Gospels as striving for the first place in the kingdom of Christ, afterward are seen in the Acts of the Apostles acknowledging the headship of Peter. The only explanation is that Christ actually gave it to him.

This headship of Peter was not a mere personal honor but, in the person of his legitimate successors, the Bishops of Rome, an unchangeable provision in the constitution of the Church. For Christ made His Church a monarchy; that is, while He remains the invisible head, one man is His Vicar and exercises supreme authority. Peter and his successors are the rock against which the powers of darkness will vent their fury in vain. The Church is one flock under one supreme shepherd. The Roman See is the practical source of the Church's unity. For "in order that the episcopacy itself be one and undivided and that the whole body of the faithful be preserved in unity of faith and communion through priests closely bound one to another, Christ put Peter over the rest of the Apostles and in him established a perpetual principle and visible basis of both unities."[21] The Bishops of Rome have always claimed supreme rule over all the Christian churches, and the churches have acknowledged that claim, so that whatever church should repudiate it is guilty of schism, of rending the seamless robe of Christ. To rationalize their position, separated churches maintain that the primacy of the Roman See is a usurpation of man and not an arrangement of God. To help

[20] Jn. 21:15–17.
[21] Vatican Council, *Den.* 1821 (*TCT,* 201).

refute this heresy Catholic scholarship offers evidence which shows that the headship of the Roman See was recognized from the earliest times. While useful, this evidence is not necessary. For the testimony of Scripture is clear, and the Church solemnly affirmed at the Vatican Council that Peter was made Prince of the Apostles by Christ Himself and given a true primacy of jurisdiction over the Church Militant, that in the Bishop of Rome Peter has an unfailing successor in the primacy.

Not only is the Roman Pontiff successor of Peter but he is, even apart from the rest of the bishops, the supreme infallible teacher of Christian beliefs. The infallibility of the Roman Pontiff is not a guarantee of wisdom in decisions of government nor of personal sanctity but solely of purity of faith — he cannot err when he acts as supreme pastor and instructs the whole Church in matters of faith and morals. This doctrine is a dogma of faith, first, because at the Last Supper Christ said to Peter: "Simon, behold, Satan has desired to have you, that he may sift you as wheat. But I have prayed for thee, that thy faith may not fail; and do thou, when once thou hast turned again, strengthen thy brethren."[22] The Peter, whose faith will not fail but will ever support the faith of his brethren, is not only Simon Peter but the perennial Peter on the throne of the Fisherman. Second, the early churches looked to the Roman See for the solution of disputes about the faith, and the Fathers of the Church assert the decisive teaching power of the Roman Pontiffs. The Councils which were held to promote the union of East and West, namely, Constantinople IV (A.D. 869), Lyons II (A.D. 1274), and Florence (A.D. 1438–1445), assert the supreme teaching power of the Roman See and its unique authority to settle all questions of faith. Finally, the infallible Church solemnly defined that the Roman Pontiff, when he acts as supreme pastor, has exactly the same infallibility which Christ desired His Church to exercise in defining doctrines of faith and morals.

Since, therefore, Jesus entrusted His doctrine to an infallible teaching body at whose head is an infallible pastor, whoever receives their doctrine receives the doctrine of Jesus. As the ultimate reason

---

[22] Lk. 22:31–32.

for religious faith is the word of God, so the immediate rule of what we are to believe is the teaching of the Church. We believe what the infallible Church says is the word of God.

How the Church teaches

The Church teaches in an extraordinary and in an ordinary way. The issue of a creed or brief summary of Catholic beliefs is the most ancient form of extraordinary teaching. The most noteworthy creeds are: (1) the Apostles' Creed, which is traceable to the Apostles and begins, "I believe in God"[23]; (2) the Nicene-Constantinopolitan Creed, which was compiled after the Councils of Nicea (A.D. 325) and Constantinople I (A.D. 381) and begins, "I believe in one God"; the Athanasian Creed which begins, "Quicumque vult salvus esse — whoever wishes to be saved."[24] The most solemn type of teaching are definitions of Ecumenical Councils. Ecumenical means universal, and an Ecumenical Council means that the episcopacy of the world meets in one place to fulfill its function of teaching. It is *The Church Teaching,* the legitimate successor of the first Apostolic body. Councils are extraordinary gatherings, summoned by the Roman Pontiff and presided over by his legates, for the purpose of combating pernicious teaching or solving acute crises. The first was held at Nicea (A.D. 325) to make plain the Church's teaching that Jesus is God.

Sometimes statements of local councils have been accepted as dogmas of faith, not on account of their origin in an infallible teaching organ, but because they have come to be received by the universal Church as exact expressions of faith. For example, what the Council of Carthage (A.D. 418) formulated on grace and original sin against the Pelagians, and what the Council of Orange (A.D. 529) formulated on grace and predestination against the Semi-Pelagians, have long been accepted as dogmatic utterances.

Definitions of dogma are also made by the Roman Pontiff alone.

---

[23] Cf. J. Quasten, *Patrology,* Vol. I, p. 24. Newman, Westminster, 1951. The Apostles' Creed arose from the ceremony of baptism in which the baptized made a profession of faith. St. Ambrose explains the apostolic symbol, *PL* 17, 1193–96. Also cf. St. Irenaeus, *Contra Haereses,* I, X, 1. *PG* 7, 550.

[24] Since the seventh century the Quicumque has been ascribed to St. Athanasius but the time of its composition and its authorship are disputed. Cf. *Bihlmeyer-Tuchle,* Vol. I, p. 259. Newman, Westminster, 1958.

In 1854 Pius IX proclaimed the dogma of the Immaculate Conception of the Blessed Virgin Mary. In 1950 Pius XII proclaimed her
Assumption into heaven.

Finally, there are Professions of Faith containing a rather full
exposition of certain doctrines which happen to require emphasis at
a particular time. Notable among them are: (1) the Tridentine
Profession of Faith (A.D. 1563); (2) the profession prescribed for
the Greeks by Gregory XIII (A.D. 1575); and (3) that which
Benedict XIV offered the Maronites (A.D. 1743).

The ordinary teaching function is carried on by the pope, the
bishops, and their assistants, clerical and lay. It is done by the
written and spoken word. The pope uses encyclicals, allocutions,
letters, radio addresses, and the like. A bishop, who is the official
but not infallible teacher in his territory, teaches by sermons, pastoral
letters, instructions to his flock, the censorship of books. In the
parishes of a diocese the same kind of catechetical instruction goes
on now as in the days of the Apostles.

What the Church teaches

The Church teaches, first, *dogmas of faith;* that is, truths which
"are contained in the word of God whether written or handed on,
and as divinely revealed and demanding belief, are proposed by the
Church either by solemn decree or through her ordinary universal
teaching."[25] To such truths we owe divine faith, and whoever rejects
such a truth is a heretic. Second, the Church teaches whatever other
truths are necessary to explain and safeguard the dogmas of faith.
In this second class are *theological conclusions,* that is, propositions
immediately derived from dogmas; *dogmatic facts,* which are not
revealed but intimately bound up with some dogmas, such as the
legitimacy of an Ecumenical Council; *truths of reason,* which are not
revealed but are necessary for the right understanding of dogma,
for example, the spirituality of the soul and the freedom of the will.
In this area the Church has "the right and duty of denouncing knowledge falsely so called lest any one be cheated by philosophy and

---

[25] Vatican Council, *Den.* 1792 (*TCT,* 66).

vain deceit."[26] The truths of this second class we call Catholic truths, as distinct from the dogmas or divine truths, and to Catholic truths we owe an interior assent of the mind on account of the infallible teaching power of the Church. Prominent among Catholic truths are the evidences of the Church's own divine mission. "For to the Catholic Church alone belongs all those many and marvelous things which have been arranged by God for the evident credibility of the Christian faith."[27]

The concern of the Church is that its teaching be a faithful image of the Apostolic faith. The primitive catechesis was simple. It told the story of Christ's life, gave an explanation of Christian morality and the rites of baptism, confirmation, and the Eucharist, taught the doctrines of the Trinity, salvation by Christ, the need of penance and faith in Christ, the second coming of Christ, the resurrection of the dead and the last judgment. The Apostolic Church deemed this instruction enough to insure the Christian living and salvation of the new converts.

Since the Church today teaches many more dogmas, the question of the development of dogma arises. There is no development in the sense that the Church adds to the deposit of faith. Nor do the contents of dogmas change with the advance of learning, so that modern man must have a concept of God, revelation, redemption, the Incarnation, and the like which is different from that of medieval or ancient man. For the Vatican Council condemns anyone who says that "on account of the progress of science a meaning must be given to the dogmas of the Church other than that which the Church has understood and understands."[28] The reason for the unchangeable character of dogmas lies in their divine origin: "Heaven and earth shall pass away, but my words will not pass away."[29]

But just as there was a growth in God's revelation which culminated in the Christian revelation, so there is development in the understanding and expression of the Christian faith. A dogma, as a human formula selected to express a supernatural reality, may

[26] Vatican Council, *Den.* 1798 (*TCT,* 78).
[27] Vatican Council, *Den.* 1794 (*TCT,* 68).
[28] Vatican Council, *Den.* 1818 (*TCT,* 83).
[29] Mk. 13:31.

not fully manifest all the reality involved. For what words of man can do justice to the unseen things of God? So in the course of time a fuller exposition of revelation necessarily results, and things which were only implicitly believed are now explicitly proposed by the Church.

The first cause of dogmatic development is the reaction of the Church to heresy. The simple statement of a Christian mystery suffices until some clever man rationalizes about it in a way so dangerous as to destroy it. The Church then issues a more exact statement. There is a necessary departure from primitive simplicity; some complication and elaboration is added to the official instruction. While the new formula makes it impossible for believing men thereafter to fall into the errors it aims to correct, yet it need not be so definitive as to settle all disputes which may arise about the matter.

A second cause of development is loving contemplation of revealed truth. Consequently what was believed implicitly now becomes an explicit object of belief. St. Thomas says: "All the articles [of faith] are contained in certain primary matters of faith, such as the existence of God and His providence over man. . . . For the existence of God includes all that we believe to exist in God eternally, and in these our happiness consists; while belief in His providence includes everything God dispenses in time for man's salvation, and these are the way to that happiness."[30]

Primary source of the Church's teaching — The Bible

Revelation is a single body of doctrine containing truths to be believed and a Christian discipline to be followed. It is all, the Council of Trent affirms, "contained in written books and in unwritten traditions, which, given by Christ Himself to the Apostles or passed on by the Apostles, as it were, from hand to hand, have come down to us through the assistance of the Holy Spirit."[31] The Church, therefore, finds her dogmas in a twofold source, the Bible and Tradition.

The Bible is that collection of sacred writings which forms the

---

[30] *Sum. Theol.* II–II, 1, 7.
[31] *Den.* 783 (*TCT*, 95).

world's outstanding book, whose burden is the ways of God to man, whose center and climax is Christ. It is human in that it is the product of the literary efforts of men; divine, in that God is responsible for it. This means, in the words of the Vatican Council, that Holy Scripture was written under the inspiration of the Holy Spirit, had God for its Author, and as such was given to the Church.

How does one explain the dogma of scriptural inspiration? Nobody today would say that the human author was the pen and God the penman, or that God dictated the words and some man wrote them down. Under inspiration, the faculties of the inspired writer operate as freely as do the faculties of other writers. Nor is inspiration a miracle. God does not take over and displace the personality of the human writer. Inspiration works like grace; the writer may not be aware of the divine action. Let us call inspiration a supernatural psychological impulse, given by God to a man, which guides the man through the whole process of composition, so that he chooses to write, he understands what is to be written, and correctly expresses all and only those materials God wants written. While everything he writes is inspired, not everything is revealed. Inspiration is the movement to write at the impulse of God; revelation is the supernatural reception of knowledge from God. God reveals only what is necessary for salvation. The inspired writer puts down many things he knows naturally.

The claim to be divinely inspired has been made on behalf of many writings. Who is to judge the claim? Since the books themselves do not give sufficient evidence of their inspired character, some public authoritative critic, external to the books, is needed. This can only be the Church Teaching. It has worked on this problem from the beginning. Among dozens of books, circulating in early Christian times and purporting to be Gospels, it has designated four and only four and rejected all the rest. While the task of designating the complete written word of God was settled in a traditional manner before the Middle Ages, this was definitively done at the Council of Trent which drew up the official list of inspired writings. The Council approved the Latin Vulgate as the official text and the

Church has since been laboring hard to bring out an edition which is textually pure, that is, as close to the original writings as scholarship can make it.

As a consequence of its inspiration the original document and all faithful copies are free from error. This inerrancy of Scripture is, says Leo XIII, "the ancient and constant faith of the Church."[32] Since the rise of the modern sciences accusations of error and contradiction have been made against the Bible. When some Catholics replied that the sacred writer is free from error when he treats of faith and morals but is liable to error in other matters, the Church rejected their solution. A preliminary answer is that truth is not formally at stake in every line of the Bible because the sacred writer not only teaches and imparts a revelation; he aims also at effects of holiness, beauty, charm, persuasion. But whenever truth is at stake, as it is in formal assertions, then error is impossible because the assertion of the sacred writer is God's assertion. The key to the problem, then, is, What does the sacred writer, as an inspired public character, intend to assert? To meet this difficult problem Catholic scholars use these principles. First, who was the writer, what were his personal habits of thought and expression, under what circumstances of time and place did he write, how did his contemporaries understand his language? Knowledge of ancient far-eastern man sheds great light on the Bible. Second, does the writer voice a judgment of his own or does he merely give an opinion, quote, or cite an idea universally accepted in his time without passing judgment on it? To be erroneous his judgment must intend to express a facet of reality which actually it does not. Third, from what point of view does he consider his materials? Remember the Bible is not a scientific treatise, not even of religion, but a means of conveying a religious message to all mankind in a popular manner. Finally, and this is of capital importance, the literary form or genre must be considered. The Bible contains popular and political history, hagiography, prophecy, poetry, philosophical essay, moral maxims, the moral fable and apocalyptic writings. Different norms are used to judge the truth of

[32] *Den.* 1952 (*TCT*, 110).

different literary forms. The whole Bible is true, therefore, and so is every part of it, but true in the sense in which various kinds of literature witness to the truth.

Does Holy Writ have various meanings? It is usual to distinguish a literal, a typical, and an accommodated sense. The literal sense is not necessarily the face value of the words but the meaning which the author intended to convey according to the rules of the literary form he employed. Thus the literal sense of a historical book is not that of apocalyptic writing. Every part of Scripture has a literal sense, and this can only be one; otherwise God speaks ambiguously. The end of sound exegesis is discovery of this literal sense. Since God is the principal Author, the complete meaning of any statement will always be that which God intended when He inspired the sacred writer. Hence commentators speak of an extension of the literal sense which they call the "fuller sense," namely, a literal meaning which God intends but the writer may not be quite aware of. Thus, says St. Thomas, "even true prophets do not know all that the Holy Spirit means by the things they . . . speak."[33] By divine ordination, certain words and events signify other events and realities in the economy of salvation. This meaning may be by way of a type — the paschal lamb is a type of Christ — or by way of allegory, or as foreshadowing some feature of the future life. This is the typical or spiritual meaning. It does not do away with the literal sense but presupposes it. St. Thomas thinks we ought not to draw theological arguments from this sense but only from the literal sense. However, nothing is lost by this restriction because "nothing necessary to faith is contained under the spiritual sense which is not elsewhere stated by Scripture in its literal sense."[34] The accommodated sense is the application of words of Scripture to a subject which God did not intend to signify by these words. It is not really a sense of Scripture but a pious use of scriptural words.

Primary source of the Church's teaching — Tradition

The second and more important source of revelation is Tradition.

---

[33] *Sum. Theol.* II–II, 173, 4.
[34] *Sum. Theol.* I, 1, 10 ad 1.

In a religious context tradition means (1) a method of handing on truths other than by inspired writings, and (2) the truths thus communicated.

1. In the first sense, Tradition is the dynamic fulfillment of the Church's obligation to preach the Gospel, the collective consciousness which the Church has of the deposit of faith. The handing on of the faith is done by the continuous preaching of the magistery, by the belief of the Church, by the Holy Spirit speaking through the living Church. Tradition is the only means by which the primitive revelation could have been transmitted. Even when revelation began to be written down in the time of Moses, oral tradition continued. Indeed it is a doctrine of faith that the Christian revelation is handed on by this means. St. Paul tells the Thessalonians: "Stand firm, and hold the teachings that you have learned, whether by word or by letter of ours."[35] He warns the Galatians: "If anyone preach a gospel to you other than that which you have received, let him be anathema."[36] The obligation which the Apostles received and fulfilled was to speak and to teach; that of the Church, to believe. The Councils of Trent and Vatican assert that revelation came from the mouth of Christ to the Apostles and from them was transmitted to us by the aid of the Holy Spirit. The instruments of this tradition are, primarily, the Apostles, popes, councils, and bishops; secondarily, those who, under the supervision of the former, preach, teach, write, or, like the whole body of the faithful, profess their faith.

2. The objective counterpart of that preaching and belief is the body of truths, received from the mouth of Jesus Christ or from the Apostles, illumined by the Holy Spirit, which have been handed on in the Church as the revelation of God. This is the deposit of faith or the objective criterion by which all doctrinal disputes are settled. For, according to the Second Council of Constantinople, our Christian Tradition is "the faith which was given from the beginning by our great God and Savior Jesus Christ to the Holy Apostles and by them preached in the world; which the Holy Fathers have confessed and explained and handed on to the holy churches."[37] This is moreover the whole faith. True, Tradition is used in a narrow sense as

---

[35] 2 Thess. 2:14.   [36] Gal. 1:9.   [37] *Den.* 212 (*TCT,* 91).

referring only to the revelations which were not entrusted to the inspired writings, but, in the proper sense, Tradition includes the entire deposit of faith. Both in the Old and the New Law revelation was handed on orally before any of it was written down, and only some of the revelation was consigned to sacred books. Nowhere does Scripture say that it contains the entire divine message. But this was given to the Church. Her teachings, therefore, embrace Scripture because She alone knows what is inspired writing, and She alone knows the proper meaning of Scripture. Finally, if we may include in Tradition, as we surely ought, those nonrevealed truths which are necessary at times for the defense of revelation, then Tradition is the living thought of the Christian community nourished and guided by the Holy Spirit.

In opposing the Protestant claim that Scripture is the sole source of revelation, one should not give the impression that the Bible and Tradition are separate and independent of each other. There is a recent expression of Catholic thought which says that the Bible is God's revelation, understanding of course that there are some dogmas which are not explicitly contained in Scripture but are closely derivable from it. The Bible and Tradition would not then be two distinct though parallel sources of dogma, but two inseparable components of revelation, the body of which is the written word, and Tradition the soul. Revelation is fully evolved from the operation of the Spirit upon Tradition and Scripture. The Spirit acts upon the living Tradition until it crystallizes into Scripture. When revelation gets written down, the Spirit interprets it and makes it live by Tradition. Hence, according to this expression, Tradition is the divinely guided and living interpretation of Scripture by the Church. This is her understanding of the divine revelation and that intelligence is always within her.

What constitutes a tradition the Church can learn by examining the organs of tradition. Foremost among these are the Fathers of the Church, the ecclesiastical writers of the first eight centuries who have been approved by the Church for their holiness and orthodox doctrine. God raised them up to be witnesses and teachers of the faith. The practically unanimous agreement of the Fathers, that a doctrine must be believed by the faithful, is a sure argument for its divinely revealed character. Another prominent organ is the theologians. If we have the morally unanimous testimony of the theologians that a doctrine is not only true but revealed, their agreement is a certain argument for its dogmatic status. Third, the sacred liturgy is to be considered; for the prayers of the Church are a norm of its beliefs. Another norm is the practice of the Church over a long period. Thus, if the Roman Pontiffs have dissolved certain types of marriages for several centuries, one must believe that they have legitimate power to act in that way. Finally, we have the universal beliefs of the faithful. For the Spirit dwells in the whole Church, not only assisting the magistery to teach, but also the faithful to believe. Hence it is impossible for the entire body of the faithful to believe what is false.

By examining all the organs of tradition the Church can (1) discover the truths living in the minds of the faithful; (2) judge the records of the past to determine if a writer substituted his personal opinion for the true voice of Christendom; (3) declare a disputed tenet to be or not to be part of the faith; (4) reaffirm all past pronouncements. But even if all monuments of past teaching and witnessing to the faith were lost, the Church could still teach by looking within and consulting her living understanding of the doctrine entrusted to her.

Therefore, as there is one object of belief and that is the revelation of God, deposited in Scripture and Tradition, so there is one proximate rule of faith and that is the living voice of the Church Teaching.

Theology

Theology takes what the Church teaches and constructs a true science. It uses as principles the basic revealed truths and in a scientific manner draws new knowledge — theological conclusions — and unites the whole into a coherent system, the theological synthesis. This book is a modest summary of that synthesis. Theology's tool is reason illumined by faith. Its subject matter is God and all things in so far as they are connected with God. It studies these matters from the point of view of their having been revealed to us in a supernatural manner. Theology is also called the science of faith: ordered knowledge about what we believe and that by which we believe. The purpose is that one may know with certainty what he is to believe and, as far as he can, penetrate to an understanding of what he believes.

Theology is not a static science. Great changes have come about since modern theology has, for the most part, left off philosophizing on the revealed data to examine its sources more closely. New insights into the meaning and development of dogmas have resulted from a more historic study of Tradition. The greatest stimulus, however, has come from the area of scriptural scholarship. There is a vast increase of knowledge about Mediterranean civilization, Semitic psychology and literary forms, the languages allied to the Hebrew, Aramaic, and Greek in which Scripture was first written. The effort to get at the literal sense has had its repercussions in dogmatic theology. Thus the text-slinging days which followed the Council of Trent are over. While timeless truths are to be found in isolated texts, it is now considered poor method to pin dogmas upon disparate sentences of Holy Writ. Reliance, says the new method, should be placed upon the great themes of the whole of Scripture and the prominent ideas of particular books. Hence we speak of a biblical theology or a method of teaching revelation which arises immediately out of Scripture. This method aims to present an exact statement of the revealed truths contained in each inspired book; then a development of the main themes of revelation from their first mention in the Old Testament to their flowering in the New Testament. Finally, a new synthesis, based on certain core ideas may be possible: the divine plan with its themes of election, covenant, and people of God; the fall with its themes of election, punishment, and repentance; redemption with its themes of mercy and salvation; and accomplishment with its themes of hope and the kingdom of God.

The new ideas are still in the stage of discussion. Hence we follow a pattern based more or less upon the sequence of dogmas found in the Apostles' Creed. The dogmas of faith readily lend themselves to this outline: (1) Who is God in Himself? (2) God made man and offered him a wondrous destiny. (3) When man rejected his destiny he was rescued from his folly by God. (4) God supplies the means of rescue for individual men and offers to reconcile them to Himself and to sanctify them. (5) If men will co-operate they will finally get what God has promised. In accordance with this plan of development we shall treat (1) of God in Himself; (2) God the Creator and Provider; (3) God the Redeemer; (4) God the Sanctifier and (5) the means of sanctification; (6) God the rewarder.

Since theology deals with the most exalted subject matter and gives with the utmost certitude the answer to man's most profound questioning, it is the supreme science and ought to be the sovereign interest of an intelligent man.

CHAPTER TWO

GOD IN HIMSELF

"I believe in God the Father Almighty"

THE big presupposition of theology is the existence of God. We are not born with knowledge of it nor is it immediately evident to us. Its establishment, however, is the high point of Christian philosophy. For example, St. Thomas argues from (1) beings in motion and change to One who must originate all change whilst He Himself is unmoved and unchanged; from (2) causes at work around us to an Uncaused Cause; from (3) beings which exist but need not exist to One who must exist; from (4) more or less limited beings to an unlimited Greatest Being; from (5) an ordered universe to a Universal Orderer. The Unmoved Mover, the Uncaused Cause, the Necessary Being, the Greatest Being, the Universal Orderer are other names for God. Pius XII has developed arguments 1 and 5 to show how the findings of modern science, far from refuting the evidence for the existence of God, support these proofs of it. There are other valid proofs. For it is a dogma of faith, declared by the Vatican Council, that the human intellect by its native power can arrive at certain knowledge of the existence of God.

With the existence of God soundly established, theology begins its exposition of the faith by making the sign of the cross and reciting the first article of the Apostles' Creed, I believe in God, assuring us meantime that this primary truth has been revealed countless times and is professed by the Church in every symbol of the faith. The truths of God's existence and His chief attributes, says the Vatican Council, have been revealed so that they may be known by all easily, with certainty, and without admixture of error. We can and must make an act of faith in the existence of God.

Modern man is constantly inquiring into the content of concepts.

In this chapter we examine that most difficult concept, *God,* which represents the mysterious Being "who dwells in light inaccessible, whom no man has seen or can see."[1] It is hard enough to know something of Him as He is reflected in nature; but we lack the natural power of knowing *Him as He is.* For "no one knows who the Son is except the Father, and who the Father is except the Son, and him to whom the Son chooses to reveal him."[2] The Son's revelation of the Godhead we summarize thus: God is one in nature and three in Person. Our exposition of the first phrase explains *what* God is; our exposition of the second, *who* God is.

We need great caution in speaking of God. When we apply to Him philosophical words such as *nature* and *essence,* remember that these apply strictly only to created things. For God is so superior to all things that He is not classifiable among them. His reality is so tremendous that it cannot be neatly fitted within the forms of human thought. When we apply *production, procession, mission,* etc. to Him, we must cleanse them of all association of defect. We use these words for the understanding of created things and when we speak of God we have no better ones: they are accommodations to our limited ways of knowing. Many of our notions about God are negative. Thus when we call Him *infinite,* we conceive of limited being and say that God is not that. We have no way of expressing this reality positively. When we apply the same word to God and to man, we do so by analogy, that is, by a meaning which is partly the same and partly different. Thus when we say that God and man are good and just, the words do not mean exactly the same in both cases. The meaning is partly the same because God and man really have goodness and justice; but the meaning is also partly different because God is good and just in a way in which we could not possibly be. We can experience the goodness and justice of man but in God there will always be aspects of His goodness and justice which will elude us. The mistake of the rationalist is to equate God with human experience. But God is incomprehensible and cannot be enfolded within the created intellect.

---

[1] 1 Tim. 6:16.
[2] Lk. 10:22.

A. *The One Divine Nature*

The Vatican Council teaches: "The holy, catholic, apostolic and Roman Church believes and professes that there is one true and living God, the Creator of heaven and earth, who is almighty, eternal, immense, incomprehensible, infinite in intellect and will and every perfection. Since He is a single, entirely simple, unchangeable substance, it must be acknowledged that He is truly and of His very nature distinct from the world, perfectly happy in Himself and indescribably above everything that is outside of Himself or that can be thought of."[3]

The usual way of presenting this doctrine is to explain (1) the essence of God, (2) His attributes, and (3) His operations.

The essence of God

Essence is that which makes a thing be what it is. What then is that most profound aspect of God which makes Him God and different from anything else? Most theologians say that it is His Self-existence. The things we experience owe their existence to something other than themselves — to a cause from which they receive existence. But there cannot be only received existence. There has to be a source of existence which owes its existence, not to another, but to itself. God is this source of existence: He is the first and independent Being and all other things have existence because they receive it from Him. Since, then, existence is the first of realities, and since the existence of God differs from the received existence of all other things, the Self-existence of God is the most significant difference between God and all other things. St. Thomas[4] derives this doctrine from the reply which God gave to Moses when he asked Him His name. "God said to Moses I am who am. . . . Thus thou shalt say to the children of Israel: He who is, hath sent me to you. . . . This is my name forever."[5] In the Old Testament the proper name of God is "He who is." True, the Hebrews did

---

[3] *Den.* 1782 (*TCT*, 355).
[4] *Sum. Theol.* I, 13, 11, and II–II, 174, 6.
[5] Exod. 3:14–15.

not have the concept of essence, but they did know that the giving of a *proper* name is the attempt to tell exactly what the being is.

The attributes of God

Attributes are permanent qualities which flow from essence — characteristics which help us identify a thing. In creatures essence and attribute are different; in God they are all one. Defect of language and of sufficient insight into God compels us to speak of them as though they were different.

God is infinitely perfect. A being is perfect when it has everything which its nature calls for. There is nothing lacking to God. He is and has all that the First Being ought to be and have. Everything we experience is of limited scope and ability; but to God's perfections there is no limit and He has all possible perfections in the most perfect way. He is the Being than whom no greater can be conceived. Why? There is nothing to limit the Self-existing Being. Surely, nothing outside Him, for all these depend on Him. Nor anything within Him, for His nature is to exist and of itself existence is unlimited. Scripture calls Him the Most High, the incomparable, the incomprehensible, the inscrutable, the all-powerful whom nothing can resist, of whose goodness, wisdom, and greatness there is no end. The Wise Man says that He is all; St. Paul, that from Him and through Him and unto Him are all things. From His infinity some people have concluded that God *is* all things. This is completely false. For the other things are not just aspects of God who will eventually absorb all things into Himself. They are utterly distinct from God; but whatever reality they may have — even human personality — exists in God without defect. For God is the inexhaustibly rich pattern after which all things are designed and from His hand they all flow.

God is one. First, in the ordinary sense that a natural being is itself, undivided in its being and distinct from everything else. Thus my mother is one, our dog is one. Second, there is one and *only one* God. "See ye that I alone am, and there is no other God beside me."[6] Since He is the Being than whom no greater can be conceived, there

---

[6] Deut. 32:39.

could not be two greatest beings, as the Dualists said. It is likely
that this is, historically, the most important of the divine attributes.
For the doctrine that there are many gods has done more moral
harm to the human race than any comparable error. The Hebrews
were prone to it until, after many lapses, they were thoroughly
imbued with monotheism or the doctrine of God's uniqueness. "Hear
O Israel! The Lord our God is one Lord."[7] Third, God is one in a
supreme, unique sense because He is utterly *simple*. He is not made
up of parts. Parts are prior to the whole, but there is nothing which
can in any way be prior to God. To have parts is to be defective
in unity and God is perfect unity. He has, therefore, no physical
parts such as body and soul; nor any quantitative parts. For, while
He has all the perfection of the material being, He has none of its
defects one of which is to be extended in space. Hence He is spirit,
Pure Spirit, completely independent of matter. God is all substance,
all God. His attributes and His substance are the same; so much so
that, while we say that a creature has life or charity, God is life,
God is charity. "Therefore God is said to be simple," says St.
Augustine, "because whatever He has is Himself."[8]

God is unchangeable.   Change means that a being becomes either
better or worse; but that is impossible in the case of the Being who
is infinitely perfect. To the substance of God — which is not an
inconceivably huge mass of most subtle matter — nothing can be
added, nothing taken away. Neither is there any change in His
knowledge nor in the choices of His will; for "with him there is no
change nor shadow of alteration."[9]

Because we change and have bodies we are inescapably immersed
in time and space. Time is the measure of change; space, the
imagined receptacle of bodies. To God these things are as nothing —
the sign of the creature's servitude. He does not exist in time but
in eternity, which expresses a duration without beginning, end, or
change. Decidedly eternity is not some superior sort of time endless
at both extremities. Our existence in time means that we live our

---

[7] Deut. 6:4.
[8] *The City of God,* Bk. XI, 10, 1. *PL* 41, 325.
[9] James 1:17.

lives in parts, in a succession of past, present, and future: God lives in an undivided present — a *now* which never ceases or changes. Hence *God is eternal;* He is the Self-subsisting Being. Scripture calls Him the Eternal One; shows Him pre-existing creation and lasting forever; He is ever the same and has an everlasting name; a thousand years are as a day in His sight. Because He is perfect spirit, He is outside of space and place. Since He can be contained or measured by nothing, *He is immense.* "Heaven and the heaven of heavens cannot contain thee."[10] This attribute has nothing to do with material size; it is rather our feeble attempt to put creation side by side with the infinity of God. Although God is not restricted to space, *He is everywhere present.* "Whither shall I go from thy spirit. . . . If I ascend into heaven thou art there: if I descend into hell thou art present. If I take my wings early in the morning and dwell in the uttermost parts of the sea: even there thy right hand shall lead me."[11] Wherever anything can be there is the divine substance. God is with and in all things; for the spiritual being is said to be where its power operates and to be in the things which receive the effects of that power. In such wise God exists in everything, not as water in a container or electricity in a wire, but as the one who brings them into existence, supports them, and supplies them with the power to do whatever they do.

Biblical theology proposes a more concrete way of considering God. The concepts of essence and attribute, it says, are products of Greek thought and foreign to the thought patterns of Scripture. Why not evolve directly from the sacred writings a description of God which is comparatively free from philosophical ideas? Represent God as the most vibrant, tremendous Personality, awe-inspiring, righteous, full of power, wisdom, and mercy. To produce this portrait our ideas of God could center about three main themes.

a) He is a holy God. Scriptural holiness means, first, a numinous or godly quality which shows God to be separate from, and wholly other than, all created things. He is immeasurably above all things. He alone is the living God, and is completely different from the gods

---

[10] 3 Kings 8:27.
[11] Ps. 138:7–10.

of the gentiles which have neither being nor life. He is so immeasur-
able that no image can depict Him. His grandeur is without rival.
His power has no bounds. The hand of the Lord is never shortened.
He is different from every agent of which we have knowledge; for
to do something, He has but to will and it is done. The word of the
Lord never returns to Him empty, but it always accomplishes that
for which it was intended. While He works with consummate wisdom,
His purposes are different from those of His creatures, and the means
which He employs are not the means men would choose. As for
comprehending Him and His ways, we can but exclaim: "Oh, the
depths of the riches of the wisdom and of the knowledge of God!
How incomprehensible are his judgments and how unsearchable his
ways."[12] The same numinous quality is attributed to whatever He
makes His own. His house among men is removed from profane use.
Where He is, is sacred ground, and there men must stand barefoot.
He dwells in His holy place and only the clean of heart shall stand
in it with Him. The things, the days, the people, set apart for Him,
share in this sanctity. His holiness is also, and perhaps especially,
His moral stainlessness. He is poles apart from any injustice, selfish-
ness, disorder. Between Him and sin no compromise is possible.
Nothing defiled shall enter His sight. He hates iniquity. In His
presence the prophet trembles at remembrance of his sinfulness. The
word God speaks is inviolable: His Law leads men to holy lives.
What more awful thing can be said of men than that they have
blasphemed the Holy One of Israel? Before so holy a God men
should cry out: "Holy, holy, holy, the Lord God of hosts,"[13] and
be confounded for their sinfulness.

   b) **He is a covenanting and electing God.** Despite the austerity of
His majesty and the abyss separating Him from men, God has an
intimate part in human affairs and directs their course by His will.
The great cosmic force is the will of God for man's good. To accomplish this beneficent will, He allies Himself to man and, in the
ancient Hebrew thought, pledges *to act as a kinsman*. He made
promises to the Fathers, and with their sons at Mt. Sinai He made

[12] Rom. 11:33.
[13] Isa. 6:3.

a solemn agreement whose substance was: "I will walk among you and be your God and you will be my people."[14] God promises to act with loving kindness and to give rewards: they promise submission to His will, which is the only thing that integrates human life, personal or social. The basic belief of Israel was that God had chosen him, and his pledge of loyalty to God was his response to the divine election and deliverance from Egypt. But why does God choose this obscure people? Such is His good pleasure: "the Lord hath chosen Jacob unto himself."[15] And the same is true of every individual who enjoys the divine favor. But by departing so often from His Law His people void the agreement and are finally rejected. On Calvary the old covenant is dropped and a new and eternal covenant is made with the whole human race. The Eucharist becomes the blood of the new covenant and the Church the new people of God. This view presents the condescension of God, His loving kindness, His fidelity. He is a strong and faithful God, keeping His covenant, faithful in all His words. Trust in God, then, is the sole support of life. Above all, His justice is manifest. Since He cannot be in the debt of anyone, this justice is not that of equal to equal but of the Supreme Lawgiver, rendering to every man according to his works. It is vindicative, punishing for sin: "Vengeance is mine; I will repay."[16] It is also rewarding: "There is laid up for me," says the Apostle, "a crown of justice, which the Lord, the just Judge, will give to me in that day: yet not only to me, but also to those who love his coming."[17]

c) **He is a saving and a loving God.** This intimate view of God, kinsman of His people, is climaxed by the notion of God, the Savior. "God is my Saviour. I will deal confidently,"[18] cries the prophet. Out of compassion God saved Israel from the bondage of Egypt. When Israel forgot the covenant and abandoned the way of God to reap the fruits of infidelity, God saved him again and again. For Israel is His son. The whole Bible story leads up to the salvation of the race wrought by Jesus, Savior. Human history is an economy of *salvation,* that is, of man's need for a rescue which only God could

---

[14] Lev. 26:12. [16] Rom. 12:19. [18] Isa. 12:2.
[15] Ps. 134:4. [17] 2 Tim. 4:8.

give. Salvation flows from mercy, the most characteristic act of God
to man. "The Lord is compassionate and merciful: long-suffering
and plenteous in mercy."[19] Whereas the Lord of the covenant is a
God of justice, the Savior is a God of love. For He is our Father,
the God of all consolation. "In the wilderness . . . the Lord thy God
hath carried thee, as a man is wont to carry his little son."[20] He is a
Father of unwearied patience who is drawn to misery, distress, and
even sin. He goes to find the prodigal. He is willing to pardon not
just seven times but seventy times seven. He rejoices more at the
salvation of one sinner than at the ninety-nine who need no repentance. From love, He gives us His most precious possession: "God
so loved the world that he gave his only begotten Son."[21] The Son is
savior and shepherd of men's souls. The group of the elect is a
spouse whom He cleanses from stain and unites to Himself in mystic
marriage. The Holy One, the Lord of Sabaoth, calls each one to
Him as the bridegroom calls his bride: He is more than kinsman;
He is lover.

The Divine Operations

Every being does something, and the highest kind of activity is
life. God eternally lives and by that life He swears, giving assurance
of the truth of what He says. He is the source of all life, and while
every kind of activity exists in God in a perfect manner, we shall
speak only of the activity of His intellect and will.

The Knowledge of God. Knowledge is that peculiar contact with
reality whereby an agent is united to an object through awareness of
it. Intellection is the knowledge of the spiritual faculty, and the union
between intellect and reality is generally explained by some kind of
spiritual representation. The thing known is re-present to the knower
when the form or image of the thing is received and expressed by the
knower's intellect. Our knowledge is imperfect because it is a process
of learning bit by bit and it is full of mistakes. God's knowledge,
however, is perfect both in its manner and its freedom from error.
He needs no images; by one sweep of insight He is aware of all
reality. He knows everything that is knowable.

[19] Ps. 102:8.   [20] Deut. 1:31.   [21] Jn. 3:16.

Practically every page of the Bible gives testimony of the depth, range, and perfection of His knowledge. The great thing He knows is Himself. He has perfect comprehension of His infinite being, and in His case the knower, the thing known, and the act of knowing are one thing — the Divine Substance. Since the Divine Nature is the pattern according to which all things are made, and since He knows all that His power can produce, He knows in Himself all things distinct from Himself. This includes all possible things, and all past, present, and future events, including the free choices of men. To know the free future with certainty belongs to God alone.

To reconcile the freedom of man with the foreknowledge of God is a problem. People say: if God knows that I am going to sin tomorrow, then I must sin and my act cannot be free. Human liberty is a fact but to safeguard it we cannot deny divine foreknowledge. The free act, which does not as yet but will exist, is something, and therefore knowable by infinite intelligence. Many think the problem cannot be solved but this much can be said. If God knows that I will go to New York tomorrow, then that act will infallibly take place and in the free manner God foresees. Otherwise God would not know all things or He would be mistaken. The foreknowledge of God, however, does not change a free act into a compulsive act. Suppose an artillery observer had his binoculars on a column of troops approaching a bend in a distant road. If his knowledge was complete he would know at what time each file of soldiers would arrive at the bend, but his knowledge would not be the cause of their arriving at that spot. He still remains an observer. So also by his *knowledge of vision* God remains an observer. While He sees what we shall do tomorrow, His foreknowledge of vision does not cause us to do these things. Origen says: "A thing will happen not because God knows it as future: but because it is a future thing, it is on that account known by God before it happens."[22]

God knows also all futurible things, that is, the actions which a man would perform if this or that condition were fulfilled. If He did not He could not, as a provident Father, direct men and wisely grant their petitions. He is the Seeing-One, the searcher of hearts

[22] *Comment. in Rom.* vii, 8. *PG* 14, 1126.

and reins; that is, He knows the intimate thoughts and feelings of all men. "All things are naked and open to the eyes of him to whom we have to give an account."[23]

God not only has the truth, as we sometimes have it, but He *is* *truth* itself. This means, first, in the sense that truth and being are one, that God is the first knowable thing. Second, in the sense that truth is a mental likeness of reality, God is the perfect picture of all things; for He is that to which things are compared to see if they are what they are supposed to be. Third, in the sense that truth is conformity between one's expression and one's thought, God is *infinite veracity*. He cannot lie.

The Will of God.   In the intelligent being the faculty of choice, desire, or love is will. God has a perfect will. Since being is good and desirable, God is the Supreme Good, the most desirable of beings. As His being under the aspect of truth is the only thing that can satisfy His intellect, so His being under the aspect of goodness is the proper object of His will. God necessarily loves and rejoices in Himself.

It is an outstanding characteristic of goodness to share itself. Since God is supremely good, He should make a communication of goodness which is worthy of Himself. As we shall see in discussing the Most Blessed Trinity, the Father communicates the Divine Substance to the Son — an infinite giving — and the Father and the Son communicate the Divine Substance to the Holy Spirit — another infinite giving. With these infinite givings the matter might have rested: the good God has shared Himself as He ought — infinitely. But so boundless is the goodness of God that He shares Himself in a finite way with things outside Himself. Without this overflow of Divine Goodness nothing but God would ever have existed. All things outside of God owe their being to the fact that God chose them to share the Divine Goodness. God, however, was not compelled to do this. He is free. He "works all things according to the counsel of his will."[24]

The freedom of God is different from the freedom of man and

23 Hebr. 4:13.
24 Eph. 1:11.

this is best seen in the relations of man and God to evil. Evil is the deprivation of good which ought to be present. In itself it is nothingness. Physical evil is the lack of well-being which properly belongs to a natural being; it is death, disease, pain, loss of limb, and the like. Moral evil is the lack of proper order toward the final end which should be in every free act. Can man and God will evil? No one, no matter how depraved, can will evil as evil. When evil is sought, it is sought as a good, real or apparent.

God wills many physical evils, not as ends in themselves, for such choices would be contrary to wisdom, but as means to some greater good. Thus He wills the destruction of lower beings for the sake of higher beings. Indeed the beauty and variety of the universe demand certain physical evils. Big fish eat little fish, cows live off grass, man can live off beef. If God were to eliminate all physical evil only one immutable creature could exist. As for physical evil inflicted on man, God can will it for the punishment and improvement of man. After the fall, the creation, which had been intended to minister to man's pleasure, shared in the corruption of sin and has become a partial source of suffering. But physical ills accepted in faith are an expiation of sin and an opportunity of virtue. In this sense the Wise Man means: "Good things and evil, life and death, poverty and riches, are from God."[25]

As for moral evil, man can but God cannot will it. The fact that man is physically free to sin is not a sign of greater liberty but of fundamental defect. Capacity to sin is not power but weakness. Man's power to sin is attributable to the defect of a will which can turn from its last end. It can do so because its final end is not in itself but in another. To sin means to turn away from the Divine Goodness. God cannot do this because He necessarily loves Himself and can never be wanting to Himself. The Council of Trent sharply rebuked those who say that God works evil works. While always forbidding sin, God allows it; that is, He respects the freedom of the intelligent creature during his probation and chooses not to interfere with his immoral choice. Why God permits men to sin we discuss when we speak of Divine Providence.[26]

---

[25] Ecclus. 11:14.   [26] See p. 65 ff.

There is the other problem of reconciling the freedom of God with His unchangeableness. Since the free will of God is the same as the unchangeable Divine Substance, how can His will be both free and necessary? The answer is that the will of God is necessary as regards love of Self but free as regards love of creatures. But if God's will to create, which is Himself, had never existed, would not a God who does not create be different from a God who does create? Theologians say that, since the presence of creatures adds nothing to God, their absence would likewise take nothing away. But when we ask *why* God is the same whether He creates or does not, we meet the distinction which says that if there were no creation God would suffer no intrinsic change but merely an extrinsic change — the loss of a relationship. All that the distinction says is that, while God remains the same, nothing exists outside Him. Quite obvious, but the mystery is hardly scratched by the distinction.

In the Old Testament God is presented as speaking, hearing, seeing, laughing. He rides the clouds, goes down to look at the Tower of Babel, closes the door of Noe's ark. He feels joy, disgust, repentance, jealousy. Such speech is understandably directed to a primitive people because it taught the lesson that God is personal, not an abstract force. We, however, should not reconstruct God in the image of a man. God has no passions but He has certain intellectual and moral virtues which are identical with His simple nature. Since we must speak about God in a human way, it is all right to talk as if these virtues were distinct. But we may not attribute to Him any virtue which implies defect. Since He has all knowledge, He cannot have faith. Since His power is infinite, He cannot hope, pray, or be humble. Since He cannot sin, He cannot practice penance.

Finally, God is both His own and our happiness. Requiring nothing, He has within Himself the source of His happiness, which He finds in the perfect and joyous knowledge and love of Himself. He calls us to share life and happiness with Him.

B. *The Three Persons in God*

God is no mere impersonal force; He is personal because He is intelligent. It would never have occurred even to the sharpest mind to inquire into the number of Persons in the Godhead because everyone would say that, as God is one in nature, so He is one Person. All our experience is thus summed up — one intelligent nature, one person. We have seen that the nature of God is mysterious enough, but, left to ourselves, we would never have suspected the deeper mystery of the infinite simple nature of God being had by three distinct Divine Persons. Yet the basic dogma of the Christian religion states that three distinct Divine Persons actually possess the same identical nature.* No one can rightly call himself a Christian who does not profess belief in this mystery.

We explain this doctrine by answering three questions: (1) Is it a fact revealed by God that three Divine Persons have the same identical divine nature? (2) How far do faith and reason go in explaining this fact? (3) What are the consequences to us of this fact?

The Fact of the Mystery

The first Christians held the Old Testament belief that the God of Israel is the one true God, and they identified Him as the Father of Jesus. Although Jewish monotheism led a few converts to deny the divinity of Jesus, the New Testament, which contains the faith taught by the Apostles, speaks of the Father, the Son, and the Holy Spirit, and presents them as distinct, as persons, and as divine. Instead of following these themes through Scripture, let us go to the documents of Tradition and see how the Church has manifested her faith in the Trinitarian doctrine as of Apostolic origin and how consistently she has clung to it, clarifying her teaching as occasion required.

The belief of the infant Church in the Triune God is discernible not only from the New Testament but also from the ceremonies of baptism, from symbols of the faith, from public prayers, from accounts of the death of various martyrs, from the writings of the Fathers. The early heresy in this field was monarchianism which held that there is only one person in God. It had these variations: (a)

---

* Nature and essence are only different aspects of the same fundamental reality. Essence is the principle of being in a thing while nature is its principle of activity. See below, p. 39, where Fourth Lateran Council identifies essence and nature.

Jesus is God, but He is the Father who became man and died; (*b*)
Jesus is a man who was given divine powers at the baptism in the
Jordan and was adopted by God; (*c*) according to Sabellius, the
Father, the Son, and the Holy Spirit are merely three aspects or
roles of the one God. The first major doctrinal crisis, however, came
to a head in the fourth century with the heresy which held that the
Son and the Holy Spirit are distinct persons but less than God. Today
we call this subordinationism. Arius began the trouble by teaching
that, although Jesus is the Logos or Word of God, He is only a
creature adopted by God. When this teaching threatened to tear
the Church apart, the first Ecumenical Council met at Nicea (A.D.
325) and proclaimed: "We believe in one only God, the Father,
Almighty, maker of things visible and invisible; and in one Lord,
Jesus Christ, the Son of God, the sole-begotten of the Father, that is
to say of the Father's substance; begotten not made, consubstantial
with the Father."[27] The Arians seized upon the word *consubstantial,*
and said it did not mean "of the same substance" but merely "like"
the Father. Some applied this doctrine of subordination to the Holy
Spirit. The whole world became inflamed with theological controversy, and world politics seemed to turn upon acceptance or rejection
of a few Greek letters. The bishops met again at Constantinople
(A.D. 381), renewed the definition of Nicea, and asserted the divinity
of the Holy Spirit. The Council of Ephesus (A.D. 431) and the Council of Chalcedon (A.D. 451) reaffirmed the divinity of Jesus. The
Trinitarian doctrine, proclaimed by the first four Councils, is admirably summarized in the Athanasian symbol: "This is the Catholic
faith that, without confusing the Persons or separating their substance, we adore one God in a Trinity and a Trinity in a unity. The
Person of the Father is distinct, the Person of the Son is distinct, the
Person of the Holy Spirit is distinct; but to the Father, the Son,
and the Holy Spirit there belongs one Godhead, equal glory and
coeternal majesty."[28] The tendency of heresy afterward was to affirm
the three Persons but to deny their true unity. Thus the Monophysites
of the sixth century, some Nominalists of the twelfth century, and

---

[27] *Den.* 54 (*TCT,* 2).
[28] *Den.* 39 (*TCT,* 6).

Abbot Joachim of the thirteenth century thought that the Father, the Son, and the Holy Spirit were alike in their Godhead as three men are alike in their human nature. Hence the Fourth Council of the Lateran (A.D. 1215) declared: "We firmly believe . . . that One alone is the true God . . . the Father, and the Son, and the Holy Spirit: three Persons indeed but one essence, substance or nature which is wholly simple."[29] For the benefit of the Eastern Churches seeking reunion with the Church, the Council of Florence drew up this mature statement of Trinitarian doctrine: "The Holy Roman Church . . . believes, professes and preaches the one true God, almighty, unchangeable and eternal, the Father, and the Son and the Holy Spirit, one in essence, three in persons: the Father is unbegotten, the Son is begotten of the Father, the Holy Spirit proceeds from the Father and the Son. The Father is not the Son or the Holy Spirit; the Son is not the Father or the Holy Spirit; the Holy Spirit is not the Father or the Son: but the Father is only the Father, the Son is only the Son, and the Holy Spirit is only the Holy Spirit. The Father alone begot the Son from His own substance, the Son alone is begotten of the Father alone, the Holy Spirit alone proceeds from both the Father and the Son. These three persons are the one God, and there are not three gods: for belonging to the three there is one substance, one essence, one nature, one godhead, one immensity, one eternity, and [in them] all things are one save where the opposition of relation occurs.

"On account of this unity the Father is wholly in the Son, wholly in the Holy Spirit; the Son is wholly in the Father, wholly in the Holy Spirit; the Holy Spirit is wholly in the Father, wholly in the Son. No one precedes Another in eternity nor exceeds in magnitude nor excels in power. Truly eternal and without beginning is the fact that the Son exists from the Father; and also eternal and without beginning is the fact that the Holy Spirit is from the Father and the Son. Whatever the Father is or has, He has not from another but from Himself; and is the principle without principle. Whatever the Son is or has, He has from the Father, and is the principle from the principle. Whatever the Holy Spirit is or has, He has from the

---

[29] Fourth Lateran Council, *Den.* 428 (*TCT*, 335).

Father and the Son together. But the Father and the Son are not two principles of the Holy Spirit but one principle: just as the Father and the Son and the Holy Spirit are not three principles of the creature but one principle."[30]

To what extent can faith and reason explain the mystery?

In exploring the infinite Being of God, we come upon the unexplorable; and in the face of august mystery the best we can do is to make imperfect comparisons with our experience, and then show that reason is not upset by any contradiction.

To understand, therefore, what we may of the mystery, let us pursue three inquiries: (1) What is the origin of the Divine Persons? (2) How are they related to one another? (3) What do they do? Theology answers the first with the doctrine of (1) *the divine processions;* the second with the doctrine of (2) *the divine relations;* and the third with the doctrine of (3) *the divine missions.*

Procession, relation, and *mission* are technical terms, but to venture an explanation of the Trinity without technical terms is futile. It is just as impossible to write about theology without technical terms as it is to write about physics. Indeed the well-read layman should be familiar with the more important technical terms of theology; at least they are easier to grasp and remember than the new chemical and medical terms.

The Divine Processions

An ordinary way of explaining a thing is to begin by the telling of its origin. But can there be origin in the First Being who has no beginning? Origin and beginning are not the same. Even in The Eternal there is origin and upon a basis of different origins we base distinction of Persons.

To inquire into the origin of Divine Persons is to ask if God is fruitful. We see fecundity in the living things we know: many kernels spring from the blade of corn; men beget children. Is it true that in the Godhead one Divine Person produces another Divine Person? Theologians shy away from that word *produce;* it is too redolent of

---

[30] Council of Florence, *Den.* 703–704 (*TCT,* 311, 312).

caused production. The Church rather says: "The Father is from no
one; He is neither created nor begotten. The Son is from the Father
alone. He is neither made nor created but begotten. The Holy Spirit
is from the Father and the Son. He is neither made nor created nor
begotten; He proceeds."[31]

Procession is the word chosen by theology to express the origin
of a Divine Person from another Divine Person. It probably came
from the Latin Vulgate where Christ says: "Ego enim a Deo processi
— for from God I came forth."[32] Procession here has nothing to do
with local motion or any kind of change but simply denotes a vital
activity remaining within the Godhead and explaining the origin of a
Divine Person. In this respect it differs from mission which produces
an effect outside the Godhead. Procession involves (1) a Person of
origin — a divine principle — who communicates the divine nature
to (2) another who exists by communication of this nature. This
Person proceeds from His principle without any dependence on His
part or any superiority on the part of the Person of origin. The Person proceeding does not come into being nor is He a caused effect,
as Arius thought, but simply that within the divine nature in which
the originating activity terminates, for example, the Son terminates
the knowledge which the Father has of Himself. In human origins,
both nature and person are produced, the produced nature is only
similar to the nature of origin, and the terms of the originating
activity are completely distinct. In the Godhead, the nature is not
produced but communicated, the nature of the Person of origin and
of the Person proceeding are exactly the same, and the terms of the
originating activity are only relatively distinct.

After considering the self-subsisting nature of God, it is easy
enough to conceive of the Father as having no origin. "Whatever the
Father is or has, He has not from another but from Himself; and is
the principle without principle." But it is not easy to conceive of a
divine origin. All our experiences of origin involve a coming into existence, a before and after, dependence on an originating principle, and

---

[31] The Athanasian Creed, *Den.* 39 (*TCT,* 6).
[32] Jn. 8:42. This text does not directly refer to the eternal procession of the
Son but to His temporal mission.

production of a caused effect which had no previous existence. The clue to our understanding of a divine origin is that it is an eternal communication. It involves no coming into existence, it denies beginning, dependence, and caused effect, and simply asserts that one Person is *from* another through communication of the divine nature.

It is an article of faith, repeatedly defined, that two Divine Persons proceed. Hence there are two divine origins and two divine processions. One is intellectual by which the Son proceeds from the Father; and the other is of the will by which the Holy Spirit proceeds from the Father and the Son.

The intellectual procession

Plants and animals produce offspring which are exterior to, and wholly distinct from, the parent stock. This is a vital but material production. When the intellect acts, there is a spiritual production, the idea, which is the resemblance of the thing known existing within the knower. As production becomes more perfect, the thing produced is necessarily vital and immaterial and is more interior to, and more like, the producing principle. In God, then, ought not "production" be wholly immaterial and perfect, a "result" which is completely interior to, and identical with, that from which it proceeds? In God does not a Father beget a Son, who is His perfect image, who is of the identical substance of the Father, and who yet abides as a distinct Person in the Godhead?

In the Bible a Divine Person constantly calls God "My Father." He says that He proceeds from God, that He has everything from the Father, that He knows all that the Father knows. This Divine Person is also called the Son, the Only-begotten, the Word, Divine Wisdom. Furthermore, in God there must be a First Person, rightly so called because He has no origin, and this Person must know. From all this we gather that the First Person is also rightly called the Father because a Second Person proceeds from Him by a real generation which is intellectual.

In God there is a real Father and a real Son because by the act of infinite knowledge whereby the First Person knows His own divine nature, the divine idea or Word is conceived. In the Godhead there must be real intellection and this intellection mysteriously originates the word. Now the conception of this word is the generation of a Son because Scripture identifies the Word as "the only-begotten of the Father."[33] The Word proceeds from the Father as from a living principle because "as the Father has life in himself, even so he has given to the Son also to have life in himself."[34] The Word proceeds that He may express the perfect likeness of the Father; for "He is the image of the invisible God."[35] Now the Divine Word is not like the word of human thought. Our ideas come and go; they are not us. In God the Word is substantial; it is the very substance of the Father. For "the Son received without diminution the substance of the Father and thus the Father and the Son have the same substance."[36] Finally, between the Father and the Son there is perfect interiority, for the Father is in the Son and the Son is in the Father. The Fathers of the Church emphasize the intellectual character of the generation of the Son, when they call Him the Splendor of Unbegotten Light, the Image of the Father, God of God and Light of Lights, Divine Wisdom. There is only one Divine Word, for Scripture and the Councils call Him "the Only-begotten of the Father."

The procession of love

Love, as we know it, is that psychic effect wrought in us by a person whereby that person becomes desirable to us. This effect consists in the approval of, the complacence in, the loved one, and this becomes the source of the desire by which we seek our loved one. The true lover wants union with his beloved through the gift of self, and when he achieves it, he rejoices in the union effected. All our emotions and all our human dynamism basically stem from love. Love, stripped of change, motion, or defect, exists in the Godhead and explains the second procession.

St. Thomas says: "Procession exists in God only according to an action which does not tend to anything external but remains in the agent itself. Such action in an intellectual nature is that of intellect and will. The procession of the Word is by way of an intellectual

---

[33] Jn. 1:14.   [35] Col. 1:15.
[34] Jn. 5:26.   [36] Fourth Lateran Council, *Den.* 432 (*TCT,* 307).

operation. The operation of the will within ourselves involves another procession, that of love, whereby the object loved is in the lover; as, by the conception of the word, the object spoken or understood is in the intelligent agent. Hence besides the procession of the Word in God, there exists in Him another procession of love."[37] Just as a mental image of the thing known is produced in us when we think, so when we love an affection or impulse toward the beloved is made in us. This impulse is the attraction of the loved one, his spiritual force at work within us. Indeed, as St. Thomas says, it is himself within us drawing us to him. In the Godhead, the mental image is the Word, and the affection or impulse is the Holy Spirit.

In God there must be love and love of God. Hence the Father and the Son eternally love the divine substance in each other; that is, their knowing the divine substance evokes from them an affection or impulse toward it. In us, love comes and goes; it is not us. In God, however, this affection is a Third Person because the love which the Father and the Son breathe or "spirate" is not transient or accidental but wholly substantial. It is God, the divine substance breathed, spirated, loved, given by the Father and the Son.

This Divine Person, the fruit of the love and the very love of Father and Son, is called Spirit, Love, Gift, Life. His most proper name is Spirit. The original name of "spirit" is wind, breath, motion. Love impells the lover to the beloved. They who love breathe their love. Hence the medieval Scholastics said that the Spirit is God in a sigh of love. Love is a divine name in two senses. In one sense love is the act of the divine will common to all three Persons, as St. John says: "God is love."[38] Here it is the *personal* love which proceeds from the Father and the Son and is the result of their mutual attraction and desire. This is the sense in which the liturgy calls the Third Person "living fount, fire, and Love." He is Gift because lovers give; the gift of self is the peak of loving. The Father gives Him to the Son and the Son gives Him to the Father, and in time God gives Him to man so that He is "Altissimi donum Dei," "Gift of God Most High." While life does not signify the Person as do the other

---

[37] *Sum. Theol.* I, 27, 3.
[38] 1 Jn. 4:16.

names, yet love is the source of a person's dynamism of which life is the highest expression, and the Holy Spirit is the principle of supernatural life in us. The creed calls Him "Lord, the Life-giver." St. Augustine says: "The Holy Spirit is not the Spirit of the Father alone . . . but of the Father and the Son. . . . *He is their common life.* . . . It was therefore their will to give us communion with one another and with themselves through that which is common to them both; to gather us together in one by this Gift which both have in common, namely, by the Holy Spirit, who is God and the Gift of God."[39]

Unfortunately some of the Greeks say that the Holy Spirit proceeds from the Father alone. While Scripture does not say in explicit words that the Holy Spirit proceeds from the Son as it says the Son proceeds from the Father, nevertheless the teaching of the Church has a sound Scriptural basis. The Holy Spirit is called the Spirit of Jesus, the Spirit of the Son. This means He is breathed or spirated by the Son. The Holy Spirit receives from the Son, but the only thing He could receive is the divine nature. Jesus tells the Apostles He will send them the Holy Spirit, but the Son could not send the Holy Spirit upon a temporal mission unless the Holy Spirit eternally proceeded from Him. For, since the Holy Spirit is God, the divine will concerning a temporal mission could not be intimated to Him unless the divine substance be eternally communicated to Him. Finally, the Second Council of Lyons says: "the Holy Spirit eternally proceeds from the Father and the Son . . . as from one principle . . . and by one spiration."[40]

It is an article of faith that the Holy Spirit is not generated; He "proceeds." The generative capacity of the divine nature is completed by the generation of an infinite Son.

Since procession remains within the Godhead, each Person is in the other. The Word abides in the bosom of the Father. "He who sees me sees also the Father. . . . Do you believe that I am in the Father and the Father in me?"[41] What here is asserted of the

---

[39] *Sermo* LXXI, 12, 18. *PL* 38, 454.
[40] *Den.* 460 (*TCT,* 308).
[41] Jn. 14:9, 11.

Father and the Son is, as we have seen, also asserted of the Holy Spirit by the Council of Florence. This is called by theology *circumincession* or the mutual indwelling of the Divine Persons. You cannot know or name one without implying the others, for they live in a mutually immanent coexistence. Since the essence of one is the essence of the others, there is a mysterious impenetration of one by the others.

Since the distinct Persons are one in nature and are in one another, it follows, first, that although there are three who are eternal, omnipotent, and infinite, yet there is only one eternal, omnipotent, and infinite God. So the Church says: "While thus the Father is God, the Son is God, the Holy Spirit is God, yet there are not three gods but one God."[42] Second, although there is a difference of origin among the three Persons, no one is superior or inferior to another. The symbol says: "In this Trinity nothing is before or after, nothing greater or less; but all three persons are mutually coeternal and coequal."[43] In the preface of the ordinary Sunday Mass the Church sings beautifully and succinctly: "In the profession of the true and everlasting Deity there is adored distinction in persons, unity in essence, and equality in majesty." Third, in all effects to be produced outside the Godhead, the three Persons act as one undivided principle. The Council says: "The Father and the Son and the Holy Spirit are not three principles of the creature but one principle."[44]

The relations in the Trinity

From the two processions arise the relationships in which theology finds its ultimate explanation for the distinctiveness of the three Persons. For when we ask what makes the Father to be the Father and not the Son or the Holy Spirit, and so of the other Persons, theology answers, Each Person is that Person on account of a real subsistent relation.

A relation is that which makes something bespeak a connection with something else. Relative is opposed to absolute, that which does

---

[42] *Den.* 39 (*TCT,* 6).
[43] *Den. ibid.*
[44] Council of Florence, *Den.* 704 (*TCT,* 312).

not bespoken a connection with another, or at least prescinds from it. A relation is real when it exists independently of thought. It is logical when it exists solely in the thinker's mind.

In God there are these relationships. The Father bears the Son the relationship of (1) Paternity and the Son bears the Father the relationship of (2) Sonship. The Father and the Son bear to the Holy Spirit the relationship of (3) Spiration and the Holy Spirit bears them the relation of (4) Procession.

These divine relations are real because the objects related are not mental fictions. There is a real Father, a real Son, a real Holy Spirit. Furthermore, these relations are based on the real fact of the divine intellection and the divine volition. Otherwise Sabellius would have been right: the Father, the Son, and the Holy Spirit are merely God under the guise of creator, redeemer, and sanctifier.

These relations are subsistent. In creatures all relations are accidental in the sense that they are not the nature of the being. Neither the nature of a man nor his person is changed by his becoming a father. Nor is being a son part of a man's essence; for it is conceivable that he come into existence in some other way than by the activity of parents. In God it is different. On account of His simplicity all His relations are identified with His nature. Whatever is in God is God. Hence these relations are subsistent. They are the divine substance.

If there are four real subsistent relationships, why is there not a Four-some in God? The answer is that only three of these relations are distinct. The Council of Florence furnishes the clue: "All is one in God save where the opposition of relation occurs."[45] Opposition is difference of origin and hence denial of identity. Of the four relationships only three manifest opposition of origin, for the spiration of the Father and the Son are not opposed to their Paternity and Sonship. Hence there are only three mutually distinct relations in the Trinity: Paternity, Sonship, and Procession.

These three relations make the Father, the Son, and the Holy Spirit to be three distinct Persons. To be a person one must be an individual intelligent substance. That the Three are intelligent and

---

[45] *Den.* 703 (*TCT*, 311).

substantial is clear. What makes them individual? Being an individual means not only that one is distinct from others but also incommunicable. The characteristic note of person is to be wholly oneself, so master of self that one is not given over to be possessed by another. When the Father communicates the divine nature to the Son, He gives Him everything he has except His Paternity. "All things that are the Father's, except His being the Father, the Father gave to His only-begotten Son in begetting Him."[46] If He gave that to the Son, He and the Son would be the same and the Son would be capable of generating His Son. When the Father and the Son communicate the divine nature to the Holy Spirit, they give all they have except Paternity, Sonship, and their common Spiration. These are incommunicable; otherwise the Holy Spirit could generate a Son or spirate another Person. That the Holy Spirit proceeds from the Father and the Son is communicated to no one; for by the generation of a Son and the spiration of the Spirit the divine production is complete. Therefore, what makes the Father a Person distinct from the Son is His Paternity. What makes Him distinct from the Holy Spirit is His Spiration. What makes the Son distinct from the Father is His Sonship. What makes Him distinct from the Holy Spirit is His Spiration. What makes the Holy Spirit distinct from the Father and the Son is His Procession.

If we say that the Father is the divine nature endowed with Paternity, the Son the divine nature endowed with Sonship, and the Holy Spirit the divine nature endowed with Procession, we must remember that Paternity, Sonship, and Procession are relative, not absolute things. They are in the divine nature, and are real, but they add nothing absolute to it. Indeed, as the simplicity of God requires, they are identified with it. But if the Paternity is the one divine nature and the Sonship is also the divine nature, why is not the Father the Son? The reason is that the Father and Son are one in that which is absolute, the divine nature, but they are not one in that which is relative, personality. But how can three distinct Persons be identically one in nature? Only God can answer that. We can but say: "Hardly do we guess aright at things that are upon the earth: and with labor

---

[46] Council of Florence, *Den.* 691.

do we find the things that are before us. But the things that are in
heaven, who shall search out?"[47]

The Divine Missions

What do the Three Persons do? Within the Trinity there is the
immanent activity of intellect and will. On account of the first, the
Father begets the Son and the Son proceeds from the Father. On
account of the second, the Father and the Son spirate the Holy Spirit,
and He proceeds from Them. But let us not imagine these as past
activities; think of them as eternal so that the Father eternally begets
the Son, the Son is eternally begotten, and the Holy Spirit eternally
proceeds. Even so, what a colorless picture of the intimate life of God!

How the Blessed Trinity, acting as one, has a causal influence
in every created effect is explained in the next chapter.

To share in the intimate life of the Trinity is the goal of mankind.
Now from the divine processions we derive the divine missions, a
most consoling doctrine because it is the dogmatic basis of our
redemption and sanctification.

A mission is the sending of a Divine Person by Another to do
something which promotes the sanctification of man. Mission has
nothing to do with local motion. It is a temporal procession and
means that a Person, who eternally proceeds, acquires in time a
new way of being present to man so that man possesses and enjoys
Him. It presupposes eternal procession and is a fuller manifestation
of the Trinity to man. Since the Father does not proceed He cannot
be sent; He gives Himself. The Son is sent by the Father and the
Holy Spirit is sent by the Father and the Son.

There are two kinds of mission. The first is invisible and takes
place only when sanctifying grace is given to the soul. God, who is
present to all things by His essence, power, and knowledge, acquires
by grace a new presence in the sanctified soul; that is, God *as He is*
dwells there as knowable and lovable. "If anyone love me, he will
keep my word, and my Father will love him, and we will come to
him and make our abode with him."[48] Through sanctifying grace
the Father comes to the soul, the Son is sent as the author of sanctifi-

---

[47] Wisd. 9:16.   [48] Jn. 14:23.

cation, and the Holy Spirit is sent as the divine Gift. The three Divine Persons dwell in the soul as in God's own temple. "Do you not know that you are the temple of God and that the Spirit of God dwells in you?"[49] A living union is effected between the soul and the Divine Persons so that the life of God as He is is poured into it. The soul now can imitate and continue that life within itself. This is the beginning in man of that eternal life which will be made perfect in the beatific vision.

The invisible mission always occurs when grace is given to a soul. This was true even in the Old Law. There occurred an invisible mission to the human soul of Christ at His conception but no subsequent one, for He was conceived full of grace. St. Thomas says that the just receive other invisible missions when very unusual graces are granted, for example, when one is moved to undergo martyrdom, to renounce all his possessions, to undertake some great work.

The second kind of mission is visible and it exists for the sake of the first. The first and most memorable mission occurred at the Incarnation when the Word was made flesh and dwelt among us. The outstanding sendings of the Holy Spirit were at the baptism of Christ in the Jordan, when He appeared in the form of a dove, and at Pentecost, when He appeared to the Apostles in the form of fiery tongues. He is also said to have been sent to Christ at the Transfiguration under the form of a bright cloud and to the Apostles on Easter night when they received the power to forgive sins. The Holy Spirit is never substantially united to any creature, but is represented in some extraordinary way by a visible sign of His presence. St. Thomas says: "The mission of the Holy Spirit was not accorded to the fathers of the Old Law because the visible mission of the Son was to be accomplished before that of the Holy Spirit; since the Holy Spirit manifests the Son as the Son manifests the Father."[50]

The consequences to us of the mystery

God has revealed this ineffable mystery because our destiny is to share in the life and happiness of the three Divine Persons. The

---

[49] 1 Cor. 3:16.   [50] *Sum. Theol.* I, 43, 7, ad 6.

more we penetrate the mystery of the Trinity, the better we prepare ourselves for happiness in heaven.

We should not, however, expect theology to explain away mysteries. After the best explanation the mystery of the Blessed Trinity remains. Theology establishes the existence of the mystery, then shows that, if it is properly set forth, it neither violates reason nor denies any attribute of God. It does not say that three natures are one or that one Person is three, but, holding that in God nature is one and absolute while Person is three and relative, it teaches that the Three Persons have one identical nature. How this can be we shall never know in this life. Even in the beatific vision, while we shall know the how and the why of the mystery, we shall never exhaustively comprehend it.

The greatest care should be exercised in explaining the Trinity. "For," says St. Thomas, "when anyone in the endeavor to prove the faith adduces reasons which are not cogent, he falls under the ridicule of unbelievers; since they suppose we stand upon such grounds and believe for such reasons."[51] Our words also must be carefully selected. Human language is at a loss in dealing with the infinite and we are compelled to use words like *produce, origin, procession.* When we use them, we must keep in mind that no connotation of defect like change, beginning, or dependence attaches to them. In the choice of adjectives and substantives those should be avoided which would either multiply the nature or deny the distinction of Persons. How carefully does the Athanasian symbol say: "The Father is almighty, the Son is almighty, the Holy Spirit is almighty: and yet there are not three almighty beings but One Almighty."[52] The Fourth Lateran Council warns us not to say that it is the divine substance which generates or is begotten or proceeds, "but it is the Father who generates, the Son who is begotten, and the Holy Spirit who proceeds: and thus is distinction in Persons and unity of nature preserved."[53] Finally, theologians have a manner of speaking about the Divine Persons which is called *appropriation.* While it is always the entire

---

[51] *Sum. Theol.* I, 32, 1.
[52] *Den.* 39 (*TCT*, 6).
[53] *Den.* 432 (*TCT*, 307).

Trinity which produces all divine effects outside the Godhead, there is a tendency on our part to attribute certain of these effects to one Person rather than another because this effect seems better to fit the Person's characteristics. Thus, since the Father is the principle without principle, we appropriate to Him eternity and the work of creation. Since the Son proceeds through the act of intellect, we appropriate to Him the works of wisdom, order, restoration. Since the Holy Spirit is Personal Love, we appropriate to Him goodness, mercy, charity, and the sanctification of man.

CHAPTER THREE

GOD THE CREATOR
AND PRESERVER

"Creator of heaven and earth"

AFTER treating of God as He is, theology turns to whatever is not God and asks what relation it has to God. Men have always wondered about the world and its people, asking, Where did it all come from? It is irrational to reply that one merely accepts a universe for which there is no explanation. Some have thought that everything is God or that the universe is the unfolding of the Divine Mind or Will into which everything will be reabsorbed. But the Vatican Council assures us that the world is utterly distinct from God.

The universe began, not by accident as some materialists claim, but as an idea in the mind of God where exist images of all the possible ways in which His infinite perfections can be imitated. Out of all possible worlds God chose one for actual existence. He implements His choice by simply willing it and things begin to exist where hitherto nothing had existed. The divine action imparting being into the first things in the universe is creation.

A. *God the Creator*

The fact of creation is recorded in the first line of Holy Writ. How apposite that the written word of God should begin with so noble a remark as "In the beginning God created heaven and earth"?[1] The universe is His. For "thine are the heavens and thine is the earth: the world and the fulness thereof thou has founded."[2] Creation by God is a major theme running through the Old and New Testaments. "For from him and through him and unto him are all things."[3] The Vatican Council says: "If anyone shall not profess that the

---

[1] Gen. 1:1.   [2] Ps. 88:12.   [3] Rom. 11:36.

53

universe and all things contained therein, both spiritual and material, were produced in their total substance from nothing by God . . . let him be anathema."[4]

To create is to make something totally out of nothing: new being arises from no pre-existent material. We can change the shape of materials already existing but only God can create. If something begins to be where before there was nothing, an omnipotent cause is required to explain it. For to bridge the gap between nothingness and something the agent must have all possible power. Since the universe once was nothing, it is accounted for only by the fact that it was brought out of nothing by God, the First Cause of all things. If, however, one were to say that there always was *uncreated* stuff, then God would not be the First Cause but a mere organizer. Thus, according to an ancient Greek view, originally there was Chaos, an indescribable mess, unformed matter agitated without rhyme or reason by obscure forces until divinity got round to putting order into the disorder. But God has to be the First Cause of all things which do not have being of themselves, otherwise their existence cannot be explained. For if their existence is not from themselves, and assuredly it is not, then they could have got it only from the Source of all being.

There was once a theory that there were two creators: one, the good God who made spiritual things; the other, an infinite principle of evil who made corporeal things. But God alone is the Creator, for the existence of two infinite beings is absurd. Isaias says: "I am the Lord, that make all things, that alone stretch out the heavens, that establish the earth, and there is none with me."[5] The Manichees imagined that under the one God good angels made the invisible world and bad angels made the visible world. But in making things the best the creature can do is give a new form to things already existent. The angels could not be even instrumental causes in creation. For instruments operate by disposing material to receive the imprint of the principal cause, but in creation no material pre-exists in which an instrument can work.

---

[4] *Den.* 1805. (*TCT*, 362).
[5] Isa. 44:24.

When did God create? At the beginning of time; that is, creation marks the beginning of time. Before God created there was neither change nor motion nor time; time is merely the measure of succession and change. Christ says there was no eternal creation: "Now do thou, Father, glorify me with thyself, with the glory that I had with thee before the world existed."[6] Revelation gives no information as to how long ago the first creation took place.

How did God create? 1. *Freely,* for the Vatican Council condemns anyone who "shall say that He did not create [the universe] by a will free from all necessity but was impelled to create by the same necessity by which He loves Himself."[7] The infinite goodness of God does not compel Him to share Himself with other things because, in the divine processions, wherein the nature of God is communicated to the Son and the Holy Spirit, God acts in accord with all the demands of infinite goodness. There could have been no other communication of good. For "whatsoever the Lord pleased he hath done, in heaven, in earth, in the sea, and in all the deeps."[8] Nor was God compelled to create *this* world on the supposition that God's creation must be the best possible. This is not the best possible world but it is best suited to God's actual designs.

2. *Wisely.* Wisdom was His counselor in the making of the world, for "thou hast made all things in wisdom."[9] God had a plan in creation which is worthy of Himself and that plan will be fulfilled with consummate skill.

Why did God create? The Vatican Council says "the universe was created for the glory of God."[10] Let us not imagine that God was motivated to create by the desire of acquiring glory from the universe. For the Council says that God acted "not to increase His happiness, not to acquire but to manifest His perfections by the good things He bestows on creatures."[11] God needs nothing and can get nothing from creatures; He can only give to them. Since God cannot be influenced by cause, His purpose in creating is not a final cause; it is merely a reason which explains His creative act. Since this reason has to be worthy of God, the Wise Man says: "The Lord made

---

6 Jn. 17:5.   8 Ps. 134:6.   10 *Den.* 1805 (*TCT,* 362).
7 *Den.* 1805 (*TCT,* 362).   9 Ps. 103:24.   11 *Den.* 1783 (*TCT,* 356).

all things for himself."[12] This is no assertion of egoism but the
affirmation of what must be. "I am the Alpha and the Omega . . .
the beginning and the end!"[13]

To understand this teaching, we distinguish between the motive
moving God to create and the objective He aims at achieving through
creation. The motive is Himself, His boundless goodness and freedom.
Only God moves God to act. The objective is finite and consists in
the glory of God. Glory is the acknowledgment and praise which is
due to excellence. God has His own internal glory which is the praise
He has for Himself in the depth of His being. In the glory of God,
which is the end of creation, we find three things. First, are the good
things which God communicates. Second, once the good things are
given, they necessarily display something of the goodness and wisdom
of God. "The heavens shew forth the glory of God and the firma-
ment declareth the works of his hands."[14] This is a basic glory which
every creature, great or small, renders by its very existence. Third,
intelligent creatures must acknowledge their place before God and
voluntarily submit to Him. Eventually all of them will submit, willingly or unwillingly, and in this submission consists the formal glory
which is the final end result of the universe.

This end result is hard to describe. How much reality will God
communicate? That depends, first, upon the capacity or willingness
of the creature to receive, but ultimately upon the divine choice.
How much glory will intelligent beings freely render God? That
depends in part upon their co-operation, but ultimately upon God's
will to give grace. How much grace will God give? That depends
upon the nature of His ultimate designs, and what these are is His
secret. However, we can be sure of this: opportunity for free service
ends for all; those who have freely submitted will be forever subject
to Him in love and will possess Him as He is; those who refused
free submission will have no capacity to receive Him and will be
subject in punishment. In either event God receives the submission
of the intelligent universe. St. Paul describes the realization of the
divine objective: "Then comes the end, when [Christ] delivers the
kingdom to God the Father, when he does away with all sovereignty,

---

[12] Prov. 16:4.   [13] Apoc. 22:13.   [14] Ps. 18:2.

authority and power. . . . And when all things are made subject to [Christ], then the Son himself will also be made subject to him who subjected all things to him, that God may be all in all."[15]

What did God create? It is impossible that God should do evil, that is, morally bad, works. Nor is this the worst possible world. There are no creatures bad in themselves for "God saw all the things he had made and they were very good."[16] According to the Nicene Creed He made an invisible and visible world. The Fourth Lateran and Vatican Councils say: "He created the spiritual and corporeal creature."[17]

The angels

In innumerable places the Bible speaks of angels or spirits, but since the Bible is the story of God's dealings with men, angels figure in it only incidentally. Hence the data of revelation about them is fragmentary. Reason, endeavoring to fill in a complete picture, derives some certain conclusions from revelation, but often, especially when it extrapolates the laws of human psychology or seeks analogies with our supernatural history, it does not get beyond probability.

The Fourth Lateran Council has defined the existence of angels. Holy Writ speaks of intelligent substances, inferior to God and superior to man, and calls them angels. They are intelligent because they announce the mystery of the Incarnation and the birth of Christ, minister to Him in the desert and the garden, guard the original paradise, speak, offer advice. They are less than God because He created them and demands their praise and service. They are greater than men. The psalmist says that man is made a little less than the angels. St. Peter attributes to them greater might. St. Paul calls them thrones, dominations, principalities, powers.

It is at least certain that angels are pure spirits and not subject to the limitations of matter. St. Thomas soundly argues that the beauty and order of the universe demand that God create spiritual substances which resemble Him more closely than does anything in

---

[15] 1 Cor. 15:24–28.
[16] Gen. 1:31.
[17] *Den.* 428, 1783 (*TCT*, 306, 356).

58   DOGMA FOR THE LAYMAN

the visible universe. It was, however, anciently thought by some that angels, especially bad angels, had subtle rarefied bodies. Being spiritual, angels are naturally immortal. Their knowledge, which most likely is infused, far surpasses ours. We must not, however, exaggerate the extent of angelic knowledge; they do not naturally know the secrets of hearts, the mysteries of grace, or the future which depends on free choice. In comparison with man's, their power is prodigious. It is St. Thomas' opinion that no individual man has all the perfection of the human species, that it takes all men to exhaust the possibilities of the human species, but that each angel is a species completing in himself all the possibilities of that species. It is certain that all angels are not of equal splendor, and it is likely that they are distributed among nine choirs. They are exceedingly numerous. The Prophet says: "Thousands of thousands ministered to him and ten thousand times a hundred thousand stood before him."[18]

As for their supernatural history, it is certain that they were not created in heaven, that is, in possession of the beatific vision. This was their destiny, but they had to pass a moral test before they got it. They were all adorned with sanctifying grace which in them too is a supernatural gift. The Fourth Lateran Council has defined that some of them sinned. St. Thomas explains that in the first act after their creation the angels chose good or evil, and such is the fixity of their nature the choice was irrevocable. Those who chose good were immediately confirmed in grace, and they now "behold the face of my Father"[19] and dwell in the heavenly Jerusalem. The bad angels fell through the influence of Lucifer, the most exalted of them all, and St. Thomas opines his sin was pride. Not that he wished to be God Himself — an impossible wish — but he desired to attain his happiness solely by his own powers. It is certain that very many sinned. It is of faith that the bad angels were cast into hell. Such is the definition of the Fourth Lateran Council and the testimony of Holy Writ. Christ says that reprobate men will go into the eternal fire which was prepared for the devil and his angels. St. Peter says

[18] Dan. 7:10.
[19] Mt. 18:10.

God did not spare the sinful angels but cast them into hell to be kept in custody until judgment.

What do the angels do? The permanent function of the good angels is the praise and service of God. The psalmist often calls upon the angels to praise God. The prophet "saw the Lord sitting upon a throne high and elevated; and his train filled the temple. Upon it stood the seraphims. . . . And they cried one to another, and said: Holy, holy, holy, the Lord God of hosts, all the earth is full of his glory."[20] A secondary function is to help in man's salvation. Holy Writ gives countless instances where angels benignly interfere in human affairs to promote the purposes of the Incarnation. For example, angels deliver the law at Mt. Sinai, bring revelations to prophets, adore the Son of God upon His entry into the world, protect the Holy Family, comfort Christ in His Passion and have a part in His resurrection and ascension. It is of faith that there are guardian angels who watch over men during their probation. "For he has given his angels charge over thee; to keep thee in all thy ways."[21] St. Peter calls them ministering spirits who are sent for the sake of those who shall inherit salvation. It is certain that every member of the true faith has a particular angel assigned to watch over him until he dies. It is likely that all men have a guardian angel.

While Satan has succeeded in having himself forgotten by the majority of modern men, yet it is of faith that there is a personal devil, the prince of demons, whose purpose is the destruction of mankind. Scripture depicts him as the father of lies, a murderer from the beginning, through whom sin entered the world. The Fourth Lateran Council has defined that Adam fell through his suggestion. Jesus came to destroy his power as prince of this world, a power which was manifest in divine worship accorded to demons, lack of faith in the one true God, demonic possession of the bodies of some men. Though Jesus triumphed on the cross and passed judgment on the prince of this world, the struggle continues. "For our wrestling is . . . against the Principalities and the Powers, against the world-rulers of this darkness, against the spiritual forces of wickedness on

[20] Isa. 6:3.
[21] Ps. 90:11.

high."[22] Since "he who commits sin is of the devil,"[23] denial of this slavery to Satan is denial of the need of salvation. Demons lure men to sin, though not all temptations are of diabolic origin. The Church is keenly aware of this struggle. She exorcises the person she baptizes, and blesses water, candles, and oil for the putting of demons to flight. She warns us in the office of Compline: Brethren, be sober and watch for your adversary the devil goes about like a roaring lion seeking whom he may devour. There will come a time when he will seem to triumph in the great persecutions of the Church and the rise of Antichrist, but at the end Satan and his angels will be cast into the lake of fire. Truly is Satan the Accursed One for whom there is no possibility of turning from evil, of ceasing to hate God. Here is the mystery of iniquity! But God uses sin and even Satan for the furthering of His designs from the scope of which absolutely nothing escapes.

The visible creation

Although the Church has not officially settled the matter, the indications are that the material creation occurred when the angels were created. This does not mean, however, that man appeared with the first material things. A great problem is the meaning of the first three chapters of Genesis. Is the creation story to be taken literally, allegorically, or symbolically? The Church steers a middle course between the extremes of Fundamentalism, which interprets with absolute literalism, and Modernism, which calls the story a fable.

In seeking the meaning of these chapters let us distinguish between the fact of divine creation and its manner. The Church has traditionally interpreted the story to mean that God created all things and is at least mediate Author of the various kinds of things there enumerated. Hence the story is not fable but history, told, however, in a popular manner accommodated to the thought patterns of those for whom it was first written. As regards the manner and order in which God created, the meaning of each item of the account, there is no traditional interpretation. St. Thomas remarks: "In discussing questions of this kind two rules are to be followed. . . . The first is to

---

[22] Eph. 6:12.   [23] 1 Jn. 3:8.

hold the truth of Scripture unwaveringly. The second is that since Holy Writ can be explained in a multiplicity of senses, one should adhere to a particular sense only in such a way that he is prepared to abandon it, if it be proved with certainty to be false; lest Holy Writ be exposed to the ridicule of unbelievers."[24] We must hold unwaveringly that these chapters tell the truth. What truth? Tradition says — the fact of creation by God.

How creation came about is an open question. Theology neither fears nor disdains science. The Vatican Council teaches that no conflict can exist between revelation and scientific truth. If conflict should appear, either revelation has been misunderstood, or that is proposed as science which is not. What about evolution? The Church has condemned materialistic evolution which says that man, body and soul, was evolved from uncreated matter. This is the evolution which has been the bogey man of some peoples' faith, but there are other theories of evolution which admit a Creator. The possibility of a God-guided evolution was admitted by St. Augustine and St. Thomas. Evolution is a question of fact. Has the universe come into its present state because the multitudinous species of things have evolved from one or a few simple species? The theory of Aristotle that there is no crossing over from one physical species to another has been pretty well discarded. Today most people would grant that after the first creation matter must have gone through progressive stages of development before it was capable of supporting a rational soul.

Theology is interested in evolution only as it attempts to explain the origins of man. The Church says that the first man was made a human being by the direct immediate action of God, action which affected his soul and body. God immediately created his soul as He creates the souls of all men. What about the origin of his body? Did God use inorganic matter or the living, pre-existing product of an ascending evolution? While science confidently asserts an unbroken continuity of life from the lowest to the highest forms, Pius XII[25] says that science has not as yet established this position with certainty. The first man could not have been the son of a brute;

[24] *Sum. Theol.*, I, 68, 1.
[25] *Humani Generis*, No. 36 (N.C.W.C. trans.).

for the brute cannot produce a body capable of sustaining a spiritual soul. God could have used material prepared by evolution for the body of the first man, but this would not have been a human body until it had been reorganized and made fit for a human soul. Let the experts, says the Pontiff, examine this and similar questions concerning human origins, but they must always be prepared to accept the decision of the Church. While evolution is now respected as a sound working principle, one is not to imagine that it has been demonstrated as an immutable truth or that no problems of harmonizing science and theology remain.

As for the origin of the first woman, the account of Genesis has been interpreted by the majority of the Fathers literally. Some interpreters see an allegory in it; others, a vision of truth. That woman originated from man by God's special action is held as certain by very many. Besides the texts of Genesis, they appeal to "He created of him a helpmate like to himself"[26]; "woman is from man"[27]; and the decision of the Biblical Commission that the formation of the first woman from man is a fundamental truth of the Christian religion. Since, however, this last is not an irreformable statement, some modern exegetes say that a symbolic interpretation of the story is possible. The sacred writer may have been inculcating the lesson that woman is not the slave of man, that marriage is indissoluble, that Adam did not supply the material but was the pattern after which Eve was made.

It is certain that all men are descended from a single pair. All the Councils which deal with original sin — Carthage (A.D. 418), Orange (A.D. 529), Trent (A.D. 1546) — speak of *one* Adam. All scriptural references on the matter present us with one man and one woman.[28] Pius XII rejects polygenism, or the theory of multiple sets of ancestors of the human race, as incompatible with the oft-defined doctrine of original sin.

All men have the same nature and constitute the single species, man. It is of faith that every man is a composite of matter and a rational soul. The Fifth Council of Lateran says that every human

---

[26] Ecclus. 17:5.   [27] 1 Cor. 11:8.
[28] Gen. 1:27; 2:5; 2:22. Wisd. 10:1. Acts 17:26. 1 Cor. 15:45.

being has an individual soul. This soul, according to the Council of Vienne, is man's formal cause, that is, the internal active principle which makes him to be what he is. The human soul is immortal and endowed with free will. It does not pre-exist its union with a particular body. According to the theory of the transmigration of souls, a soul successively informs various animal and human bodies. This is false because each soul is created when it is infused into the body. On account of his powers of reason, man is the image of God. "Let us make man to our image and likeness."[29] All visible things, less than man, are only the footprints of God and exist for man's sake. God affirms man's pre-eminence in the primeval blessing: "Increase and multiply, and fill the earth, and subdue it, and rule over the fishes of the sea, and the fowls of the air, and all living creatures that move upon the earth."[30] The age of the human race is a scientific question upon which revelation does not enlighten us.

While man shares the destination of the universe to the glory of God, he has his own peculiar destiny to attain. Now the end of any nature is its state of perfect well-being, and the perfect state of man is the happiness arising from the full and enduring possession and love of God which accords with his nature. Man's natural possession of God is by perfect knowledge which is rational and discursive. Such would have been the actual destiny of man, but, the Council of Vatican says: "God out of His infinite goodness, ordained man unto a supernatural end which consists in such a share in the divine benefits as to completely surpass the grasp of man's intelligence."[31] Benedict XII calls this supernatural end the beatific vision — the clear, immediate, face-to-face sight and enjoyment of God as He is.

Consequently theology must repudiate the modern lay dogma that the supernatural cannot exist. The natural is that which is required for man to exist, to live well and attain the fullness of his natural endowments. The natural order of human existence would be the right arrangement of everything necessary for the attainment of man's faculties, the divine assistance required for these activities, the natural moral law. Man, however, has the power to receive gifts which are above his nature. The supernatural, then, is that which

29 Gen. 1:26.   30 Gen. 1:28.   31 Den. 1786 (TCT, 59).

exceeds the nature of man; it is required neither for man's existence nor the development and proper activity of his faculties nor the attainment of a natural destination. It is not opposed to the natural; it presupposes and perfects it. So the supernatural order is the reasoned arrangement of everything required for man's attainment of a supernatural destiny. Chief among these things are the super- nature of sanctifying grace, divine revelation, the Church, the sacra- ments, actual grace, and divine positive law.

Man has always lived in a supernatural dispensation. The first man and woman, says the Council of Trent, were established in holiness and justice. This means (1) that God called them to the beatific vision. This, however, He was not to give them as an out- right gift but as an earned reward. To enable them to accomplish so exalted a destiny, God (2) gave them sanctifying grace, which is a share in His own nature and life. Such is the teaching of St. Paul who says that Christ restored what Adam had lost. Since Christ restored "the new man created according to God in justice and holiness of truth,"[32] such was the blessed state of the first man. The grace given the first man is a supernature, something to which he had no claim, as the Church has asserted against the Jansenists who said that Adam had a right to it. This supernature made our first parents live with God's own life as His adopted children, His heirs and living temples. Through this supernature they could exercise the activity which would win them the beatific vision. In addition to this essential grace God gave them other gifts to which they had no natural claim: *integrity,* which is the absence of concupiscence, the absolute subordination of sense appetites to reason and will; and *immortality,* immunity from bodily death. From these endowments resulted freedom from pain, a mental and bodily well-being, and the utmost felicity of social intercourse. This blessed state was the music of the spheres and the melody of the morning of creation when a virginal earth served man harmoniously, man was master of his soul and all his movements, and, resplendent with reason and grace, he fixed his total being on God. This blissful condition was original justice and God intended it to be the lot of all men.

---
[32] Eph. 4:24.

B. *God the Provider*

Having made the universe God does not leave it to its own devices as the Deists claim He did. For the tenuous being of the creature depends on God, not only that it may begin to be, but that it may continue to be, to act, to reach its due perfection. How does God manage His creation? His general care of all things is (1) His providence whereby He foresees and supplies the needs of the universe. The supply of these needs requires (2) that He maintain all things in existence, (3) that He enable creatures to act by acting with them, and (4) by His government of the world fulfill the decrees of His providence.

1. *Providence*

There is no such thing as fate, for nothing happens in the world by chance. Everything has been foreseen, and whatever happens takes place because God wills it or allows it. Everything has its place in the divine scheme, for the Vatican Council teaches: "All the things God has made He safeguards and governs by His providence."[33] Divine providence means that God, having established a general goal for all things and proper ends for all classes of being, likewise ordains the means by which these ends are to be attained by all individual things. Holy Writ is full of this idea: God makes the rain to fall and the grass to grow, He feeds the beasts and young crows, and not a sparrow falls without His nod. He has a special care of men. "The very hairs of your head are numbered . . . you are of more value than many sparrows."[34] He who made both great and small has equally care of all. As clay is in the potter's hand, so is man in the hand of Him who made him. Finally, God has a very special providence over the elect and allows nothing to prevent their death in the state of grace.

People argue against divine providence, first, that an efficient provider will exclude all evil from his charge and, since evils abound in the world, God does not seem to care. The case is different, answers St. Thomas, with a particular provider and with the universal

---

[33] *Den.* 1784 (*TCT,* 357). [34] Mt. 10:29–31.

provider. The first "excludes all defects from what is subject to his care as far as he can; whereas, one who provides universally allows some little defect to remain, lest the good of the whole be hindered."[35] The captain, who holds a tiny sector of a five-hundred mile battle line, may not allow the overwhelming of his company if he can prevent it; the general-in-chief may, for the sake of ultimate victory, allow the loss of a number of companies. So God, the universal provider, now allows seeming setbacks in order to secure His ultimate purposes. This is the lesson of the parable of the tares or weeds: the servants are to allow the tares and the wheat to grow to the harvest lest, in rooting up the tares, they harm the wheat.

But some people are emotionally disturbed by the problem of evil. They rail against personal calamities, the sufferings of the innocent, the prosperity of the wicked. They call this an irrational world in which there is so much senseless suffering. Now we have seen that the beauty and harmony of the universe demands certain physical evils which God wills not as ends but as means. However, human suffering is ultimately the result of sin. God cannot will sin. He may allow it if He is not compelled to stop it, and if His tolerance of it can be made to serve His ultimate purposes. God is not obliged to stop men's sins. He could have a sinless world by not creating free beings but what a loss to have a world in which there are no men and no moral excellence! He could refrain from creating those men who He foresees will be sinners, but He is not obliged to; otherwise His independence is limited and He is subordinate to ill will. Since He creates such people, He must know how to accomplish His purposes despite their sins. Hence God allows sin only that some greater good may come of it. Egyptian Joseph expressed this idea to his newly found brethren: "Can we resist the will of God? You thought evil against me: but God turned it into good, that he might exalt me . . . and might save many people."[36] From the catastrophe of original sin God draws the incomparable good of the Redeemer. The human race was a long time shut up in unbelief simply that God might have mercy on all. We may not know the greater good God

---

[35] *Sum. Theol.* I, 22, 2 ad 2.
[36] Gen. 50:19–20.

has in mind when He allows nations to fall from the faith; it is enough that God does.

But could not God obtain His glory and the free service of man without sin and punishment coming into the world? Undoubtedly. He could confirm every man in grace and lavish upon him stupendous graces. Why does He not? Obviously the grant of such grace does not fit in with God's over-all goal in the universe. We do not know the precise nature of that goal, but whatever it is, this world of sin and suffering is the divinely chosen means of attaining it. Even though he cannot dot all the i's and cross all the t's in this problem, the man of faith is satisfied with such a general answer. It is only at the Last Judgment that the divine plan will be clear, and then all will adore the wisdom of the Creator. Meantime men must trust God. For there will always be a certain mystery about iniquity. Sin is nothingness and St. Augustine remarks that "one cannot know what nothingness is."[37] Nor do we fully appreciate the worth of suffering; it is part of the folly of the cross. These obscurities are part of man's probation, of the darkness of his faith.

The special providence which God has toward men is manifest, first, in His sincere desire for the salvation of all men. God wishes no man to be lost; for the prophet says He does not desire the death but the conversion of the sinner. The will to save is even positive. "I urge," says St. Paul, "that supplications, prayers, intercessions and thanksgivings be made for all men. . . . This is good and agreeable in the sight of God our Savior, who wishes all men to be saved and come to the knowledge of the truth. For there is one God and one Mediator between God and men, himself man, Christ Jesus, who gave himself a ransom for all."[38] The Church has condemned as heretical the Jansenistic statement that Christ died only for the elect. The divine will to save is no empty wish such as, "God would like all men to be saved." This will is sincere because He does something to effect it: He gives His Son for man's redemption and sends the Holy Spirit to sanctify the redeemed. It is certain that God gives every adult grace sufficient for salvation. Although theologians have

---

[37] *De Libero Arbitrio,* II, 20. *PL* 32, 1269.
[38] 1 Tim. 2:1–6.

trouble explaining how God's will to save includes children who die without baptism,[39] God has neglected nothing and can say through the prophet: "What is there that I ought to do more to my vineyard that I have not done to it?"[40] God's will to save, however, is not absolute; otherwise all men would be saved. His benign will is conditioned upon the use which men make of the opportunities of salvation. Some will co-operate with grace and be saved; some will not co-operate and will be lost. However, as long as a man is capable of receiving grace, God sincerely desires his salvation.

The very special providence which God exercises over the just brings in the topic of *predestination*. Whereas providence means the ordering of means to an end, predestination means such an efficacious ordering of means that in the case of some men the end is actually attained.

It is revealed doctrine that God has eternally predestined certain persons to eternal happiness. St. Paul says: "For those who love God all things work together unto good, for those who, according to his purpose, are saints through his call. For those whom he has foreknown he has also predestined to become conformed to the image of his Son. . . . And those whom he predestined, them he has also called; and those whom he has called, them he has also justified, and those whom he has justified, them also he has glorified."[41] Only those are saved who die in the love of God. Who are they? Those whom God has foreknown and predestined! God calls them, He sanctifies them with graces which He has made ready for them, and finally He glorifies them. To this process there is no exception.

The will of God to sanctify and glorify the elect cannot be frustrated. For "my sheep . . . shall never perish, neither shall anyone snatch them out of my hand. What my Father has given me is greater than all; and no one is able to snatch anything out of the hand of my Father. I and the Father are one."[42] The number of the elect is fixed, and God knows with infallible certainty how many

---

[39] See discussion on Limbo, pp. 191–192, 199.
[40] Isa. 5:4.
[41] Rom. 8:28–30.
[42] Jn. 10:27–30.

and which men will be saved. How great is that number and who are included is the secret of God. While there are good conjectural indications of one's election, no one can be certain of it without a special revelation. He who imagines he will stand should take heed lest he fall. For it is part of our probation that we work out our salvation in fear and trembling.

To those who worry about their predestination St. Augustine says that it has been prepared for others; you be like these others and it is prepared for you.[43] The Church assures us that, if we do the best we can with the grace we get and pray unremittingly for perseverance, our petition will be heard.

As there is predestination of the elect so there is reprobation of the nonelect. In the preview of the general judgment the Judge says to those on his left hand, "Depart from me, accursed ones, into the everlasting fire which was prepared for the devil and his angels. . . . And these will go into everlasting punishment."[44] Reprobation differs from predestination in this respect that predestination is the reason why the elect receive grace in this life and may expect glory in the next; whereas reprobation is the reason why the reprobate may expect punishment in the next life, but it is not the reason why they sin in this life. This is due to their own bad will according to the prophet: "Destruction is thy own, O Israel."[45]

It is of faith that God infallibly knows and decrees the salvation or damnation of every man. How does theology explain these decrees? According to Pelagianism, which holds that salvation depends entirely on man, predestination consists merely of God's foreknowledge of man's use of his free will. According to Calvinism, God simply picks some men for heaven and predestines them to grace and glory; others he predestines to sin and hell. Man is not free under the influence of grace and there is no merit or demerit to human acts. Nothing that a man can do in life affects his salvation or damnation; God has fixed it beforehand without any reference to his deserving.

Between these heretical explanations theology steers its course. Any solution must safeguard these truths: God's will to save is

---

[43] In Ps. 136, 18. *PL* 37, 1772.   [44] Mt. 25:41–46.   [45] Osee 13:9.

universal and seeks the damnation of no one; God offers sufficient grace to all adults so that those who are lost deserve hell; men are free to accept or reject grace; the first grace and the final grace of perseverance are gratuitous gifts. The central problem of predestination is then, Does God predestine a man with or without consideration of his future merits or demerits? Theology has no certain answer. Nor is this surprising, since the Council of Trent says the problem is an unfathomable mystery.

2. *Conservation*

The first thing which providence demands of God in time is that He keep His creatures in existence. As they could not begin to be unless He brought them from nothingness, so they would lapse into nothingness if God ceased to pour being into them. This constant divine support is *conservation*. It is an absolute necessity because, if creatures could go on existing without it, they would be independent of the source of all being, and that they can never be. Scripture says: "How could anything endure, if thou wouldst not? or be preserved, if not called by thee?"[46] This doctrine is defined by the Vatican Council.

3. *Co-operation*

Divine co-operation means that as created beings depend on God for their being, so they depend on Him for their activity. God's co-operation can be (*a*) mediate; that is, He gives and conserves for the creature the power to be active; or (*b*) immediate; that is, when the creature acts, God must act with it. Although the Church has made no pronouncement, theologians are generally agreed that God must immediately co-operate in every act of the creature. Since the action of the creature has a being distinct from the power whence it flows, it too, as being, must be derived from God. The prophet says: "Thou hast wrought all our works for us."[47] St. Paul says: "In him we live and move and have our being."[48] In explaining how God concurs with free acts care must be taken not to destroy human freedom or to withdraw the created act from its due dependence on

---

[46] Wisd. 11:26–27.   [47] Isa. 26:12.   [48] Acts 17:28.

God. This dependence on God, however, cannot make God the author of sin. True, man can do nothing unless God produces the act with him. In the case of a sin God produces the physical entity of the act which is good; but in so far as the act is morally deficient, it is attributable solely to man's wrong choice. God tolerates the choice: He does not make it.

4. Government

That God alone is the ruler of the universe has been defined by the Vatican Council. His government is the execution in time of the decrees of His eternal providence. As His providence, so His government extends to the least things — the lilies of the field, the birds of the air, the hairs of our head. God, however, does not have to do everything Himself: "for He governs things inferior by things superior, not because of any defect of His power, but by reason of the abundance of His goodness, whereby the dignity of causality is imparted to creatures."[49] Angels have a function in regard to the visible world; man is caretaker of the earth; in the family, State, and Church, some men have a share in the divine authority. Thus, through the medium of secondary causes, God is directing His universe to the appointed end that He be all in all to all things.

---

[49] St. Thomas, *Sum. Theol.* I, 22, 3.

CHAPTER FOUR

GOD THE REDEEMER

"And in Jesus Christ, His only Son, our Lord,
who was conceived of the Holy Ghost, born of
the Virgin Mary, suffered under Pontius Pilate,
was crucified, died and was buried. He descended
into hell. The third day He arose again from the
dead. He ascended into heaven and sitteth at
the right hand of God, the Father Almighty."

THE first outpouring of divine goodness upon man was his creation
for a supernatural destiny. More wondrous still was God's rescue of
man from the folly of rejecting that destiny by sin. This great mercy
is our redemption.

A. *The Need of Redemption, Original Sin*

According to His ordinary providence God irrevocably bestows
supernatural blessings only as an earned reward. Thus He gave the
beatific vision to the angels who chose good and refused it to the
angels who chose evil. The human race underwent a test in the person
of the first man. Adam was not only the physical source whence
natural life would flow to his descendants; he was also the trustee
of the gifts of original justice so that permanent possession of these
favors by the race depended on Adam's fidelity to his trust. Hence
God put him to the proof as head of the race by laying on him a
command sanctioned with threat of death: "Of the tree of knowledge
of good and evil, thou shalt not eat. For in what day soever thou
shalt eat of it, thou shalt die the death."[1]

God judges the creature He tests by this norm: good acts are
proof that the reward should be given; evil acts are the reason why

---

[1] Gen. 2:17.

the reward is withheld. Evil acts are also sins; that is, they are not only bad for the agent and destructive of his good, but they transgress the divine command. A sin, then, is any deliberate act which violates the eternal law and cannot be directed to man's last end. The sinful act produces a habitual sin or sinful state which consists in a wrong relation of the sinner to his last end. When this relation is complete severance of the man from his last end, the sin is mortal; for it kills sanctifying grace which is the supernatural life of the soul and robs the man of his chance of heaven. He whose sin is a rejection of God can no longer share the proper life of God through grace. The sin is venial when the relation to the end remains substantially intact despite the violation of the divine command.

The human race required redemption on account of original sin, a term which means two things. The first is the transgression of Adam who, through the temptation of the devil and the solicitation of his wife, broke the divine command. It is an article of faith that Adam sinned in paradise and sinned grievously. Whether the external sin was the eating of a piece of fruit is not certain. Some of the ancients said it was a sexual sin. Some modern exegetes say it was perversion of the conjugal union whereby our first parents submitted their conjugal life to mystic fertility rites and hoped to be as gods, masters of the force of life. While these explanations are unlikely, St. Thomas is on solid ground when he says the disobedience was motivated by pride or inordinate desire for spiritual good. It is not easy to explain Adam's sin. He was not impelled by bad habits or inward corruption. The allure to sin had to arise from without but this could not becloud his intellect, for its clarity was such that he knew full well he was doing wrong. He could sin only by turning away from reason and concentrating his attention on some inordinate object of desire, expressible in the words: "You shall be as gods, knowing good from evil."[2] He did not aspire to impossible equality with God; rather he wished to resemble God in that "by his own natural power he might decide what was good and what was evil for him to do."[3] Adam could choose an inordinate

2 Gen. 3:5.
3 St. Thomas, *Sum. Theol.* II–II, 163, 2.

object because the created will is defectible; its end and norm of rectitude are not within, but outside, itself.

To Adam the consequences of his sin were dire and swift. He "immediately lost the holiness and justice in which he had been established and by the offense of this sin he incurred the wrath and indignation of God and consequently the death with which God had beforehand threatened him, and along with death servitude beneath the sway of him who henceforth held the empire of death, that is the devil, and on account of this offense the whole Adam was changed for the worse in body and soul."[4]

Original sin, in its second meaning, is the sin with which everyone is born; for "the sin of Adam harmed not only himself but also his descendants, and the holiness and justice which he had received from God and lost, he lost not for himself alone but also for us. . . . Defiled by the sin of disobedience he transmitted to the whole human race not only bodily death and punishments but also a sin which is the death of the soul."[5] This definition is the teaching of St. Paul who says: "As through one man sin entered into the world and through sin death, and thus death has passed into all men because all have sinned."[6] Hence original sin in us is not, as the Pelagians said, the sins by which we imitate Adam's fall. Rather it is something we inherit; it is "one by origin, and transmitted to all by natural generation, not by imitation, it exists in each as his own."[7] This sin is real and makes us guilty. It is not, however, any personal wrongdoing of our own but a sinful state which consists in the loss of the grace which God had intended for us if Adam had been faithful. This state is sinful, first, because loss of grace cuts us off from our supernatural end; and second, it was induced by Adam's sin as head of the race. If Eve alone had sinned, calamity would not have come to the race. The sinful state is *ours,* not because we willingly joined Adam in his sin, but, since we were present in his seed when he fell, we suffer the evil consequences of his sin just as

---

[4] Council of Trent, *Den.* 788 (*TCT,* 372).
[5] *Ibid. Den.* 789 (*TCT,* 373).
[6] Rom. 5:12.
[7] Council of Trent, *Den.* 790 (*TCT,* 374).

we would have profited from his fidelity. The solidarity of the human race makes the sin of its head the sin of the race. Hence it is shared by all of Adam's seed, the solitary exception we know being the Blessed Virgin Mary. But there is no injustice in our being penalized on account of Adam. For we are deprived of nothing to which we have a right by nature but only of supernatural gifts to which we have no claim.

The over-all consequence to the race was that the happy bond of communion with God, established by original justice, was severed. Since, therefore, Adam lost holiness for all, whoever dies infected by original sin is excluded from the vision of God, as the Council of Florence teaches. Since the sin incurred the anger of God, we are born "by nature children of wrath."[8] We lost integrity and inherit concupiscence; that is, our lower appetites rebel against reason, intellect and will have been weakened, and we suffer an inward conflict of good and evil tendencies. We lost absolute dominion over irrational nature and are subject to pain and death. Finally, the race became, in a manner, captive to Satan. We are not, however, totally corrupt as Luther and Calvin held.

Could the work of sin be undone? Man could not set himself right with God again because all men "were slaves of sin and under the power of the devil and death to such an extent that neither the Gentiles by the power of nature nor even the Jews through the letter of the Mosaic law could free themselves and rise therefrom."[9] Left to himself man perishes. Among the various alternatives open to God, He chose this course of mercy: He will restore the lost gifts, each in its own time, if man will offer compensation for sin. Since fallen man cannot fulfill this condition, God will give the race a new head, capable of undoing the work of the first Adam. Therefore, for the work of reconciling man with God, God chose His only Son: "God so loved the world that he gave his only-begotten Son, that those who believe in him may not perish, but may have life everlasting."[10]

---

[8] Eph. 2:3.
[9] Council of Trent, *Den.* 793 (*TCT*, 557).
[10] Jn. 3:16–17.

The history of man falls into two parts: before Christ the Redeemer and after Christ. Before Christ is the corruption of the human race and its enslavement to Satan who became the prince of this world, the strong man in armor who guards his courtyard. It is also the time of preparation for the Redeemer, the stronger one who will overcome Satan and strip him of his armor. The preparation consisted in prophecy about the Redeemer, the kindling of faith in Him, and the selection and nourishing of a people of God who would produce Him in the flesh. With this people God made a solemn but temporary agreement and delivered to them The Law. When the Redeemer would come, the Law and its covenant would become obsolete and would be supplanted by an everlasting covenant made with all men, the New Law.

B. The Incarnation . . . His only Son . . . born of the Virgin Mary

"When the fulness of time came, God sent his Son, born of a woman, born under the Law."[11] He is known in history as Jesus of Nazareth, the son of the Blessed Virgin Mary, who conceived Him of the Holy Spirit when the power of the Most High overshadowed her. Jesus is the fulfillment of the messianic prophecies of the Old Law. The chief teaching of the Church about Him is that He is true man and true God.

Jesus is true man. Under the misapprehension that the flesh is altogether evil, early heretics said He had only the appearance of a body. But Scripture records His genealogy, birth, and circumcision. Other heretics said He came from heaven with a spirit-form body and passed through the body of His mother without taking anything from it. But the Athanasian Symbol says He was born into the world from the substance of His mother. It is precisely through His birth from a daughter of Adam that He is incorporated into the human race and made our Brother. Unless He is one with our flesh, there is no redemption. In the statement, "The Word was made flesh,"[12] we have the classic Scriptural record of the fact of the Incarnation. This means that the Word of God assumed a real human

---

[11] Gal. 4:4.   [12] Jn. 1:14.

nature from Mary whom the New Testament so explicitly refers to as the mother of Jesus. The human nature of Jesus did not pre-exist its union with the Word but began to be when Mary agreed to be the mother of a heaven-sent Son. The Council of Ephesus says: "The Word of God the Father is united to the flesh in a personal union and . . . Christ is one with His own body."[13]

The Council of Chalcedon says He is perfect in humanity. In His life on earth He had (and still has) a rational soul, a body of flesh, and every human faculty. It is heresy to say that in Him the function of a rational soul was performed by the Divine Word. His humanity was an instrument fit in every way for the purposes of the Incarnation. It had no defects ascribable to original sin or personal fault. His soul was full of grace and untainted by concupiscence, His will free and sinless, His intellect without error and perfect in all human knowledge, As man, however, He was not omnipotent or omniscient; "for the Father is greater than I."[14] Although we cannot pierce the mystery, He both enjoyed the beatific vision and was subject to our common miseries and capable of suffering and dying.

Jesus is true God. Christianity is the religion which is based upon confession of the divinity of Jesus. Whoever denies this truth does not deserve the name of Christian. The testimonies to His divinity in Holy Writ and Tradition are numberless.

First, the Apostles said He was God and died for that belief. They present Him as the Author of life, the Judge of the living and the dead, the Giver of the Holy Spirit, the Lord of all, the fount of grace, He who sits at the right hand of God. St. John says: "In the beginning was the Word and the Word was with God and the Word was God. . . . And the Word was made flesh and dwelt among us."[15] John wrote his Gospel explicitly to prove the divinity of Jesus: "These are written that you may believe that Jesus is the Christ, the Son of God, and that believing you may have life in his name."[16] St. Paul told the Colossians: "All things have been created through and unto him . . . it has pleased God the Father that in him all his fullness should dwell."[17] He told the Philippians: "Have this mind in

---

[13] *Den.* 114 (*TCT,* 401).   [15] Jn. 1:1, 14.   [17] Col. 1:16, 19.
[14] Jn. 14:28.   [16] Jn. 20:31.

you which was also in Christ Jesus, who though he was by nature
God, did not consider being equal to God a thing to be clung to, but
emptied himself, taking the nature of a slave."[18]

Second, Jesus said He was the natural Son of God. He claimed
divine honor: "Father, glorify me with thyself, with the glory I had
with thee before the world existed."[19] He claimed divine power: "As
the Father raises the dead and gives them life, even so the Son also
gives life to whom he will. For neither does the Father judge any man,
but all judgment he has given to the Son, that all men may honor
the Son even as they honor the Father. . . . As the Father has life
in himself, even so he has given to the Son also to have life in himself."[20] Jesus asserted power over His own life and death: "No
one takes life from me, but I lay it down of myself. I have the power
to lay it down, and I have the power to take it up again."[21] Jesus
identified Himself with God: "He who sees me also sees the Father . . .
All things the Father has are mine."[22] Like God, Jesus is the object of
man's heavenly happiness: "This is everlasting life, that they may
know thee, the only true God, and him whom thou hast sent, Jesus
Christ."[23]

The Jews understood His claim to be God and tried to kill Him
on account of it. When He claimed to be the Lord of the Sabbath,
the reaction of the Jews was swift and venemous. "The Jews were
seeking the more to put him to death; because he was not only break-
ing the Sabbath, but was also calling God his own Father, making
himself equal to God."[24] When Jesus said: "Amen, amen, I say to
you, before Abraham came to be, I am,"[25] the Jews took up stones
to throw at Him. By Jewish law a blasphemer was put to death by
stoning and these Jews thought Jesus was blaspheming by arrogating
to Himself the peculiar name of God, "I am who am."[26] Again, when
the Jews petulantly asked Him, "If thou art the Christ, tell us
openly," and Jesus said, "I and the Father are one," the Jews went
to stone Him. Jesus remonstrated with them: " 'Many good works
have I shown you from my Father. For which of these works do you

---

[18] Phil. 2:5–7.
[19] Jn. 17:4.
[20] Jn. 5:21–27.

[21] Jn. 10:18.
[22] Jn. 14:8 and Jn. 16:15.
[23] Jn. 17:3.

[24] Jn. 5:18.
[25] Jn. 8:58.
[26] Exod. 3:14.

stone me?' The Jews answered him, 'Not for a good work do we
stone thee, but for blasphemy, and because thou, being a man,
makest thyself God.' " If the Jews had misunderstood Him Jesus
should have corrected their wrong impression, but far from toning
down what He had said, He replied: "Is it not written in your law,
'I said you are gods'? If he called them gods to whom the word
of God was addressed (and the Scripture cannot be broken), do you
say of him whom the Father has made holy and sent into the world,
'Thou blasphemest,' because I said, 'I am the Son of God'? If I
do not perform the works of my Father, do not believe me. But if I
do perform them, and if you are not willing to believe me, believe the
works, that you may know and believe that the Father is in me and
I in the Father."[27]

On account of His claim to be divine He was put to death. "The
high priest said to him, 'I adjure thee by the living God that thou
tell us whether thou art the Christ, the Son of God.' Jesus said to
him, 'Thou hast said it. . . .' Then the high priest tore his garments,
saying, 'He has blasphemed; what further need have we of witnesses?
Behold, now you have heard the blasphemy. What do you think?'
And they answered him, 'He is liable to death.' "[28]

Christian apologetics has proved the truth of these claims by
showing that He worked true miracles, uttered prophecy, and rose
again from the dead.

The first dogma ever defined by an Ecumenical Council was, as
we have seen, that of the divinity of Jesus. The definition of Nicea
was repeated by the First Council of Constantinople (A.D. 381).
The Council of Ephesus (A.D. 431) proclaimed Him to be both
God and man. The Council of Chalcedon (A.D. 451) said He was
perfect in His Godhead, perfect in His humanity.

But how are the human and the divine united in Christ? For three
hundred years after Nicea controversy raged on this question.
Nestorius said that Jesus is both a human and a divine Person, that
the Blessed Virgin Mary is the mother of a human person, Christ,
but not the Mother of God.

Jesus is one Divine Person. The Council of Ephesus condemned

---

[27] Jn. 10:24–39.   [28] Mt. 26:63–67.

Nestorius by declaring that Mary is the Mother of God, that Christ is only one Person and that divine. Then to explain the one Person in Christ, Eutyches fell into the error that the human nature of Christ was so absorbed by the divine that there resulted one divine nature and one divine Person. The Council of Chalcedon condemned Eutyches, saying: "We teach . . . that one and the same Christ, Son, Lord, Only-begotten must be acknowledged as existing in two natures without confusion, change, division, separation, that the difference between the two natures has not been destroyed by their union but rather that the characteristics of each nature have been preserved."[29] Finally, it was argued that since personality is manifest in will and action, there can be only one will and operation in Christ; therefore He had no human will. This error was condemned at the Third Council of Constantinople (A.D. 680) which said that in Christ there are two natural wills which are never at variance, two natural operations.[30]

This then is the mystery of the Incarnation: while Jesus Christ has a human nature and a divine nature He is only one Person, His humanity having been assumed by, and inseparably united to, the Person of the natural Son of God. It is the second mystery of the Christian revelation, less in importance only to the mystery of the Most Blessed Trinity.

To grasp what we may of the mystery, let us understand a nature to be the ultimate principle of activity in a being, and a person to be the intelligent, independent subject to whom is attributed whatever the being has and does. "Christ has two natures" means that He has two separate sources of activities which are exceedingly different. On account of His divine nature He can create; on account of His human nature He can suffer and die. "Christ is one Divine Person" means that all He has and does belongs to the Divine Word; whether the actions arise from His human or divine nature, they are ascribed to Him. Thus we can say that God died for us.

What then did the Word take to Himself? Some said a human person; some a man; and others a separate soul and a separate body.

---

[29] Den. 148 (*TCT*, 414).
[30] Den. 291 (*TCT*, 451).

St. Thomas disposes of these views by showing that He assumed a human nature; not human nature in the abstract nor the human nature of all men, but this concrete human nature supplied by the Blessed Virgin Mary, fecundated by the Holy Spirit. The moment of the fecundation of the womb of Mary was the moment of the Incarnation. The Word descended into the human by taking the human to Himself; a man was not elevated to the divine.

But, the reasoning mind inquires, since He has two intelligent natures, why is He not two persons? First, if He were two persons, Scripture and Tradition have erred in presenting Him as one undivided thing. It is absurd to say that Christ is two things. So, to be one thing He must be one Person. Since He is already a Divine Person He cannot be a human person. His human nature has been assumed by the Word, but a person is incommunicable. But what became of His human personality? According to the explanation given above He never had one. It is supplied for by the Word. Remember that "personality" is here used in the philosophic sense of that which makes an intellectual substance incommunicable; it is not used in the modern sense of a psychological "personality," the sum of one's psychic characteristics. Christ had a human "personality" in this latter sense. Second, if Christ were two persons there could only be a moral connection between them and it would be impossible to say that God died for us. That the activities of His human nature be attributable to God, there must be some common ground of *identity* between the human and the divine in Him. This is found only in His Person. The mystery, therefore, is not so much that Christ is one Person but rather that, being one Person, He exists in two natures. How that can be we can no more understand than how three Persons can possess one and the same nature.

Why did the Word become incarnate? The Nicene Creed replies: "For the sake of us men and for the sake of our salvation He descended from heaven." St. Paul says: "Jesus Christ came into the world to save sinners."[31] Would He have come even if man had not sinned? We do not know.

Theology calls the union of the human and divine in Jesus

---

[31] 1 Tim. 1:15.

hypostatic or personal. It is unique and without parallel. It is a union closer than that of body and soul. The Divine Word thoroughly penetrates His human nature, even though remaining distinct from it. Since it is perpetual, the hypostatic union was not dissolved when Christ died. It is the greatest gift God can bestow on a created being. In bestowing this gift, the Word lost nothing of His divinity. Indeed, as immutable God He suffers no change whatever by the Incarnation. We must be careful, however, not to misinterpret the phrase of St. Paul, "He emptied himself."[32] This does not mean that He surrendered His Godhead, but that the outward manifestations which should accompany it were withheld during the mortal career of Christ, except for brief moments like that of the Transfiguration. While the hypostatic union makes it possible for the human race to satisfy God for sin, yet, the God-Man, who results from this union, can in no sense be called, as we are called, the adopted son of God. If He were also the adopted son of God, He would be two persons, but He is always and only the natural Son of God.

The hypostatic union has two important consequences. First, the human nature of Christ, as the personal instrument of Christ, is worthy of divine honor. For "when he brings the firstborn into the world, he says, 'And let all the angels of God adore him.' "[33] Every part of the Sacred Humanity may be adored. The outstanding conclusion from this doctrine is the liturgical devotion to the Sacred Heart of Jesus wherein His heart of flesh, united to the Word and symbol of His human and divine love, is the object of divine adoration.

Second, Jesus Christ is the sole natural Mediator between God and men. "For there is one God, and one Mediator between God and men, himself man, Christ Jesus."[34] He is a natural Mediator because He is God and man. He is the sole Mediator because no man can do for mankind what He does, namely, reconcile man with God by paying the price of sin. His unique mediation, however, does not exclude lesser mediators who, united to Him, dispose men for union with God by acting as instruments of Christ.

His function of mediation Jesus fulfills as Prophet, Advocate,

[32] Phil. 2:7. [33] Hebr. 1:6. [34] 1 Tim. 2:5.

King, and Priest of the human race. He is Prophet because, above all others, He announced the revelation of God to men. He is the Advocate who takes our part and pleads for us: "He is able at all times to save those who come to God through him, since he lives always to make intercession for them."[35] He is true King. The prophecies of the Old Law present Him as King in Sion to whom the Gentiles are given as an inheritance. The angel of the Annunciation says He will reign in the house of Jacob forever. When Pilate asked Him if He were a king, He answered that He is. His is a supernatural rule over all men: "a kingdom of truth and life, of sanctity and grace, of justice, love and peace."[36] It is the kingdom of God on earth, and in heaven and He will rule over it "until he has put all his enemies under his feet."[37] At the end He will judge it and deliver it to God the Father that God may be all in all.

Above everything else Jesus is The Priest. A priest is a public person called by God to act on behalf of society as its mediator with God, especially by offering Him the supreme worship of sacrifice. According to the Council of Ephesus, "the divine Scripture records that Christ was made the high priest and apostle of our faith . . . when He was made flesh and a man like us."[38] At the moment of the Incarnation God said to Him: "Thou art a priest forever according to the order of Melchisedech."[39] Thus He was appointed to offer gifts and sacrifice for sin. He was called to this dignity as had been Aaron, who was priest of a temporary covenant and head of a perishable priesthood. The priesthood given to Jesus, however, was far more glorious. For Jesus, the High Priest, is "holy, innocent, undefiled, set apart from sinners, and become higher than the heavens."[40] His priesthood is eternal, and He does not serve an earthly but "the true tabernacle which the Lord has erected and not man."[41] "He has obtained a superior ministry, in proportion as he is mediator of a superior covenant, enacted on the basis of superior promises."[42] While the blood of bulls and goats sealed the old covenant, the new covenant is sealed by the blood of the High

[35] Hebr. 7:25.
[36] Preface of Feast of Christ King.
[37] 1 Cor. 15:25.
[38] *Den.* 122 (*TCT,* 409).
[39] Hebr. 5:6.
[40] Hebr. 7:26.
[41] Hebr. 8:2.
[42] Hebr. 8:6.

Priest Himself. Finally, the sacrifices offered by Aaron's priesthood
were ineffectual, for the blood of bulls and goats cannot take away
sin. "But Jesus, having offered one sacrifice for sins . . . has perfected
forever those who are sanctified."[43]

By offering sacrifice as the priest of the race, Jesus fulfilled the
grand purpose of the Incarnation. It is this one offering which re-
deems mankind, that is, restores the race to its original supernatural
community of life with God.

C. The Redemption . . . He suffered under Pontius Pilate, was crucified, died

All the creeds and many Councils teach that Jesus is the Savior
and Redeemer of the human race. The Fourth Lateran Council says:
"[He] likewise suffered and died upon the wood of the cross for the
salvation of the human race."[44] The Council of Florence says: "Our
Lord Jesus Christ . . . alone brought low the enemy of the human
race by His death and . . . re-opened the gates of heaven."[45] The
instrument of redemption is "His most holy passion on the wood
of the cross."[46] The death of Jesus on the cross is the most important action within the cycle of human history. For theology teaches
that on the cross Jesus (1) offered a propitiatory sacrifice as (2)
Head of the human race, and by this means He (3) merited for
Himself and us and redeemed us by (4) destroying sin and (5)
restoring the supernatural order.

1. A sacrifice is the offering to God of a visible gift in token of
man's complete dependence on Him. It is propitiatory when the gift
is destroyed for the express purpose of regaining the divine favor
lost by sin. On the cross Christ offered His life to the Father as
a sacrifice: "Christ also loved us and delivered himself up for us,
an offering and a sacrifice to God."[47] The reason for the offering
was that "He might redeem us from all iniquity."[48] In God's mysterious plan, however, the accomplishing of this purpose required the
death of the victim. Jesus had to die; as He says: "All things must

---

43 Hebr. 10:12–14.   46 Council of Trent, *Den.* 799 (*TCT*, 563).
44 *Den.* 429 (*TCT*, 455).   47 Eph. 5:2.
45 *Den.* 711.   48 Titus 2:14.

be fulfilled that are written in the Law of Moses and the Prophets
. . . concerning me. . . . Thus it is written; and thus the Christ
should suffer, and should rise again."[49] And the death accomplished
this purpose because "God has set [Him] forth as a propitiation by
his blood through faith. . . . God in his patience remitting former
sins."[50]

2. Christ offered His sacrifice as the new Adam who had united
the human race to Himself at the Incarnation. By the same principle
of solidarity whereby all men fell in Adam and needed redemption,
so by Christ's sacrifice all men died and were uplifted. "For just as
by the disobedience of one man the many were constituted sinners,
so also by the obedience of the one man the many will be constituted just."[51] The sacrifice, however, did not automatically sanctify
each individual. To be sanctified each one has to approach the cross
and take to himself its saving power.

3. By freely laying down His life out of obedience to His Father
and out of love for us, Christ earned certain rewards for Himself
and for us made one with Him. For Himself He merited the glory
of the Triumphant Messias. The Council of Trent says He won two
great things for us. The first is redemption: "The sin of Adam . . .
can be taken away by no other remedy than through the merit of
. . . Jesus Christ who reconciled us to God in His blood."[52] The
second is justification, or the gifts of grace and glory: "Jesus Christ
. . . merited for us justification by His most holy passion."[53]

4. The over-all notion of redemption is that the Redeemer sets
us right with God again after we have sinned. Its primary though
negative aspect is *destruction of sin*. For God to be pleased with us,
it is first necessary to destroy in us the sin which has caused His
wrath and to cancel the handwriting of the debt which was against
us. Christ had first to snatch us from the powers of darkness and
then transfer us into His kingdom. It is a fundamental dogma that
Christ overcame sin on the cross. How was this done?

We must explore the depths of sin because there are as many
elements in redemption as there are distinct facets to sin. First, sin

---

[49] Lk. 24:44–46.   [51] Rom. 5:19.   [53] *Den.* 799 (*TCT*, 563).
[50] Rom. 3:25.   [52] *Den.* 790 (*TCT*, 374).

is man's evil. To sin is "nothing else than to stray from the good of our nature."[54] The ultimate good of man is possession of God and by sin man turns from God and establishes his end in a creature; and thereby man is corrupted. Second, sin denies the truth of what God is to man and destroys the relationships founded on that truth. Hence Holy Writ presents the sinner as disobedient to the Supreme Lawgiver, as ungrateful to the Fount of all good, as the servant who rises against his Lord, as the criminal who despises his Judge, as the adulterer who rends the bond which binds him to his Spouse, as the idolator who worships the creature in place of the Creator. Sin is the greatest possible evil because it is the attempt to inflict evil on God. It is an injustice which denies God His right to our service; it is personal contempt of God because the sinner chooses the creature and rejects the Creator. Hence it has an infinite malice which alienates man from God, making him guilty, an enemy of God and liable to punishment. The function of the Redeemer is to free man from these noxious effects, so that his relations with God are henceforth harmonious, and to give him a remedy for the wounds inflicted by sin, so that he may be sound and whole.

There is some difficulty in explaining just how the Redeemer destroys sin. Some theologians explain redemption as an act of ransom, the buying back of a slave for a price. The Council of Trent says: "We were slaves of sin and under the domination of the devil and death."[55] From this bondage the Redeemer released us; for "you have been bought at a great price."[56] The price was the blood of the Redeemer; for "you were redeemed . . . not with perishable things, with silver or gold, but with the precious blood of Christ."[57] So far the explanation agrees with revelation, but if we would complete the picture of ransom, we must ask, To whom does the Redeemer pay the price? Assuredly not to Satan who has no rights whatever in man. To God the Father? One may say that the price is paid to God in the sense that He is propitiated by the sacrifice, but if we follow through with the idea of price, we convert the

---

[54] St. Thomas, *Sum. Theol.* I–II, 109, 8.
[55] *Den.* 793 (*TCT*, 557).
[56] 1 Cor. 6:20.
[57] 1 Pet. 1:18–19.

beauteous gift of sacrifice into a commercial transaction and have God selling back to God the human race for a consideration.

Others advocate a theory of substitute punishment according to which a propitiatory sacrifice is the substitution of an innocent victim for the guilty party. In that view God made the Redeemer our substitute, and having inflicted on Him the punishment of sin, we, the guilty, are let free. It is true that Isaias says: "He was wounded for our iniquities, he was bruised for our sins . . . and by his bruises we are healed."[58] St. Paul also says: "Christ redeemed us from the curse of the Law, becoming a curse for us."[59] Christ is evidently our substitute in the sense that, guiltless of sin, He suffered on account of it. He is not, however, a substitute in the sense that He is a stranger, that there is no solidarity between Him and us. Granted then that we are one with Christ, it becomes necessary for the supporters of this theory to show that the sufferings of the Passion are juridic penalties intended by God for the human race and accepted by Christ in its stead. It would be difficult to support that statement from revelation. Moreover, if it were true ought not men to be released from the necessity of dying? Nor can it be proved that the Father inflicted on Christ in His Passion the torments of the damned so that we might be spared them. This theory of substitute punishment has the unseemliness of God pursuing God with the apparatus of punitive justice, of God being the ultimate author and deviser of the pains of the Passion.

It is closer to revelation to say that the effects of sin, which poisoned man's relations with God, were taken away because Christ made adequate satisfaction for sin. The Council of Trent says: "Our Lord Jesus Christ, through the exceeding great charity by which He loved us though we were enemies, merited for us justification and made satisfaction for us to God the Father by His most holy passion on the wood of the cross."[60]

How does satisfaction wipe out sin? God must hate sin and hold the sinner an enemy. If the sinner will not or cannot wipe out the sin, then both he and his sin will be eradicated. Eradication consists in the sinner suffering punishments against his will whereby he be-

---

[58] Isa. 53:5.   [59] Gal. 3:13.   [60] *Den.* 799 (*TCT,* 563).

comes as though he were not. For the punishment of sin is death of the body and the second death of hell. In hell the sinner goes on existing, but such is the frustration of his whole being that cessation from existence would be a more desirable lot. If, on the other hand, the sinner willingly withdraw his offense and freely offer God honor which makes up for the dishonor of sin, God will again be favorable to the sinner, and the sin is wiped out. This sorrow for the offense, and the offering of voluntary compensation so as to unite the offender and the offended party, is satisfaction.

Fallen man is incapable of making satisfaction. He could be sorry for the offense, but he could not offer God honor equivalent to the full malice of sin. If then proper satisfaction was to be made by mankind, a Divine Person, whose actions have an infinite value, had to take flesh and assume man's responsibility for satisfaction. Consequently, the Son of God took over man's burden of guilt, not in His proper Person for He is impeccable, but as representative of the race. He then directed to the Father His death (which not God but sinners had devised) for the wiping out of man's offense. "Christ also has suffered for you . . . himself bore our sins in his body upon the tree, that we, having died to sin, might live to justice; and by his stripes you were healed."[61] By this act of love and submission He placated God for us. "For when we were enemies we were reconciled to God by the death of his Son."[62] And we also died with Christ, for satisfaction can wipe out the offense only if the offending party have part in the satisfaction. If then all men sinned in Adam, all men had to die in Christ. St. Paul says: "We have come to the conclusion that, since one died for all, therefore all died."[63]

Christ offered His satisfaction in the name of, and for the sake of, all men, living and dead, damned and elect. "He is the propitiation for our sins, not for ours only but also for those of the whole world."[64] Christ's dying for all does not mean that all men are actually saved, or that they who were in hell when Christ died could have been freed, but it does mean that within reach of absolutely every man during his mortal career is put the means of liberation

---

[61] 1 Pet. 2:21, 24.
[62] Rom. 5:10.

[63] 2 Cor. 5:14–15.
[64] 1 Jn. 2:2.

from sin. These means are and were available at all times and in all
places. They became available immediately after Adam's sin, and
all who were saved before the coming of Christ were saved by His
death.

Christ offered His satisfaction chiefly for original sin but also for
all actual sins. On account of the great love wherewith He suffered
and the dignity of the life He laid down, His satisfaction was "good
measure, pressed down, shaken together, running over."[65] God was
more honored by Christ suffering from love and obedience than He
is dishonored by the sins of all men.

5. Whereas the negative aspect of redemption is destruction of
sin, its positive aspect is *reconciliation*. The Council of Trent says:
"[Jesus Christ] reconciled us to God in His blood, having become
for us justice, sanctification and redemption."[66] Jesus is our justice
who makes men just again because He *restores the supernatural
order.*

For the race, restoration of the supernatural order means that
the lifeline, communicating divine life to mankind and severed by
Adam's sin, is repaired. Human destiny can be achieved. Since the
race is wedded to His Son and the price of sin is paid, God is
pleased with mankind. Perhaps it is more accurate in this context to
substitute for "mankind" "the spouse of Christ," the Mystical Body
born from the side of Christ and washed in the laver of regeneration.
But the cross did not put everything back exactly as it was before
the fall. We remain a fallen race though now uplifted. The way to
heaven has been reopened, but not all men will become members of
Christ. Some of the effects of Adam's sin — death and the inward
conflict — will not be taken away until the Last Day. However,
these are not mere punishments; they have been transformed into
remedies conducive to eternal life. By personal suffering men can
participate in the redeeming sufferings of Christ, as St. Paul says:
"What is lacking of the sufferings of Christ I fill up in my flesh for
his body, which is the Church."[67]

For the individual, restoration of the supernatural order means
opportunity of salvation. The Council of Trent says: "The heavenly

---

[65] Lk. 6:38.   [66] *Den.* 790 (*TCT,* 374).   [67] Col. 1:24.

Father . . . sent to men Christ Jesus, His Son . . . that all men *might*
receive the adoption of sons."[68] Although all men are born dead to
God, the cross gives them the opportunity of being reborn through
Christ. If they are reborn, they become the adopted sons of God and
the essential things of grace in this life and a chance for glory in the
next are restored. The cross, however, is not an automatic guarantee
of salvation.

In order to destroy sin completely the Redeemer must not only
take away the enmity of God and man's guilt and liability to punishment, but He must also offer man a remedy for the wounds which
sin inflicted on his nature. We have seen that Jesus merited for man
all the gifts of grace and glory. How each one must go to this infinite treasury of grace bequeathed us by Christ and make some of
it his own, we tell in the next two chapters when we speak of man's
sanctification and the sources of grace.

And was buried. He descended into hell

The burial of Jesus is a dogma of faith which emphasizes the
reality of His death and resurrection. Without a burial there is no
empty tomb. By descending into hell — not the hell of the damned —
Jesus conveys the effects of His Passion to the just who had died
before His sacrificial death. While His body lay in the tomb, His
soul proceeded to Limbo, to the abode of these dead, and overcame
death. In the liturgy of His burial the Church celebrates this triumph:
"O death, I will be thy death; O hell, I will be thy bite."[69] He freed
the prisoners of death by giving eternal happiness to the souls of the
just who, until then, were deprived of the vision of God. Since ex-
clusion from paradise is the prime penalty of sin, no one could
attain paradise until the penalty had been paid.

The third day He rose from the dead

That Jesus rose the third day is a basic dogma, fully set forth in
Scripture and asserted in all the symbols of the faith. While the
resurrection did not merit our release from sin, yet without it the

---

[68] *Den.* 794 (*TCT*, 558).
[69] Osee 13:14.

cross is incomplete. Hence it belongs to the completeness of the Redemption and is therefore associated by Holy Writ with the cross as one complete whole. Thus St. Paul says: "Jesus was delivered up for our sins and rose again for our justification."[70] We are justified when we are made right with God and restored supernaturally. This is possible only by union with Christ. While the race as such is united to Him by the Incarnation, the individual requires in addition faith and baptism. Without the resurrection, however, faith and baptism have no power to unite us to Christ. The foundation of our faith is the resurrection; for "if Christ has not risen, vain then is our preaching, vain too is your faith."[71] Therefore, unless Christ is risen we could not believe in Him. Between baptism, which is our rebirth to God, and the Resurrection the connection is this: baptism is a symbol of our dying with Christ to sin and our rising with Him to a new life, but if He has not risen, baptism is a piece of superstition.

The Resurrection promotes our justification also because it is the basis of our hope. Since Christ, our Head, has triumphed over sin and death we hope to do the same thing through Him. His rising is the instrument and model of our rising from the dead. Furthermore, it is only through the Resurrection that Jesus became "a life-giving spirit,"[72] that is, permanently capable of giving others the life of grace. What He communicates is His glorious life. It is the *risen* Christ who gives us "the power of becoming sons of God."[73] While He had the fullness of the Holy Spirit during His mortal life, a condition for His dispensing the Spirit to us is His death and Resurrection. While He was alive, "The Spirit had not yet been given, seeing that Jesus had not yet been glorified."[74]

By rising Jesus begins a glorious life which is the pattern of the entire life of the Christian: of the present life, in that, dead to sin, he should walk in newness of life; of the life to come, in that he too will rise to a life of glory.

He ascended into heaven

As He rose by His own power, so by His own power He ascended

---

[70] Rom. 4:24.   [72] 1 Cor. 15:45.   [74] Jn. 7:39.
[71] 1 Cor. 15:14.   [73] Jn. 1:12.

into heaven. He took with Him into heaven the souls of the just freed from Limbo. All the actions of Christ are means of salvation. The salvific value of the Ascension is that it is the exaltation of human nature, so that whither the Head has gone, thither it is the hope of the members also to go.

He sitteth at the right hand of God

To sit at the right hand of God is to share His power and honor; hence the Sacred Humanity is exalted to the throne of God. For salvation this means, first, the presence of the Sacred Humanity in the heavenly places is perpetual intercession for men, and second, we in union with Him will one day share His exaltation in proportion to our merits. This mystery summarizes the glory of the Triumphant Messias, which is the glorification of His body, the exaltation of His holy name, the acquisition of the members of His mystical Body, and the right to rule and judge them. From the right hand of the Father He will come to judge the living and the dead.

Summary: The sin of Adam destroyed the state of original justice; the death, Resurrection, and Ascension of the Redeemer is His victory over sin which produced the state of fallen and redeemed man. The Redeemer's remedy for sin is complete: the offense is wiped out by satisfaction; the closing of paradise, by the reconciliation of man with God; the wounds and weakness in man, by grace merited on the cross. St. Paul epitomizes the situation: "God, who is rich in mercy, by reason of his very great love wherewith he has loved us even when we were dead by reason of our sins, brought us to life together with Christ . . . and raised us up together, and seated us together in heaven in Christ Jesus."[75]

By way of epilogue we note how the munificence of God turns the catastrophe of sin into an occasion of greater benefit. Since the satisfaction of Christ was superabundant, God was more glorified by the redemption than he was dishonored by the sin. Man gained more through Christ than he lost through Adam. "For if by the offense of the one the many died, much more has the grace of God, and the gift in the grace of the one man Jesus Christ, abounded

---

[75] Eph. 2:4–6.

unto the many. . . . For if by reason of the one man's offense death reigned through the one man, much more will they who receive the abundance of the grace and of the gift of justice reign in life through the one Jesus Christ."[76] Aptly then does the Church sing: "O happy fault, which has won for us so great and so wonderful a Redeemer!"

D. *The Mother of the Redeemer*

Mary, the Mother of Jesus, holds a unique position in theology because she is the Mother of God according to the flesh. This singular privilege is the root of her importance and the basic principle of all theologizing about her. Since God predestined her to play a unique and splendid role in the universe, He provided her with all the qualities necessary for the sublime task she willingly assumed.

God prepared her soul by making it utterly free from sin and full of grace. Her freedom from sin involves, first, her Immaculate Conception. From the first moment of her existence in the womb of her mother Anna, she was endowed with sanctifying grace and free from concupiscence. While the doctrine is not explicitly stated in Scripture, some of the Fathers and many great theologians find it implicit in the story of the fall related in Genesis, as Pius IX notes in his bull proclaiming the dogma. The feast was celebrated in the East as early as the seventh century and in the West in the ninth century. Unfortunately some writers presented this doctrine as meaning that Mary had no need of redemption, and therefore St. Bernard and others denied it. In the thirteenth century the Franciscan theologian, Scotus, resolved the seeming conflict of doctrines by showing that Mary had need of redemption and was preserved from the effects of Adam's sin through anticipation of her Son's merits. They who denied the doctrine steadily lost ground. The Council of Trent explicitly excluded her when it decreed that all men inherit original sin from Adam. After Trent the Popes forbade the denial of the doctrine to be taught and finally, December 8, 1584, Pius IX solemnly proclaimed that

At the first instant of her conception, through the grace and privilege of God Almighty and in view of the merits of Jesus

[76] Rom. 5:15–17.

Christ the Savior of the human race, the Virgin Mary was preserved and exempted from all stain of original sin.[77]

It is also a truth of faith that Mary never committed an actual sin. The Council of Trent says: "If anyone shall say that a man once justified . . . can in the whole course of his life avoid all sin, even venial ones, except by a special privilege of God, such as the Church holds in the case of the Blessed Virgin Mary, let him be anathema."[78]

Gabriel saluted Mary, "Hail, full of grace," using that form of greeting in place of her name. As Solomon is called the Wise Man and the Messias the Just One, so Mary is named *Full of Grace*. Since the sanctifying grace in a soul is proportioned to the love God bears that soul, the grace of Mary, even at the beginning of her existence, surpassed that of any man or angel except the fullness of grace which was in the human soul of Christ. His was the fullness of grace befitting the Head of the human race and the soul joined to God in a personal union. God so prepared the soul of Mary from the first moment of her creation that, even before she consented to be the Mother of the Redeemer, she was fit for such intimate association with the God-Man. She is the Lily of Israel; the perfection of grace attained under the Old Law. But the fullness of her grace was not static; her habitual grace ever increased through the wisdom and singular perfection of her daily life until she rose to the greatest heights reached by a human person. As for other supernatural privileges, we may assert with confidence that she had to the highest degree whatever was compatible with being a wayfarer, with the perfection of sanctity, with her sex, and with her essential function as Mother of the Redeemer.

The Mother of the Redeemer is the Mother of God. The Council of Ephesus says: "If anyone shall not confess that God is truly Emmanuel and therefore the Holy Virgin is the Mother of God; for according to the flesh she begot the Word of God become flesh, let him be anathema."[79] The definition means, first, that Mary is a real mother, since she supplied to the body of Christ what every mother gives to the child she begets. Second, the child she conceived, bore

---

[77] *Den.* 1641 (*TCT*, 510).   [79] *Den.* 113 (*TCT*, 400).
[78] *Den.* 833 (*TCT*, 506).

in her womb, and gave birth to is the Son of God. St. Cyril explains that Mary is not mother of the divine nature (the pagans believed in a mother of the gods), but through human generation she is Mother of a Son who is God; she is not Mother of a man who became united to God but of a man who, from the moment of His conception, was personally God; nor is she Mother merely of the flesh of Jesus but Mother of a Divine Person who subsists in that flesh.

The Divine Maternity gives Mary a function and dignity which lift her above all created persons. Thereby she enters into unique relations with the Persons of the Most Blessed Trinity. She is called and is the spouse of the Holy Spirit. The Word of God calls her mother. While on account of grace the baptized soul can say, My God is my Father, in a more real sense she can say, My God is my Son. She has this unique thing in common with the Father that each of them can say of the Divine Word, This is my beloved Son.

It is a dogma of faith that Mary is both mother and virgin. St. Leo I said: "He was begotten by a new kind of birth because inviolate virginity [that] knew not concupiscence supplied the materials of His body."[80] The Second Council of Constantinople calls her "ever virgin." Paul IV spells out the doctrine: "The Blessed Virgin . . . preserved the integrity of virginity always, that is, before giving birth, during birth and ever afterwards."[81] The object of belief is threefold: (1) Mary conceived by the Holy Spirit without the co-operation of man. In the conception of Jesus the paternal function of generation was filled by the act of the Most Blessed Trinity, which we appropriate to the Holy Spirit. When Mary inquired of the angel how her maternity would be accomplished, he replied: "The Holy Spirit shall come upon thee and the power of the Most High shall overshadow thee; and therefore the Holy One to be born shall be called the Son of God."[82] (2) Mary bore her Son without any violation of her virginal integrity. Her giving birth to Jesus was miraculous, bloodless and painless. This is the doctrine of the Virgin birth, which some people confuse with Mary's

---

[80] *Dogmatic Epistle of Leo to Flavian, Den.* 144 (*TCT,* 413).
[81] *Den.* 993 (*TCT,* 507).
[82] Lk. 1:35.

Immaculate Conception. Some theologians say that the Virgin Birth is not a historical event transmitted to us by Scripture, but a mystery whose existence the intuition of faith finds implicit in the revealed deposit. Others reaffirm the classic proof of the Fathers which is based on Scripture. Isaias prophecied that Emmanuel will be born of a virgin: "Behold a virgin (a young marriageable girl) shall conceive and bear a son, and his name shall be called Emmanuel."[83] The reference is to one who remains a virgin in the very act of birth because the prophet is offering a most extraordinary sign, a sign "unto the depths of hell or unto the heights above." Now Emmanuel is Christ and St. Matthew says that prophecy is fulfilled in His birth: "She shall bring forth a son, and thou shalt call his name Jesus. . . . Now all this came to pass that there might be fulfilled what was spoken by the Lord through the prophet, saying, 'Behold, the virgin shall be with child and shall bring forth a son; and they shall call his name Emmanuel.' "[84] (3) Mary remained a virgin ever afterward. The gospel reference to the brethren of Jesus is no argument that Mary did not remain a virgin. These brethren were cousins of Jesus and in Holy Writ kinsmen are frequently called brothers.

Mary's part in the economy of salvation did not end with her giving birth to the Redeemer. For the mother of the Head is also spiritual mother of the members of the Head. This is a dogma found in the universal teaching of the Church and received by the faithful; it follows from our solidarity with Christ. For by agreeing to be the mother of the Redeemer, Mary assumed a peculiar responsibility for the redeemed. At the foot of the cross she was acknowledged to be Mother of the mystical Body, as many Popes have taught. Thus Benedict XIV says: "The Catholic Church, under the tutelage of the Holy Spirit, has ever taken great pains to profess and cultivate filial devotion to Mary . . . to a most tender mother, bequeathed to her by the last breath of her dying Savior."[85] As a consequence she fosters the salvation of all men, especially of the faithful, as mediator, intercessor, and advocate.

What is the nature of her mediation? Assuredly it is subordinate

---

[83] Isa. 7:14.   [84] Mt. 1:22–23.   [85] Bulla *Gloriosae Dominae.*

to that of Christ and in no way conflicts with the dogma that Christ is sole mediator between God and men. Christ alone is the principal, independent, and all-sufficient Mediator, for He alone satisfied for sin. His sole mediatorship, however, does not exclude secondary mediators who are close to Him and dependent upon Him.

What is the power and extent of her mediation? Since power of intercession is in proportion to one's holiness, Mary full of grace is more powerful in intercession than all God's saints. Indeed the liturgy has hailed her as Mediatrix of All Graces. This title may be understood in two ways. First, inasmuch as she gave us the Redeemer, the Source of Grace, she is the channel of all graces. To this all Catholics agree. Second, some theologians go farther and call her Co-redemptrix. Although as daughter of Adam she required redemption, yet by her close association with her Son and her moral support she had a part granted to no other mortal in achieving the objective redemption. As Christ is the new Adam, she is the new Eve. As Eve enticed man to his fall and by her generative function transmitted sin to all, so Mary paved the way for and had at least a remote effect upon redemption. To this statement, again, all would agree.

The theologians in question see her as having an *immediate* effect upon redemption; that is, she is a moral co-cause, subordinate to her Son, in that she made her own the divine will to redeem. Thus the Incarnation waited upon her consent which she gave in the name of the race; in the mystery of the Purification she accepted all the pains demanded by her part in the redemption; and at the foot of the cross she offered her Son to the Father for our redemption and so suffered in spirit as to win the title "Queen of Martyrs." Since she did so much to win redemption, she should have her share in the disposal of it. Therefore, they say that no grace is given us except through her intercession. This does not mean that we must ask her for all favors, or that, in the nature of things, all grace must pass through her hands, but that, by God's positive ordination, the grace of Christ will actually be given only through Mary. It is not unlikely that this doctrine of her universal mediation, so favored by the Pontiffs of the past two centuries, may some day be defined. St.

Pius X says: "From this close union of sorrows and wills between Mary and Christ, 'she most assuredly deserves to become the restorer of a lost world,' and hence the dispenser of all graces which Jesus won by His death and blood. . . . Since she outshines all in sanctity and close connection with Christ and has been associated by Him with the work of human salvation, she . . . is the chief dispenser of graces."[86]

Mary, close associate of Jesus in achieving the redemption, shares His glory as triumphant Messias. Her first glory is her Assumption. As her Son by His own power rose and ascended into heaven, so by His power Mary was taken into heaven body and soul. Though she knew no sin, she shared our common lot of mortality. However, the object of belief in the doctrine of the Assumption is not that Mary died, but that her glorious body, which had borne the Eternal Word, was not suffered to corrupt in the grave, there to await the general resurrection. Shortly after her death, body and soul were reunited and borne in triumph to heaven. Her glorification is commemorated by her most ancient liturgical feast, as is found in the Sacramentary of Gregory I, in the Gallo-Gothic missal, and in the Mozarabic missal of the sixth century. This truth was called in question by a few in the early Middle Ages, especially by Usard's martyrology, but the pious faithful have always believed it, and it was proclaimed a dogma of faith by Pius XII, November 1, 1950.

Her second glory is that she reigns in heaven Queen of angels and of men. Her sovereignty is founded on her Divine Maternity and her unique part in our redemption, as Pius XII says: "As Christ, the new Adam, must be called King not merely because He is the Son of God, but also because He is our Redeemer, so, analogously, the Most Blessed Virgin Mary is Queen not only because she is the Mother of God, but also because, as the new Eve, she was associated with the new Adam."[87] The constant belief of the Church in Mary's sovereignty is manifest in the glorious mysteries of the Rosary and was crowned with new recognition on November 1, 1954, when

---

[86] *Den.* 1978a (*TCT,* 514).
[87] Encyclical Letter, *Ad Caeli Reginam* (trans. *On the Queenship of Mary,* N.C.W.C. ed., p. 9, No. 38).

Pius XII instituted the liturgical feast of The Queenship of the Blessed Virgin Mary.

On account of her utterly singular position, her matchless dignity, and the part she played in the salvation of men, Mary is accorded religious honor. That worship, however, is essentially less than the adoration paid to God but of a higher type than the honor given to any angel or holy man. Some heretics accuse the Church of giving Mary divine honor and refuse to credit her when she says that she carefully distinguishes between the worship due to God and the honor paid to Mary. Be it so. But it is a sure sign of orthodoxy to know by instinct the right thing to say of Mary, just as it is characteristic of heresy to fear Mary and be unwilling to render her what God expects she should have.

CHAPTER FIVE

GOD THE SANCTIFIER

"I believe in the Holy Ghost, the holy Catholic Church, the Communion of saints."

FROM consideration of man's redemption we pass to that of his sanctification. What Jesus did to save us and the merits He won for us are, in theological terms, the objective redemption. The individual, however, does not automatically share in these benefits. It is not enough that the price of sin be paid for the race. In addition every man must be purified of the effects which sin has had upon him and be made over supernaturally. He must be reborn to God through union with Christ, be healed of the wounds of sin, be made fit for the vision of God. This process is his sanctification or the subjective redemption.

God demands human co-operation in the work of sanctification. For, as St. Augustine observes: "He who made you without your knowing it, does not justify you without your willing it."[1] Therefore, every man must freely approach the means of salvation won by the cross and apply them to himself. If anyone, however, is incapable of a rational act, some other man must act for him. But even this co-operation in his own sanctification lies beyond man's natural power. To be recreated in justice, live a supernatural life, and die in the friendship of God, a man needs special help from God. Hence salvation is the work of God in us. The beginning, middle, and happy end of man's journey to the vision depend upon a mysterious combination of God's action and man's co-operation.

We treat now of God's part in the personal venture which constitutes the central story of everyman's life — his attainment of heaven. For the sanctification of every man God provides a Divine Person who sanctifies, a sanctified and sanctifying Church, and grace.

---

[1] *Sermo,* 169, ch. xi. *PL* 38, 923.

A. *The Divine Person who sanctifies*

Some of the Fathers interpret the parable of the Good Samaritan allegorically. The unfortunate man who went down from Jerusalem to Jericho and fell among robbers is the human race. The priest and levite who passed by are the Old Law unable to render effectual help to sinful man. Christ is the Good Samaritan who poured oil and wine into his wounds and brought him to the inn of the Church. Having rescued the man the Redeemer arranges for his convalescence which — and here is the undeveloped part of the allegory — is the care of another Divine Person. The divine work of mercy, begun by the redemption, is completed by the Holy Spirit who sanctifies.

The divine task of saving men is not neatly divided among the Persons of the Most Blessed Trinity, for it is the total Godhead who produces all divine effects among creatures. The work of sanctification is, however, rightly appropriated to the Holy Spirit. For He is the Person breathed or spirated by the divine will. As the Son is the expression of the divine intellect, so the Third Person is the expression of the divine will whose object is always holy — either God who is holiness itself, or created holiness which is approach to and participation in God. Hence the Divine Person who is spirated expresses the divine sanctity and is both Holy and Spirit. Among men his task is to breathe into flesh, made dead by sin, the power of loving God. Since He is the Divine Gift in the Trinity, the Love uniting Father and Son, He is also the Gift of God to man. He is given to man to enable him to give himself to God in perfect love.

The sanctifying mission of the Holy Spirit began with the anointing of the God-Man, the solemn dedication to the task of redemption of Him "whom the Father has made holy and sent into the world."[2] At the moment of the Incarnation the human nature of Christ was made full of grace. Jesus is truly *The Christ,* the Anointed One. On another occasion "God anointed [Him] with the Holy Spirit and with power";[3] that is, at the baptism in the Jordan the Holy Spirit came upon Him with all the charisms necessary for His public messianic mission. Henceforth the Third Person may be called the

---

[2] Jn. 10:36. [3] Acts 10:38.

Spirit of Jesus, as St. Paul often does. This is an apt name because at the Last Supper Jesus promised to send Him to the Church and He is given to us personally only through Jesus.

The temporal mission of the Holy Spirit, comparable to the mission of the Word of God, took place on Pentecost, fifty days after the Resurrection. Under the form of fiery tongues the Third Person came to those who believed that Jesus is God in order that this little flock might become "a spiritual house . . . a holy nation,"⁴ filling the earth. This group was the Church of Christ, made manifest to men, now that the Holy Spirit had anointed and sanctified it. As the Apostles are sent as witnesses of the Resurrection, so also, as Jesus says: "[The Spirit] will bear witness concerning me."⁵ He comes as "the Spirit of truth whom the world cannot receive,"⁶ because it is bound fast by the father of lies. Therefore, "He will convict the world of sin, and of justice, and of judgment"⁷; that is, He will prove it to be guilty of unbelief, of the injustice of rejecting the Redeemer, and hence already condemned with Satan. He will illumine the Church concerning the doctrine of Christ because "He will teach you all things and bring to mind whatever I have said to you."⁸ He comes as the Paraclete, the advocate whom one calls to his side in a difficult lawsuit; as Consoler who renders every sort of spiritual aid. He will protect the Church in trials and inspire its members what to say when they are brought before kings and councils for the sake of Jesus. From the Paraclete will proceed the charisms and signs proclaiming the divinity of the Church, and He will dwell in it forever.

B. *The Sanctified and Sanctifying Church*

In a general sense the Church is the assembly or community of believers in the true God. The first such community was formed when God segregated Israel from all other peoples and gave this people the true religion, based on belief in a Redeemer to come. He made with them the covenant of the Old Law sealed with the blood of calves. The agent of this covenant was Moses who "took

---

⁴ 1 Pet. 2:5, 9.   ⁶ Jn. 14:17.   ⁸ Jn. 14:26.
⁵ Jn. 15:27.   ⁷ Jn. 16:8.

the blood and sprinkled it upon the people and he said: 'This is the blood of the covenant which the Lord has made with you.' "[9] But the death of the Redeemer canceled this imperfect covenant, made with one people, and in its stead an everlasting covenant, whose High Priest is Jesus and whose seal is His blood, was made with all mankind. For, instituting the Holy Eucharist the night before He died, Jesus said: "This is my blood of the new covenant."[10] The rending of the veil in the temple of Jerusalem was a great sign that the wall of separation dividing Jew from Gentile was broken down. And to St. Paul was given the honor of announcing a mystery hidden for ages — God's marvelous plan of salvation whereby all men without distinction of race may be saved by being united to Christ. By His death Jesus won for Himself the new people of God which consists of all who believe in Him and are baptized. For the formation of God's final religion, the Gentiles were called out of darkness into His marvelous light: "You who in times past were not a people . . . are now the people of God."[11] This, the new Israel, we shall now consider, first, as a juridic thing or society, and second, as a mystical thing or the Body of Christ.

The Church a perfect hierarchic society and the true religion

It is a fundamental dogma of Christianity that Christ founded a Church for the sanctification of men. The Vatican Council says: "That He might have perpetually available the salutary work of redemption, the eternal Shepherd and Bishop of our souls determined to build the holy Church wherein, as in the house of the living God, all the faithful might dwell united by the bond of one faith and charity."[12] Upon the foundations of Israel, therefore, Jesus erected a new religious society to be the perfect flowering of Israel, as the true religion and as God's final arrangement with wayfaring man.

That Christ did not found a visible external society, either because He thought the end of the world was at hand, or because He wanted only an internal union of men with God, is asserted by modern

---

[9] Exod. 24:8.
[10] Mt. 26:28.

[11] 1 Pet. 2:10.
[12] Den. 1821 (TCT, 201).

rationalists and rejected by the whole Christian tradition. He gathered followers, gave them a social purpose, and set up an enduring organization endowed with all necessary means of functioning.

First, He commissioned His Apostles to complete the mission His Father had given Him: "As the Father has sent me, I also send you."[13] Then He gave them His threefold powers as prophet, pastor, and priest. We have already seen that He made them the depositary and infallible interpreter of his doctrine. He gave them also the power to rule when He said: "Whatever you bind on earth shall be bound also in heaven; and whatever you loose on earth shall be loosed also in heaven."[14] A third power of sanctifying was given them: "Go, therefore, and make disciples of all nations, baptizing them in the name of the Father, and of the Son, and of the Holy Spirit, teaching them to observe all that I have commanded you."[15] He likewise commissioned them to forgive sins, renew the Eucharist, and make priests. And thus the Apostles acted, considering themselves ambassadors of Christ and dispensers of the mysteries of God.

Second, Christ commands men to join a religious organization when He tells them to submit to the sacred powers of the Apostles. In a general way Christ says: "He who hears you hears me; and he who rejects you rejects me; and he who rejects me rejects him who sent me."[16] But more particularly He imposed an obligation of: (a) believing the Apostles: "He who does not believe shall be condemned";[17] (b) of obeying their mandates: "Teaching them to observe all that I have commanded you"; (c) of receiving baptism: "Unless a man be born again of water and the Spirit, he cannot enter into the kingdom of God."[18]

Since these powers and obligations are perpetual, the organization in which they are fulfilled is likewise perpetual. The religious needs of men are perennial. Furthermore Christ promised that He would assist the teaching function for all time, that the Holy Spirit would dwell in His organization forever, that the gates of hell would not prevail against it because it was built on the See of Peter. The Council of Trent says that the bishops are the legitimate successors of the

13 Jn. 20:21.   15 Mt. 28:19.   17 Mk. 16:16.
14 Mt. 18:18.   16 Lk. 10:16.   18 Jn. 3:5.

Apostles "appointed by the Holy Spirit to rule the Church of God."[19] The Vatican Council has defined that Peter had the primacy of jurisdiction over the Apostles, that his lawful successors are the Bishops of Rome to whom the whole Church is subject, not only in matters of defining faith and morals, but also of discipline and government. Here then is a true society, a social arrangement designed by Christ Himself who established its constitution, determining that it be a hierarchic, perfect, and visible organization, the ark of salvation, and readily identifiable as the true religion.

Since the Church consists of teachers and taught, of rulers and ruled, it is not a democratic but a hierarchic society, as the Council of Trent has defined. For the sacred power to teach, rule, and sanctify is not in the hands of the community but of superiors dependent on a supreme head who receives his authority immediately from Christ.

A perfect society is subordinate to no other organization because it aims at a universal good and has all the means proper to realizing its end. It is of faith that the end of the Church is Salvation — the same purpose which brought Christ to earth: "The Son of Man came to seek and to save what was lost."[20] The Church also has all the necessary means which are infallible doctrine, authority, and the sacraments. Hence, on account of the sublime scope of its purpose and the adequacy of means at its disposal, the Church is independent of any human authority.

The Church is the messianic kingdom, the kingdom of God on earth. This kingdom is assuredly an internal union of men with God, as is clear from the doctrine of the Mystical Body. But it is also a visible human organization. It is heresy to hold that the real Church is an invisible union of the saints or predestined, and that the external Church is purely human, subject to change and destruction. The real Church is external, as we have just seen; that it consists of men with human weaknesses is clear from the parables of Christ. It will contain sinners and just, wise and foolish. Weeds of heresy will be sown in it. It will suffer schisms and scandals. Nevertheless

---

[19] *Den.* 960 (*TCT,* 843).
[20] Lk. 19:10.

it is divine in its origin, powers, purpose, and indestructibility; for by the promise of Christ it will last until His second coming.

The Church is man's chief external help to salvation. Boniface VIII compares it to the ark in which Noe and his family were saved from the flood. But the Church is more than a help; it is sheer necessity on account of the demands which Christ makes on men to believe His doctrine, obey His rulers, and use His means of grace. Only by belonging to the Church can these obligations be satisfied. Hence the Fathers teach that they have not God for a Father who have not the Church for a Mother. Since the Church is Christ continued, and since no one is saved except by union with Him, whoever is apart from the Church is not united to Him. Many popes and councils have defined the necessity of the Church. Thus the Council of Florence defines that "all those who are not members of the Catholic Church, not just pagans but also Jews or heretics and schismatics, cannot become sharers of eternal life . . . and no one, no matter what almsgiving he may have practiced, even if he shed his blood for Christ, can be saved unless he shall have remained within the bosom and unity of the Catholic Church."[21] It would not be correct, however, to condemn the persons just enumerated on the ground that they are not *external* members of the Church. What then is the meaning of the controversial dogma, outside the Church there is no salvation?

Membership in the Church is necessary for two reasons. First, it is the ordinary means of salvation. In it alone the true faith is found and the means of grace abound. St. Irenaeus says: "Where the Church is, there is the Spirit of God; and where the Spirit of God is, there is the Church and all grace."[22] Second, Christ commands it. Can any exceptions, real or apparent, be pleaded against these reasons? Concerning the first reason, it is said than an extraordinary means may sometimes be substituted for an ordinary means; as for the second reason, invincible ignorance or impossibility of fulfillment excuses from a command. Thus Pius IX says: "They who are invincibly ignorant of the true religion are not in the eyes of the

---

[21] *Den.* 714 (*TCT*, 165).
[22] *Contra Haereses*, III, 24, 1. *PG* 7, 996.

Lord guilty of the sin [of being outside the Church]."[23] That without
which salvation is utterly impossible is possession of sanctifying
grace. Either through perfect love or the valid reception of a sacrament, one can die in the state of grace who is not in external communion with the Church. The person, however, has grace only on
condition that he desires to do all that God requires for salvation.
Since membership in the Church is one of these requirements, he
must have an implicit desire to belong to it. If then he has grace,
he is united to Christ, and consequently in some way to the Church.
However, the exact and felicitous way of expressing his connection
with the Church has not yet been found. But no one is saved who
is not in Christ and whoever is in Christ is in some way in the
Church. Therefore there are no real exceptions to the dictum that
salvation is impossible outside the Church.

One becomes a member of the Church by baptism and maintains
membership by professing the faith of the Church, obeying her
lawful superiors, and using her sacramental system. One ceases to
be a member when he is cut off by the Church or when he externally
renounces the faith and obedience he professed.

Since the Church is so necessary, Christ has provided that the
man of good will should be able to find it without difficulty. It is
the city set upon the mountaintop, distinguishable from all other
religions because, in the words of Pius IX, "the true Church of
Christ . . . by divine authority is constituted and recognized by a
four-fold mark."[24] This distinguishing mark is, in the words of the
Nicene Creed, that the true Church is one, holy, catholic, and
apostolic.

The Church is *one* because Christ founded only one Church which
endures the same forever. There are not many Churches of Christ.
Pius IX has condemned the notion of a general, loosely jointed
Church with several disparate branches. The Church is one undivided organization in which there is one teaching body, one authority, one sacramental system. Christ, the Shepherd of souls, has one
flock. Christ, the Spouse, has one Bride. Christ and the faithful form

---

[23] *Den.* 1647 (*TCT*, 174).   [24] *Den.* 1686 (*TCT*, 181).

one Body. For Christ "is the head of his body, the Church,"[25] and "we, the many, are one body in Christ."[26] No other religion has a unity which can be expressed by the formula, one faith, one obedience, one baptism. The final reason for the unmistakable unity of the Church is that the Church is Christ and Christ is one.

The Church has a *holy* purpose, the union of all men with God, and she has all the means of holiness, a divine doctrine and a sacramental system. In at least some of her children she produces exquisite fruits of holiness attested by miracles. She and she alone is sealed with the mark of God — the perennial gift of miracles. She is holy because she is the Bride of Christ, and history is the working out of Christ's purpose which is to present her eventually to the Father without spot or blemish.

The Church is *catholic* or universal because she is meant for all men of all time. Therefore, as one and the same thing, she is diffused through the world and spread through time. From the time of St. Augustine, who popularized the phrase, she has been called The Catholic Church to distinguish her from the sects which imitate her or fall from her and fade away.

The Church is *apostolic* because Christ founded her upon the Apostles and, since she is changeless, she must always be apostolic. At any given moment in history, she is the religion which derives its origin from the Apostles, teaches the full doctrine of the Apostles, and has for rulers those who legitimately trace their authority to the Apostles. She is "The Old Church" which goes back in unbroken continuity to apostolic days.

Since the Roman Catholic Church alone possesses these four marks, she alone is the Church of Christ. Pius IX says: "Each of these marks is so closely interconnected that one cannot be without the others; therefore, that Church which truly is, and is called Catholic, must at the same time shine forth with the marks of unity, sanctity, and apostolic succession. Hence the Catholic Church is one with a unity which is unimpaired through the world and among all nations, with a unity indeed whose principle, root, and unfailing origin is the supreme authority and superior rulership of Blessed Peter, Prince

---

[25] Col. 1:18.   [26] Rom. 12:5.

of the Apostles, and of his successors in the Roman See. No other Church is Catholic except the one which, founded on the one Peter, grows into one body compacted and fitly joined by unity of faith and charity."[27] No non-Catholic sect has these marks; each is man-made and history can point to the time when it arose and to the man by whose influence it was severed from the Vine which is Christ. Indeed, as the Council of Vatican teaches, the Catholic Church her-self is her own apologetic, for "on account of her marvelous propaga-tion, her exalted sanctity and her inexhaustible fruitfulness in all that is good, on account of her catholic unity and unshaken stability, the Church herself is the great and perpetual motive of belief in her and the irrefutable proof of her divine mission."[28]

The Church the Mystical Body of Christ

The Church is incomparably more than a social organization. She is a spiritual edifice built of living stones, the people of God, the new Israel, the Bride of Christ. This last intimate relation the prophet Osee foretold: "I will espouse thee to me forever."[29] St. Paul tells the Corinthians: "I betrothed you to one spouse, that I might present you a chaste virgin to Christ."[30] He tells the Ephesians that Christ is the head of the Church as the husband is the head of the wife, that Christ loves and sanctifies her as a husband loves and takes care of his wife. Hence, as Eve came forth from the side of the sleeping Adam and was flesh of his flesh, so the Church came forth from the side of the dying Christ. As the human race has sprung from the marital union of Adam and Eve, so all the reborn of God are the fruit of the mystic marriage of Christ and His Church.

St. Paul says the union of Christ and the Church is a great mystery, for they form a supernatural organism which has no parallel in the universe. The organism lives by the divine life which is in Christ and which flows from Him to vitalize and sanctify the Church. It is like a vine into which men are engrafted by baptism. As branches, they are to partake more and more of divine life and bring forth more everlasting fruit. Those are living branches who have sanctifying

---

[27] *Den.* 1686 (*TCT*, 181).   [29] Osee 2:19.
[28] *Den.* 1794 (*TCT*, 68).   [30] 2 Cor. 11:2.

grace. Those are dead branches who are in mortal sin but are still united to Christ by faith and hope. Those who are guilty of apostasy, heresy, or schism fall from the vine and wither. "If anyone does not abide in me, he shall be cast outside as the branch and wither; and they shall gather them up and cast them into the fire."[31]

St. Paul best illustrates this organism by calling it the Body of Christ. Today we add the qualification "mystical" to distinguish "the Body of Christ" from a moral body like the State, from the physical body He received from the Blessed Virgin Mary, and from the sacrament of the Eucharist.

As a body is a living unity of diverse and ordered parts, each having different functions but all co-operating toward a common well-being, so all the baptized are part of one supernatural body. Each member contributes his due share to the good of the whole which consists, first, in the well-being of the individual members, second, in the good condition of the body as such, and finally, in the glory of Christ and God. The first purpose means that, while each baptized person retains his personal identity, he is to become another Christ. The second end is a perfect Church which is attained when "we all attain to the unity of the faith . . . to perfect manhood, to the mature measure of the fullness of Christ."[32] Finally, Christ gets His glory when at length He claims the Church as His unspotted Bride. God gets His glory when the number of the elect is completed, the Bride shines in grace and splendor, and is presented to the Father that God may be all in all.

The well-being of the Body depends on the efficient functioning of the parts which are many, as is clear from the hierarchic nature of the Church. Although the most important parts are the members of the sacred hierarchy, functioning is not confined to the priesthood or to those who have special gifts. Absolutely everyone of the faithful has an internal and external role to play in the kingdom of Christ. He asks the co-operation of His members, not out of weakness or indigence, "but because He has so willed it for the greater glory of His unspotted Spouse."[33]

---

[31] Jn. 15:5.   [33] Pius XII, *Mystici Corporis,* 46 (Paulist Press trans.).
[32] Eph. 4:12–13.

Christ and His members form the Total Christ, the Christ persisting through the ages. For Christ and His Church are identified. "The doctor of the Gentiles in his letter to the Corinthians affirms this when, without further qualification, he called the Church 'Christ,' following no doubt the example of his Master who called out from on high: 'Saul, Saul, why persecutest thou me?' "[34] The Total Christ has one head, one soul, one food, and a common activity.

Christ is the Head of the Body because, as its author, He deserves to rule it. He acts as Head by guiding the Body both in a hidden and extraordinary way and in a visible ordinary way through His Vicar on earth. He is also the direct source whence life-giving grace is dispensed through all the veins and nerves of the Body. Hence we are to "grow up in all things in him who is the head, Christ. From him the whole body . . . derives its increase to the building up of itself in love."[35] Furthermore He supports the Church by laboring in it without ceasing. For it is He who through the ministry of the Church baptizes, preaches, rules, teaches, looses, binds, prays, and offers sacrifice.

The soul or principle of life in the Body of Christ is the Spirit of Jesus. The same Holy Spirit, who sanctified His human nature at the Incarnation, Jesus merited for us on the cross, breathed on His Apostles on the night of the Resurrection, and bestowed on the whole Church on Pentecost. The role of the Spirit in the Body of Christ is communication of supernatural life. In all His fullness He dwells in the Head and from Him and through Him the Spirit diffuses blessings to the members who receive according to the measure of the giving of Christ. The Spirit is present to the whole Church and dwells in its living members, for He is the principle of unity which binds the members to one another and to the Head. He illumines the Church teaching that it may recognize and explain God's revelation, He strengthens it in persecution, He assists it in governing, He inspires it to choose the proper means of sanctifying souls. He vitalizes with supernatural life whatever action, worthy of eternal life, is anywhere performed in the Church. Thus He renders the

[34] *Ibid.*, 57.
[35] Eph. 5:15–16.

sacraments fruitful, He inspires individuals to believe, to profess the faith and lead a sacramental life. That which lifts the Church above all natural societies, the State included, is the Spirit of God who fills and unifies it, who penetrates every part of its being, and is active in it without ceasing.

The supernatural food of the Mystical Body is the Eucharistic Body and Blood of Christ. By eating this food the members nourish a life, which is not entirely their own, nor altogether separate from that of the others but in a way common to all. By eating the bread which has come down from heaven the Church achieves ecclesiastical and mystical unity. "Because the bread is one, we though many, are one body."[36]

The eating of a common food nourishes a common activity. This is the ferment of the vine producing everlasting fruit, or the salutary activity of the members which is both exterior and interior. Exterior activity is the care of souls: the apostolic work of the clergy and the Catholic Action of the laity. By the Christian rearing of children the fathers and mothers of families have a prominent part in this exterior work. Interior activity is the co-operation of the members with grace. Some think this has a direct influence on the distribution of supernatural help. "This is a deep mystery . . . that the salvation of many depends on the prayers and voluntary penances which the members of the Mystical Body of Jesus Christ offer for this intention . . . to our Divine Savior as though they were His associates."[37] But whether one adverts to it or not, everyone plays an indispensable role through his reaction to grace. The holy life of one member benefits the whole Church just as the sinful life of another hinders it. As in the body healthy organs help sickly parts, so the members of Christ do not live to themselves alone but they help one another by good works and thus assist in the building up of the whole Christ.

The Church of time is in process of becoming the everlasting family of the predestined. The growth of the whole Christ by mutual interchange of benefit transcends life and time, as is clear from the doctrine of the Communion of Saints. A saint is anyone who lives

---

[36] 1 Cor. 10:17.
[37] Pius XII, *Mystici Corporis*, 46 (Paulist Press trans.).

with the life of Christ, and saints fall into three classes: the faithful
on earth, the Church Militant, who are not yet confirmed in Christ;
the souls in Purgatory, who are confirmed in Christ but are not yet
fully united to Him, the Church Suffering; and the blessed in heaven,
the Church Triumphant, who are forever united to Christ in glory.
Each division shares in the blessings of the Body of Christ and the
members of each mutually assist one another. Thus we honor and
ask the help of the saints in heaven and we pray for the release of
the poor souls; all these in turn intercede for us.

All the predestined will one day be as sons in their Father's house.
They will not be a mere society but a true community of persons in
full communion with one another and with the Triune God. God
calls the individual to share the mystery by putting on Christ. "He
chose us in him before the foundation of the world, that we should
be holy and without blemish. . . . He predestined us to be adopted
through Jesus Christ as his sons."[38] While the mercy of God touches
each individual personally, he is also caught up in the people of God,
predestined by Him to be one great family sharing His intimate life.

C. *Grace*

The Holy Spirit is sent and the Church exists so that man may
become holy, fit for union with God. The process of sanctifying him
includes these stages: his reconciliation with God or his justification;
his perseverance or increase in holiness; the crowning of his holiness
with the beatific vision. With these three things the rest of theology
is concerned.

By justification the sinner is restored to a condition of harmony
with God. In the words of Holy Writ the just man is holy and holiness is justice. Now every kind of justice is an equality, and in this
case it is the equivalence between what a man is and what God
wants him to be. God's enduring wish for man is that he live with
God's life and be God's son. But since, on account of Adam's sin,
he is born without that life, man must be revived or *made just* again.
Thus St. Paul tells the Colossians: "You, when you were dead by
reason of your sins, he brought to life."[39] Hence the Council of Trent

[38] Eph. 1:4–5.   [39] Col. 2:13.

says that justification is "the passing from that state in which a man is born a child of the first Adam to the state of grace and adoption among the children of God through the second Adam, Jesus Christ, our Savior."[40]

According to Luther God effects this transfer by a sort of juridic process. The sinner was essentially corrupted by original sin and a sinner he always remains. If, however, he is clothed in the merits of Christ and has confidence that Christ will save him, God will regard him as just. Justification, therefore, is the imputation to the sinner of the merits of Christ. The Council of Trent rejects this teaching because "justification . . . is the sanctification and renovation of the interior man through the voluntary reception of grace and the gifts."[41] The sinner's renovation involves, first, a real removal of sin. According to Holy Writ our sins are not merely hidden from God; they are washed away, taken away, removed, eradicated, etc. Second, the sinner is reborn to God, he is a new creation, he is transferred from death to life, from darkness to light, he is given a new supernatural life.

God effects this change, says the Council, by the grant of grace. Grace, in general, is a gift whose source is the good will or favor of the donor. In theology, it is an out-and-out gift, given by God to man with a view to his obtaining the beatific vision. Since man has no right to the vision, the offer of it is gratuitous, and any help from God which leads one to the vision is a grace. This grace could be a created or uncreated gift. The uncreated gift is the Holy Spirit, sent to the person on a mission of holiness. The created gift is something, usually but not necessarily, supernatural effected by the Holy Spirit in or for the man. This could be external to the man, as a miracle or a sermon, or it could be internal, a benefit directly received in the man's soul. The Holy Spirit sometimes gives wondrous powers called charisms, such as the power to heal or speak strange tongues, and these are for the benefit of the Christian community. Finally, there are internal gifts whose purpose is the sanctification of the recipient by giving him supernatural power. These can be passing or permanent.

[40] Den. 796 (TCT, 560).   [41] Den. 799 (TCT, 563).

What is the grace which sanctifies? Some thought it was the uncreated Gift, the Holy Spirit, but the Council of Trent says that "it is the justice of God, not that whereby He is just, but that whereby He makes us just."[42] While the Holy Spirit is given whenever we are justified, He is not our justice; He is the Author of it. Our justice is something created. Nor is it something external because that which sanctifies effects the interior renewal of the man. Obviously the grace which sanctifies is not given for the benefit of the community but of the person. Nor is it a mere passing touch of God's supernatural influence because the justified man is a new creation, a rebirth, the seed of God in whom the very life of God is present. Since he has new supernatural life, the grace which justifies him must be a supernatural life-principle. To this created, supernatural, internal, and permanent gift theology gives the name *sanctifying grace,* and the Council of Trent says that it and it alone is the divine gift which justifies.

Sanctifying grace

This is the most important creature in the personal life of the wayfarer, first, because it takes away his sinful state: "There is therefore now no condemnation for those who are in Christ Jesus."[43] Second, it gives him God's life and puts the beatific vision within his reach. By one and the same action — the infusion of sanctifying grace — the sinner is both justified, reconciled to God, and sanctified, made like to God. Grace endows us with a share in God's own nature. "He has granted us the very great and precious promises, so that through them you may become partakers of the divine nature."[44] Grace admits us to fellowship with God because by grace divinity is imparted to us. For grace is the seed of God, as St. John says, and when it comes to final fruition in us, "we shall be like him."[45] Grace deifies us, gives us the power to know and enjoy God as He is, and makes us members of the family of Father, Son, and Holy Spirit. For we are "born not of blood, nor of the will of the flesh, nor of the will of man, but of God."[46] Our rebirth to God is real.

---

[42] *Den.* 799 (*TCT,* 563).   [44] 2 Pet. 1:4.   [46] Jn. 1:13.
[43] Rom. 8:1.   [45] 1 Jn. 3:2.

This does not mean that we are transformed into God, or that a mere moral connection now exists with God, but we are raised to a supernatural likeness to God and in a physical manner share His life.

As a consequence we are the adopted sons of God. "You have received a spirit of adoption as sons, by virtue of which we cry, 'Abba, Father!' The Spirit himself gives testimony to our spirit that we are the sons of God."[47] Our adoption is no mere legal fiction. We are not now strangers but we have been engrafted into Christ. We are not, however, sons as the Word is. He is the substantial image of God; our likeness to the heavenly Father is imperfect. While our generation from God only resembles the generation of the Only-Begotten, it allows us truly to call God our Father, and He sees in us His true seed. "But if we are sons, we are heirs also: heirs indeed of God and joint heirs with Christ."[48] Thus grace puts the beatific vision within reach of our striving by making us brothers of Christ and sharers in His inheritance. Our inheritance of course will be finite and proportioned to the merits we achieve on earth, but grace is the true beginning of eternal life. All that is required for the justified soul's entrance upon its inheritance is perfect cleansing from the remains of sin and the light of glory after death.

Grace gives the soul an unimaginable splendor. We are now worthy of God's friendship, not because we deserve it, but God makes us lovable. Because the soul has been made so attractive, Father, Son, and Holy Spirit make their abode in it. "If anyone love me, he will keep my word, and my Father will love him, and we will come to him and make our abode with him."[49] The soul can now entertain God as guest and friend, and as proof of God's friendship the soul receives the uncreated gift: "The charity of God is poured forth in our hearts by the Holy Spirit who has been given to us."[50] Since sanctification is the work of divine love, it is appropriated to the Holy Spirit: "Do you not know that your members are the temple of the Holy Spirit?"[51] In explaining this mystery of the divine indwelling, we are warned by Pius XII not to talk as if the just soul acquires something which belongs to God alone, but we can say that

---

47 Rom. 8:15–16.   49 Jn. 14:23.   51 1 Cor. 6:19.
48 Rom. 8:17.   50 Rom. 5:5.

God is in the just soul by a special presence. This is, first, a pledge of eternal life. By grace we are "sealed with the Holy Spirit . . . who is the pledge of our inheritance."[52] He makes a mark upon the soul which is assurance that the Blessed Trinity, now given to us, will be, if we are faithful, our eternal possession. Second, the Spirit abides in the soul as the continuing source of divine life, comfort, and assistance. Finally, His presence is a real beginning of the beatific vision because, by grant of the virtues and gifts, we can, even in this life, know and enjoy God experientially. While God is present to all creatures by His essence, power, and knowledge, He remains inaccessible to them. The best that the intelligent agent can do of himself is to reason to that presence, but the just soul by means of the gifts can know and love Him experientially.

What is sanctifying grace in itself? Although Christ compares it to a wedding garment, it is not a substance but a supernatural quality, resembling a habit and inhering in the soul, distinct from the soul and its powers and probably also from charity. A helpful analogy is made between grace and man's natural life. The principle of man's natural life is his soul, which operates through faculties like reason, will, sight, etc., and thus produces the activity which completes his natural being. So grace is his principle of supernatural life and it operates through the supernatural faculties of the virtues and the gifts. By means of them the just man produces that supernatural activity which brings him the fullness of his supernatural being. Equipped, then, with grace and the gifts, he is capable of working out his supernatural destiny.

Faith, hope, and charity are the terms employed in the New Testament to signify permanent principles of action, abiding in the soul, and given by God as part of the endowment necessary for living the supernatural life; for example: "He who is just lives by faith,"[53] and, "Let us put on the breastplate of faith and charity."[54] The Council of Trent teaches that "when a man is justified, along with the remission of his sins, he receives through Jesus Christ in whom he is implanted all these gifts: faith, hope and charity."[55]

---

[52] Eph. 1:13.   [54] 1 Thes. 5:8.
[53] Rom. 1:17.   [55] *Den.* 800 (*TCT,* 564).

The first of these is *faith*. Acceptance of God's revelation is the foundation of salvation for "without faith it is impossible to please God."[56] A man is to direct his whole life to the beatific vision, but he could not do this unless he accepted as real God's supernatural economy. He can know about these things only through the word of God and the only proper reaction to that word is belief. That a man's faith be adequate it is not enough that God should make a revelation and give him the actual graces to make acts of faith. Something more is required — a permanent supernatural power of believing. In the ceremony of baptism the adult catechumen is asked: "What do you ask of the Church of God?" He answers: "Faith." Assuredly he already believes, but in the sacrament he receives a gift which will make his faith firm as a rock. Just as reason has the natural facility of accepting as true realities proposed to it through evidence, so this gift of faith is a permanent bent inclining the soul to adhere to the Christian revelation. By means of this theological virtue the believer can cling to revelation with more tenacity and certainty than he does to natural truths. This permanent power is necessary because obstacles to belief are multiple. We have a tendency to be skeptical. We are subjected to the pressure of an unbelieving world. We could not, therefore, continue to accept dogmas, which are in themselves obscure and often impose personal hardship, unless we were given a power from above.

No one could constantly direct his life to the beatific vision unless he sincerely desired it and had confidence of eventual success. Divine *hope* supplies the desire and the confidence. So steeped in material values is the natural man, that he could not of himself entertain the wish to possess the unseen God, much less strive after union with Him. Nevertheless that desire is almost ineradicable from the baptized. The state of grace is not assurance of glory. Hence the Council of Trent warns the just that "they are reborn, not yet in glory, but in the hope of glory."[57] Grace can be lost and is lost by every mortal sin. No one is certain even that he is in the state of grace unless he has a divine revelation to that effect. Hence salvation is a difficult enterprise on account of human weakness, but it is

---

[56] Hebr. 11:6.   [57] *Den.* 806 (*TCT*, 570).

attainable through the divine assistance. Lest we be overcome by faintheartedness, we need a source of courage which enables us to keep struggling on. Divine hope makes us confident that God will give us eternal life and all the necessary means. Since hope is not confidence in self but in God, it partakes of the certainty of faith: "No one hath hoped in the Lord and hath been confounded."[58] The basis in God for our hope is manifold. Our desire for Him rests upon the fact that He is our reward. Our confidence is especially supported by His fidelity: "Let us hold fast the confession of our hope . . . for he who has given the promise is faithful."[59]

By faith we cling to God, the first truth. By hope we seek Him as the source of our happiness. By charity we love Him as He is for His sake. If any activity requires a permanent supernatural principle it is *charity*. For friendship between God and the creature is naturally impossible, and charity is the love of friendship which exists between God and the just. "No longer do I call you servants . . . but I have called you friends."[60] The whole supernatural economy exists that we may be friends with God. God makes us lovable so that we may love Him and live with Him in personal fellowship. "Let us therefore love, because God first loved us."[61] We are obliged to love God above all things. This is not a love of sentimentality nor an emotional drive but preference for God founded upon faith's appreciation of Him as infinitely lovable. The core requirement of this love is preference for His will above the love of any created being. "If you love me, keep my commandments."[62] Charity is perfect when we do the will of God in all things for His sake and, as far as we can, seek Him with all the affection of the heart. Furthermore, since God is actually or potentially united to all intelligent beings who are not confirmed in malice, we are to see God in the neighbor and love him for God's sake. The characteristic command of the New Law is: "A new commandment I give you, that you love one another: that as I have loved you, you also love one another."[63] A distinctive mark of Christianity is the practice of charity: "By this will all men know that you are my disciples, if you have love for one another."[64] Charity

---

[58] Eccu. 2:11. [60] Jn. 15:15. [62] Jn. 14:15. [64] Jn. 13:35.
[59] Hebr. 10:23. [61] 1 Jn. 4:19. [63] Jn. 13:34.

is the greatest of virtues: "There abide faith, hope and charity, these three; but the greatest of these is charity."[65] Charity is the sign that God has chosen the soul to be His spouse.

It is likely that the moral virtues of prudence, justice, temperance, and fortitude are also infused. The just man receives new supernatural power to fulfill the moral demands made on a member of Christ. Natural virtue, which makes one a perfect citizen, is not enough. The just man has a higher ideal of conduct — the putting on of Christ. The acts of these virtues are to be motivated by charity and by it be directed to man's last end.

The virtues are active powers which enable a man to assume the initiative in upright conduct. There are, however, more profound and valuable powers which perfect the virtues by rendering the soul more docile to the inspirations of the Holy Spirit. These are the gifts of the Holy Spirit: wisdom, understanding, counsel, fortitude, knowledge, piety, and fear of the Lord. As the soul becomes more holy, its direction is taken over more and more by the Holy Spirit operating through the plenitude of the gifts. Without abandonment to the Holy Spirit and the potentialities of His gifts high sanctity is impossible.

Christ says that the tree is known by its fruits. He who constantly submits to the Spirit will eventually produce the fruit of the Spirit, conduct which is both virtuous and delightful. St. Paul enumerates some of them as "charity, joy, peace, patience, kindness, goodness, faith, modesty, continency."[66] These gracious actions, produced with ease by the sanctified soul, are the final outcome of the work of the Holy Spirit in the soul. They show that the members of Christ have crucified their flesh with its passionate cravings.

Actual grace

Besides sanctifying grace, which produces the permanent state of holiness, there is another internal supernatural grace of transient character called actual grace. It is given for the performance of *salutary acts* — those which lead in a positive manner to the beatific vision. To the question, What can fallen man do of himself to become and remain justified, one heresy said, Everything, another said,

---

[65] 1 Cor. 13:13. [66] Gal. 5:22.

Nothing. Between these extremes lies the Catholic doctrine on actual grace.

In the fifth century the Pelagians denied the whole supernatural order. Under the influence of Stoic philosophy, Pelagius said that by sheer strength of will a man can avoid sin, attain faith, justification, and the beatific vision; that the help which he got from Christ was merely external — good example. To this impiety the Catholics, under the championship of St. Augustine, opposed the words of Christ, "Without me you can do nothing,"[67] and said they meant that no one could be saved without the *internal* help of God. The Pelagians replied that the internal help of grace merely gave a knowledge of, and made easier, a task which, without grace, would be difficult but not impossible. The Catholics appealed to St. Paul who demands grace (1) for *every salutary thought:* "Not that we are sufficient of ourselves to think anything, as from ourselves, but our sufficiency is from God"[68]; (2) for *every salutary resolve:* "There is question not of him who wills nor of him who runs, but of God showing mercy"[69]; (3) for *every salutary work:* "It is God who of his good pleasure works in you both the will and the performance."[70] The Council of Carthage (A.D. 418) declared that the grace of Christ not only gives knowledge of God's commandments but imparts help to keep them, that without this help it is impossible to keep them.

A compromise was attempted by some ascetics of Provence, who later were called the Semi-Pelagians, namely, that while grace is needed after a person gets the faith it is not necessary for his getting it, that God gives faith as a reward for natural goodness and the merits one acquired in unbelief, that once justified a man can persevere to the end by his own power. The Church replied that no one can utter a salutary prayer unless God moves him to it: "No one can say 'Jesus is the Lord' except in the Holy Spirit"[71]; that all our salutary goodness is the gift of God according to St. Paul: "What hast thou that thou hast not received"[72]; and: "By the grace of God I am what I am."[73] The Council of Orange denied that grace

[67] Jn. 15:5.
[68] 2 Cor. 3:5.
[69] Rom. 9:16.
[70] Phil. 2:13.
[71] 1 Cor. 12:3.
[72] 1 Cor. 4:7.
[73] 1 Cor. 15:10.

can be deserved by purely natural prayer or that God waits upon man's good will in order to give grace. It asserted that the desire of salvation is formed in us by the Holy Spirit; that the increase of faith, the beginning of faith, and the very desire for it is a divine gift; that "it is through the interior infusion of the Holy Spirit that we believe, will, or are able to do all these things as we ought."[74]

Luther, on the other hand, said that the unjustified man could do nothing but sin, and he was condemned by Leo X. Jansenius said that all the acts of unbelievers were sins, and he was condemned by Alexander VIII. Hence the Church teaches that a man without sanctifying grace or faith can perform some naturally good acts. In the face, however, of prolonged temptations against the more difficult commands of the moral law such a man, left to himself, will fall; not because he has no free will or power of resistance, but such is the hold of concupiscence on him that he will not avoid sin in these circumstances unless, as St. Paul tells the Romans, he is supported by grace. What is the nature of this grace? Since it is given to heal the wounds of sin, it is a healing grace. Since the *sinner* needs it to avoid more sin, it is different from sanctifying grace. Since it is given for the performance of a good *act,* it is a transient help, an actual grace. However, since the sinner can avoid sin by performing merely naturally good acts, some think that healing grace need not, though it may, be in itself supernatural. For the observance, then, of the whole law over a long time unregenerate man absolutely needs at least transient internal help from God.*

From these controversies three dogmas emerge. (1) Unregenerate man is capable of performing some morally good acts without special help from God. (2) He absolutely needs internal supernatural help to perform any salutary act. Of himself he can overcome some temptations but these actions have merely the negative value of keeping him from becoming more immersed in sin. They have no value with regard to eternal life. For if an action is to be a positive contribution toward the attainment of the beatific vision, it must have

---

[74] *Den.* 179 (*TCT,* 546).

* Modern theologians are quite generally agreed that no one will keep the whole law for long unless, in addition to actual graces, he has also sanctifying grace.

a supernatural character. Of himself unregenerate man is totally unable to do anything supernatural. (3) This supernatural help from God is utterly gratuitous, a pure mercy of God. Whenever the communion of supernatural life does not exist between God and man, it depends on God alone to give the help which leads to its establishment. We do not say that no grace can be merited. For if God gives a grace, a man can use it to merit more, but the first grace leading to conversion can never be deserved by anything a man does. St. Paul devotes a good part of the Epistle to the Romans to expounding the gratuitous character of grace: neither the Jewish converts by fidelity to their law nor the Gentiles by observance of the natural moral law merited their call to the faith.

Actual grace, then, is a passing help, a temporary elevation of mind and heart which enables one to perform acts which positively tend to salvation. This grace consists in a pious thought and a holy movement of the will whose principal cause is the Holy Spirit and whose purpose is the recipient's performance of salutary activity. It is God at work within us. First, He "works in us but without us" when He produces indeliberate acts of knowledge and will. This is antecedent grace[75] or arousing grace. Second, God and man produce the deliberate salutary act, for "whenever we do good, God operates in us and with us that we may act."[76] The influence of the grace which alerted us follows through and assists us in performing the salutary act. The role of actual grace in a man's salvation is seen in the process (1) by which the sinner is justified and (2) in the just man's increase and perseverance in justice.

How the sinner is justified

Standing upon their doctrine of the complete corruption of man by original sin, the Reformers denied the possibility of man preparing himself for justification. It is of faith, however, that the sinner can and must prepare himself through actual grace. To be reconciled with God, unregenerate man must be aroused by actual grace and

[75] The Latin *gratia praeveniens* is misleadingly translated as "preventing grace."
[76] Council of Orange, *Den.* 182.

co-operate with that grace. The initiative of grace and the need of human co-operation is explained by the Council of Trent: "In the case of adults justification must begin with God's antecedent grace through Jesus Christ, that is, a divine and utterly unmerited call. The purpose of this call is that they who had been turned from God by sin may, awakened and assisted by grace, be disposed to turn to their own justification by freely assenting to and co-operating with that grace. The result is that, when God touches the heart of man with the illumination of the Holy Spirit, the man is not inactive since he accepts an inspiration which he can reject; on the other hand, however, by his own free will, without God's grace, he cannot take one step toward justice in God's sight."[77]

Christ says: "No man can come to me unless the Father who has sent me draw him."[78] How is the man drawn? If he is immersed in sin, he needs healing grace to overcome temptation. Once the obstacle of habitual sin is in the main removed, God will offer him supernatural graces the first of which is the call to faith. This faith is not a mere trust in God nor is it a personal conviction of salvation; it is dogmatic faith, acceptance of divine revelation. This is "the beginning of man's salvation, the basis and root of all justice."[79] Next he realizes he is a sinner; and turning from a salutary fear of divine justice to a consideration of God's mercy, he is encouraged to hope. He begins to love God as the source of all blessings and to hate his sins, turning to that penance which must be done before baptism. Finally, he resolves to do the will of God, lead a new life, and accept baptism. Not all of these steps may be taken or in the order mentioned, but in every instance there must be faith and sorrow for sins committed. Without the illumination and inspiration of the Holy Spirit none of these steps is possible, but when the sinner takes them, he prepares himself for the great climax of justification of which God is the sole Author.

Increase in justice

Once justified a man is not to become supernaturally inactive. For

---

[77] *Den.* 797 (*TCT*, 651).   [79] Council of Trent, *Den.* 801 (*TCT*, 565).
[78] Jn. 6:44.

either he will produce supernaturally good works or he will in time cease to be just. But because concupiscence remains in the just, some have imagined that the just man cannot help but sin especially when he acts from a motive of the reward of heaven; hence they cling to a blind trust in God and deny the need of good works. But no doctrine is more opposed to common sense and the word of God. In His preview of the last judgment Christ says the just are saved for having done the works of charity and the damned are lost for having neglected them. Good works, then, are necessary that we may increase in justice and persevere to the end.

The Council of Trent says: "When faith works along with their works, the justified increase in the very justice which they have received through the grace of Christ and are justified the more, as it is written: 'He who is just, let him be just still.' "[80] The daily aim of the Christian is to do the truth in charity and thus grow up in Him who is the Head, Christ. If then, as children of God, we act toward Him with love, we win an increase of His love and become more like Him. In order to do these works of love the just man needs actual graces. It is not defined doctrine, but it is commonly held that for the performance of *all* salutary acts the just require, besides sanctifying grace, also particular actual graces. The Council of Trent seems to be describing actual grace when it says: "Christ Jesus Himself . . . pours His strength into the justified incessantly, a strength which precedes, accompanies and follows their good works and without it the good works cannot be pleasing to God or meritorious."[81]

Perseverance in Justice

Can the just avoid mortal sin and thus persevere to the end? Some heretics considered this a false problem. They said that the just are incapable of sinning, that the sin of a man is proof that he has not yet been justified; and hence the truly just need not bother about observance of the commandments. This heresy contradicts St. Paul: "Let him who thinks he stands take heed lest he fall."[82] No one, therefore, is to think himself confirmed in grace unless God reveals

---

[80] *Den.* 803 (*TCT*, 567).   [81] *Den.* 809 (*TCT*, 573).   [82] 1 Cor. 10:12.

this to him. On the other hand, it is also heresy to say that some of God's commandments are impossible of fulfillment or that the just man sins in everything he does. For God does not command the impossible; His yoke is really sweet and His burden light. He never forsakes those who have once been justified unless they first desert Him.

It is then an article of faith that the just man can persevere to the end. Whence comes this power? Against the Semi-Pelagians who thought the just man had this power of himself, the Council of Orange said: "The divine assistance ought always to be implored even by the reborn and the justified that they may come to a good end or persevere in good works."[83] The Council of Trent teaches that perseverance requires a special gift of grace. Christ and St. Paul exhort the faithful to pray unceasingly for this grace. The need of it arises from the weakness of the human will which, on account of the revolt of the flesh against the spirit, has not in itself the power always to stand fast in virtue.

How does the just man obtain this grace? Can he merit it by his good conduct? He can merit a sufficient grace, which of itself is potent enough for victory over temptation, but which, through his lack of co-operation, may be void of result. What he needs is an efficacious grace, one that insures victory. This kind of grace he cannot merit; otherwise, once justified, he could never fall. The key to perseverance is the predilection of God giving grace which He foresees will have its salutary effect. Such grace is the gift of God who alone "is able to make him who stands, stand perseveringly."[84] While one's good actions cannot merit this grace, he will infallibly get it who prays for it properly.

This prayer ought to be most confident because God exercises a special providence over the just. On account of it the just man can avoid mortal and all deliberate sins. Without, however, a very special privilege, such as was given to the Blessed Virgin Mary, no one can avoid semideliberate falls: "In this mortal life, however holy and just men may be, they sometimes fall at least into slight daily sins."[85]

---

[83] *Den.* 183.
[84] Council of Trent, *Den.* 806 (*TCT,* 570).
[85] *Ibid. Den.* 804 (*TCT, 568*).

Since only he is saved who perseveres to the end, the Council of Trent calls final perseverance The Great Grace. It is not one but a series of efficacious graces. As the unregenerate cannot by natural merit win the first grace which leads to justification, so neither can the just merit the happy conjunction of the state of grace and the moment of death. It is always God who begins and brings to blessed completion the work of salvation. We ought then to have most secure hope in the help of God; "for unless men are uncooperative with His grace, God will bring the good work to perfection, just as He began it, working both the will and the performance."[86]

Distribution of Grace

There is an unending need of actual grace: the unregenerate man needs it to prepare for justification; the just man to persevere in justice; the sinner to recover it. How does God meet these needs?

Since He sincerely desires the salvation of all, God offers all an opportunity of salvation which is real. In the case of adults this means the grant of grace with which a man can co-operate and be saved. Hence the unbeliever is offered grace to keep the moral law and come to the faith: "I desire not the death of the wicked, but that the wicked turn from his way and live."[87] The believer who falls is offered grace to repent: "The Lord does not delay in his promises, but for your sake is long-suffering, not wishing that any should perish but that all should turn to repentance."[88] The just man gets grace to avoid sin and persevere: "God is faithful and will not permit you to be tempted beyond your strength, but with temptation will also give you a way out that you may be able to bear it."[89] Hence the adult who perishes is lost through his own lack of co-operation and not through any defect in the grace given him.

Moreover, if a man does what he can with the grace he gets, God will not deny him any further grace he needs. The unbeliever, who co-operates with grace to avoid sin and accept the faith, will be offered the grace of justification. The just man who co-operates with ordinary graces will be offered richer graces.

---

[86] *Ibid. Den.* 806 (*TCT*, 570).
[87] Ezech. 33:11.
[88] 2 Pet. 3:9.
[89] 1 Cor. 10:13.

Having said this, however, theology admits that the distribution of grace is a deep mystery intimately connected with divine pre-destination. The Semi-Pelagians thought that God gave equal grace to all so that the difference in holiness among men is due to human co-operation alone, but it is certain that some men receive more and better graces than others. Why? Previous co-operation with grace is a partial but not a complete explanation. The Spirit breathes where He will, sometimes granting great holiness at the dawn of reason, sometimes converting great sinners at the moment of death, sometimes leaving others obstinate in their sins. "Therefore he has mercy on whom he will, and whom he will he hardens."[90] This is not to say that God acts in an arbitrary, whimsical fashion. His grant of grace is according to deep counsels of His wisdom, all of which He has not made known. He keeps us in the dark in this regard that we may realize our complete helplessness without Him and that our childlike trust in Him may be complete.

Grace and Human Freedom

When the Reformers said that under the influence of grace man was not free, the Council of Trent branded as heretical the statement that "man's free will . . . in no way co-operates when it assents to God, who arouses and calls it . . . and that it cannot dissent if it wishes but like some inanimate thing does nothing and remains merely passive."[91]

How do we explain human freedom under the influence of grace? Are we to say that God must wait and see how man will react to grace? That is Semi-Pelagian thought. Before any grace is given God knows how man will react. That which man accepts is efficacious grace; what man rejects is sufficient grace. Those who are saved are saved because they got efficacious grace; the grace of those who are lost is merely sufficient. The heretics who denied that man is free under the influence of grace said that a merely sufficient grace is useless and pernicious; but the Church teaches as of faith that it is a real gift from God and a true benefit to man. Our Lord said:

---

[90] Rom. 9:18.
[91] *Den.* 814 (*TCT*, 578).

"Jerusalem, Jerusalem . . . how often would I have gathered thy children together, as a hen gathers her young under her wings, but thou wouldst not!"[92]

It is clear that man is free under the influence of sufficient grace, for he can reject it. But how explain man's freedom under efficacious grace; that is, how does man freely co-operate with a grace which will infallibly produce the effect God intends by it? Catholic theologians are not agreed. Some say that the divine initiative in man's salvation requires God to put something into efficacious grace which assures man's consent and which He omits from sufficient grace. Others say that this something would destroy man's liberty, that a sufficient grace in itself is no different from an efficacious grace. They explain the efficacy of grace on the ground that God, who knows how the man would react to all possible grants of grace, graciously offers him the one which is suited to his concrete situation and therefore certain to elicit his consent. The Church has never settled this debate.

Merit

A final conclusion from the presence of grace in man is that the just man can merit before God. Merit means that one freely confers on another a benefit which calls for a reward from the one benefited. Merit is real or condign when the benefit is evaluated as deserving the reward; otherwise, it is merely fitting or congruous, dependent on the generosity of the donor.

The Reformers condemned personal supernatural merits as derogating from the value of grace and the merits of Christ and as making men self-centered and pharisaical. But the notion of a heavenly reward runs through the New Testament. Our Lord promises rich rewards to the poor in spirit, to the meek, to those who suffer for Him or do the works of mercy. The parables deal with this theme constantly. St. Paul bids us "be steadfast . . . always abounding in the work of the Lord, knowing that your labor is not in vain in the Lord."[93] The Council of Trent says that the good works of the just are both the gift of God and the merit of the just man.

---

[92] Mt. 23:37.   [93] 1 Cor. 15:58.

What is the basis in God of our merit? While we can confer no real benefits on God by our service which indeed already belongs to Him, yet God can bind Himself to reward the good actions of His children. Our merit rests upon the divine promise. The basis in us of merit is (1) the state of grace. "The worth of the work," says St. Thomas, "depends on the dignity of grace, whereby a man, being made partaker of the Divine Nature, is adopted as a son by God, to whom the inheritance is due by right of adoption."[94] (2) The action must be performed before death, the "night when no man can work."[95] (3) The action must be free, morally good, performed with the help of grace, and in some way directed to the beatific vision. It is likely that all the deliberate acts of the just which are not sinful are meritorious.

Christ, as the Head, is the only one who can truly merit for others. The just man can truly merit only for himself. The Council of Trent enumerates the chief objects of condign merit: (1) *Life eternal.* "For this is that crown of justice which the Apostle says is laid up for him after the fight and the race; the crown that will be given him by the just Judge, and not to him alone but to all who love His coming."[96] (2) *Increase of grace:* "Justice which has been received . . . is increased through good works. . . . Such good works . . . are the cause of the increase."[97] (3) *Increase of glory.* Present increase of grace means a corresponding increase of glory hereafter. Our enjoyment of God in the vision is proportioned to our present love of Him, for "each will receive his own reward according to his labor."[98]

---

[94] *Sum. Theol.,* I–II, 114, 3.
[95] Jn. 9:4.
[96] Council of Trent, *Den.* 809 (*TCT,* 573).
[97] *Ibid. Den.* 834 (*TCT,* 598).
[98] 1 Cor. 3:8.

CHAPTER SIX

THE   SOURCES   OF   GRACE

"The Forgiveness of Sins"

THE first goal of the Christian is to live and die in the state of sanctifying grace. His second aim is to obtain the efficacious graces which will enable him to resist temptation, practice virtue, and grow in the friendship of God. To get these graces he must pray and have recourse to the sacraments.

A. *Prayer*

Prayer is the elevation of mind and heart to God, the conversation which faith enables a man to hold with God. Prayer is not the work of man alone but the combined work of God and man, the initiative always being with God. The first grace to an adult is the grace to pray or ask for help; hence prayer is man's first reaction to God drawing him to Himself. While a man can pray in order to adore, thank, and placate God, the chief reason for it is to ask for blessings. The bases of prayer are the nothingness of man and the unbounded benevolence of God. For the fulfillment of his needs man must go to the source of his good, which he does spiritually, by prayer. Since prayer is the unavoidable declaration of man's complete dependence on God, it comes easily to the faithful and is the most familiar act of the virtue of religion. While God, who is so liberal, can and does give many things unasked, yet the supreme thing, salvation, and most of the graces necessary for salvation, He gives on condition that we ask.

Scarcely anything has been more clearly expressed in Holy Writ or better understood by the faithful than the need and power of prayer. Christ insists: "Ask, and it shall be given you. . . . For everyone who asks, receives; and he who seeks, finds."[1] Asking is

---

[1] Mt. 7:7–8.

made a condition for the grant of favors, not for God's sake, as if He needed our prayers or would be unaware of our wants unless we asked, but for our sakes, that we may go to Him with confidence and recognize Him as the Author of all our good. The motive of our prayer, however, is not that we may change the dispositions of Providence, but that, by our prayers, we may obtain what God has appointed.

We may pray for anything whose fulfillment is no sin. While we may ask for temporal favors, as the Lord's prayer encourages us to do, our requests ought to be conditioned on the capacity of such favors to help salvation. The unconditioned requests are grace and glory for oneself and the neighbor.

Does God always hear the prayers of the faithful? Some prayers are not heard because, as St. James says: "You ask and do not receive, because you ask amiss, that you may spend it upon your passions."[2] Christ, however, assures us that every prayer properly said will be heard. The conditions are: (1) humility — we must sincerely recognize our dependence on God; (2) perseverance — our prayer should continue for as long a time as God deems fit; (3) faith — "All things whatsoever you ask for in prayer, believing, you shall receive."[3] This means that prayer must proceed from belief in God as He is and we must ask for something that conduces to life eternal. (4) Union with Christ — "If you ask the Father anything in my name, he will give it to you. Hitherto you have not asked anything in my name. Ask, and you shall receive."[4] Since Christ is the suppliant whose requests the Father always grants, our prayers will always be heard if they are united to His prayers. He always presents our petition to the Father if it proceeds from faith, humbly and perseveringly, and if we ask for what promotes our salvation. St. Thomas adds the further consideration that we ask for ourselves,[5] for the promise of being infallibly heard has been made to the *petitioner*. Moreover, even as we cannot merit salvation for the neighbor, so also our prayers for him may not always be answered. Nevertheless "we ought to desire good things not only for ourselves

2 James 4:3.   4 Jn. 16:23–24.
3 Mt. 21:22.   5 St. Thomas, *Sum. Theol.* II–II, 83, 15, ad 2.

but also for others; for this is essential to the love we owe our neighbor. . . . We ought to pray even for sinners that they be converted, and for the just that they persevere and advance in holiness."[6] God also hears the sinner; that is, He gives him actual grace to pray, and if the prayer fulfills the proper conditions, He grants it, "not out of justice, because the sinner does not merit to be heard, but out of pure mercy."[7]

While it is God alone who can grant grace and glory, yet we may also pray to the saints in heaven, asking them to intercede for us so that we may be heard on account of their intercession and merit with God.

Since salvation is through Christ, in Christ, and with Christ, the life of a Christian is a supernatural partnership with Him. The two together achieve whatever supernatural results are credited to the man. Now in the obtaining of grace, the man plays a more or less prominent part when he prays, and the graces so obtained are usually proportioned to the faith and charity of his prayer. When, however, he uses a sacrament, the chief results are due to Christ acting on him by means of sanctified matter — chosen instruments of holiness. The sacraments are a unique legacy from Christ to the Church which possesses nothing more holy than these sources of grace. They are the outstanding means by which the passion of Christ is applied to man.

B. *The Sacraments*

The word *sacrament* is from the Latin *sacramentum* which meant a sacred thing, like the oath of a soldier. It also translates the Greek *mysterion,* a hidden religious truth. In a broad sense a sacrament is any sacred symbol but, as it is technically applied to Christian ritual, it designates those symbolic rites which produce holiness in men. Hence St. Thomas says a sacrament is "the sign of a holy thing in so far as it makes men holy."[8] The Council of Trent calls a sacrament a "symbol of a sacred thing and a visible form of invisible grace."[9] Today a sacrament is generally presented

---

[6] *Ibid.* a. 7.
[7] *Ibid.* a. 16.

[8] *Ibid.* III, 60, 2.
[9] *Den.* 876 (*TCT,* 721).

to the faithful as an outward sign instituted by Christ to give grace.

Outward sign

It would be difficult to think of a religion which had no external rites expressing hidden truths. Thus the Old Law had circumcision, the eating of the paschal lamb, purifications, expiations, etc. The Christian ritual has many significative rites among which the sacraments are outstanding. A Christian sacrament, then, is first an external rite consisting of symbolic words and actions. As a rite, baptism is the pouring of water on the head of a person while the pourer recites a formula; as a symbol, it signifies the complete cleansing from sin of the person being baptized. The Holy Eucharist signifies the nourishing of the soul; Extreme Unction, the strengthening of the soul.

While there is a certain amount of natural symbolism in the sacramental rites, yet their full symbolic power derives from the will of Christ. He saw in certain rites a certain symbolic fitness and chose them to represent certain spiritual effects.

To produce the sign, which is a sacrament, three things are required according to the Council of Florence, namely, things which are the matter, words which are the form, and the minister who intends to do what the Church does.[10] The Church has borrowed the terms *matter* and *form* from Aristotle who teaches that a material being consists of two internal principles, one passive, the other active. Matter is the passive principle because it is vague and capable of more precise determination. Form is the active principle because it is precise and makes the material being this determined thing. Thus, when a form is united to a portion of matter, the result is an atom of iron, a molecule of salt, a plant, a cat, a man. Comparing the sacraments to these natural beings, St. Thomas says that "in the sacraments words and things, like form and matter, combine to make one symbolic thing."[11] The things used and the actions done are the matter of the sacraments because they are capable of receiving more precise meaning. The form of the sacraments is the words used because they impart to the total rite its full precise mean-

---

[10] *Den.* 695 (*TCT*, 663).   [11] *Sum. Theol.*, III, 60, 6, ad 2.

ing. Thus, since the pouring of water may signify cooling, irrigation, or cleansing, the symbolism of this action in baptism is not clarified until the words are spoken which say that a cleansing of the soul is intended.

Inward Grace

The purpose of the sacraments is not merely to stir up faith nor to be a sign of one's union with Christ. For they are more than symbols: they cause the spiritual effect they signify. In this respect they differ from other signs. Thus, while the light burning before the tabernacle is a sign of Christ's presence, it does not cause His presence. The words of eucharistic consecration, however, not only signify but cause His presence. Sacraments, therefore, are meant by God to produce supernatural changes in the souls of those who receive them, and it is in this unique function of producing grace that the essential value of the sacrament lies. Hence the most significant teaching about the sacraments is that they contain the grace they signify and confer it upon all who receive them properly. The sacraments of the Old Law did not cause grace but were only a figure of the grace which was to be given through the passion of Christ.[12]

For the rationalist the sacraments are a form of magic comparable to the wearing of a rabbit's foot for good luck. For him no religious rite can have a supernatural effect. He is blinded by his dogma that the supernatural cannot exist. Hence he will not see that the sacraments are saved from being superstitious by their divine origin. For Christ has promised that this rite, properly performed and properly received, will produce this effect of grace and He, God and Creator, works by means of the rite to produce the holy effect. The sacraments are God's tools, sanctified matter, which He uses for the sanctification of men.

Contrary to Calvin who taught that the reprobate get no grace, the Council of Trent[13] says that grace is *always* given to whosoever worthily receives a sacrament. This grace is, first, sanctifying grace, the primary effect of every sacrament, and it is given when the sac-

---

[12] Council of Florence, *Den.* 695 (*TCT,* 663).
[13] *Den.* 850 (*TCT,* 671).

rament is worthily received; second, it is actual grace which is given over as long a period as the purpose of the sacrament is realizable. Each sacrament produces the effect it symbolizes, and since each sacrament is different, a different effect of grace is produced by each sacrament. Since we have no reason for thinking there are different kinds of sanctifying grace, the difference of sacramental effect is to be sought in the sacramental grace peculiar to each sacrament. This sacramental grace consists in "a certain divine assistance for obtaining the end of the sacrament."[14] Most theologians agree that this divine assistance consists in giving the recipient a rightful claim to all the actual graces necessary for the accomplishment in him of the purposes of the sacrament. Thus, from the sacrament of holy orders or matrimony one acquires the right to receive, as occasion arises, all the graces necessary to lead a holy life in the priestly or married state.

Some theologians say that in addition to this right a permanent vigor is imparted to the soul by the sacrament. Grace from a sacramental source, they say, has powers which do not accompany grace from a nonsacramental source. Chief among these is the power to repair the ravages of sin, because, "after sin the soul . . . needs to receive something from corporeal things in order that it may be perfected."[15] This something is sacramental. For the supreme remedy for sin is the Passion, and the sacraments are the direct means of applying it to us. Hence sacramental grace is a special energy given to reduce the power of sin latent in us. Emanating from the cross, the sacraments become a partial substitute for the gift of integrity, lost by sin, inasmuch as little by little they weaken concupiscence and prepare us for glory.

How do the sacraments confer grace?   The second most significant teaching about the sacraments is the declaration of the Council of Trent[16] that they confer grace *ex opere operato* on those who receive them rightly. Neither the minister nor the recipient are the cause of the proper effect of the sacrament, for no mere man can bring into

---

[14] *St. Thomas, Sum. Theol.,* III, 62, 2.
[15] *Ibid.* III, 61, 2, ad 2.
[16] *Den.* 851 (*TCT,* 672).

being that share in the divine nature which is sanctifying grace. If the effect of the sacraments depended on the subjective dispositions of minister or recipient, the sacraments would work *ex opere operantis,* that is, on account of the goodness and merit of the act considered subjectively; but when the Church says they work *ex opere operato,* she means they work *by force of the action itself,* that is, in virtue of the divine power implanted in the objective act. It is the objectively valid sacramental sign which produces sacramental grace and not the meritorious acts of minister or recipient. Nor does God merely give grace upon the occasion of the performance of the rite: the rite itself has a supernatural causal effect which theologians explain in various ways. Therefore, once the minister places the valid sacramental sign, the effect is infallible — grace is given provided the recipient puts no obstacle to its flow. Certainly the sacrament depends on the minister for its coming into being, but its proper effects do not depend on his faith or moral goodness. Thus, if he has a right intention and does everything he should, an atheist could baptize, an apostate bishop ordain, a priest in mortal sin absolve from sin.

How does the recipient put an obstacle to grace? This question is different from the issue raised later on page 141 ff. that certain conditions existing in the recipient prevent a *valid* reception; for example, being a woman makes it impossible for one to receive holy orders. Here we speak not of a valid but a fruitful reception. Supposing then the sacrament is valid, defective dispositions of the recipient can prevent it from having its effect of grace. Thus, one may receive baptism without repentance for personal mortal sin. The sacrament is produced, some effect is had for the sacramental seal is given, but grace is withheld. Remove the obstacle of lack of repentance, and the sacrament which had been given, now gives grace. The sacrament is quaintly said to "revive." The same is said of holy orders and matrimony and, with probability, of the other sacraments with the certain exception of penance and the Holy Eucharist.

Since we live in time and space, it is fair to ask, How much grace do the sacraments give? Since, however, we deal with supernatural realities, the question means, How deeply does sacramental grace penetrate the being and character of the recipient? Since some sacraments are nobler than others, the nobler sacrament confers more grace. Thus, the Holy Eucharist, which contains the Author of grace, confers more grace than any sacrament. The measure of grace conferred by the same sacrament on different recipients accords with the fervor of the faith, hope, charity, etc., of each recipient. A better disposition is a greater capacity to receive grace. St. Thomas[17] says it is like approaching a fire which gives forth heat equally upon all but they who approach nearer receive more heat.

Two sacraments are intended to give grace to souls in whom it is presumed not to exist. These are baptism and penance, and they are called sacraments of the dead, for their purpose is to recall the soul from the death of sin. The other sacraments are called sacraments of the living because they presuppose the existence of grace in the soul, and their purpose is to increase it. However, it is possible for one who already has grace to receive a sacrament of the dead and it is likely that, if a person who is in mortal sin should receive a sacrament of the living and not be aware of his sinful state, he would be cleansed of his sin by this sacrament, if he has some sorrow for his sin.

The Council of Trent[18] teaches that, besides grace, the sacraments of baptism, confirmation, and holy orders produce a character or spiritual indelible mark on the soul, and consequently, none of these sacraments may be given to the same person more than once. This character or seal denotes an irrevocable consecration to God and consists in the imprint of Christ the Priest, signifying that the soul is deputed to the worship of God and is given some share in the priesthood of Christ.

There is another effect of the sacraments, namely, the integration of the recipient into the organism of the Church. By sacraments Christ receives men into Himself living in the extension of Himself, which is the Church, and entrusts them with a special social function. Hence by a sacrament one receives a more or less permanent status in the Church, together with the rights and obligations which belong thereto. Thus baptism makes one a member of the Church. Con-

---

[17] *Sum. Theol.*, III, 69, 8.   [18] *Den.* 852 (*TCT,* 673).

firmation admits one to a share in the apostolate of the Church. Penance is reconciliation not only with God but also with the Church. Extreme unction proximately prepares the members of the Mystical Body for its consummation in glory hereafter. The Eucharist is the sacrament of ecclesiastical unity. Holy orders confers the rights and obligations of the ministers of the Church. Matrimony gives the right to multiply the faithful and to expect from the Church the helps necessary to rear one's children as Christians. The theologians of our day are exploiting more thoroughly the social aspects of the sacraments.

Institution by Christ

All created effects produced by God are the work of Father, Son, and Holy Spirit. Hence, since only God can grant a share of the divine nature, the Triune God is the sole principal cause of the sacraments and of all graces imparted by each reception of a sacrament. For the institution of the sacraments God used the sacred humanity of Christ. His Passion and death are the meritorious cause of all sacramental benefits; that is, they won for us the divine assistance dispensed through the sacraments. The Council of Trent says that the sacraments were instituted by our Lord Jesus Christ.[19]

This statement of faith is interpreted to mean that He chose the effects to be produced by the sacraments, the meaning to be conveyed by the sacramental sign, and imparted to it the power of producing grace. Since He did this Himself and not through others, He is the immediate Author. But whether He designed the signs themselves in a general manner which left room for modification or in a detailed unalterable manner is disputed. The question, however, has practical bearing and means, What is the power of the Church with regard to sacramental rites? That she can make rules for their worthy reception and add prayers and sacramentals which precede or follow the sacrament is clear. But can she change the rite itself? The Council of Trent says she has no power over the substantials of the sacraments.[20] These surely include anything that Christ or-

---

[19] Den. 844 (TCT, 665).
[20] Den. 931 (TCT, 678).

dained, namely, the meaning, the grace, and the effects of the sacraments. But did He fix for all time the words and actions which
make up the sacramental sign? Some say He did so with regard to
nearly all the sacraments. Others say that, while He may have fixed
the rite with regard to one or other sacrament, He did not do so with
regard to all, and consequently the Church has made and therefore
can make changes in the rites which Christ did not fix, provided the
change leaves the meaning intact. In this view the Church has some
power "to settle what symbols, considering time and place, adequately carry the substantial meaning which [Christ] had fixed."[21]

Since God can sanctify the soul without recourse to material instruments, He did not have to invent a sacramental system. He deals,
however, with His creatures according to their natures and the condition they are in. Since man is matter as well as spirit, it is easier
for him to be sanctified if God uses material means. The sacraments
are the outward perfecting of man's inward faith. They externalize
what he believes and give him something concrete to hold on to in
his quest of God. Furthermore, since by sin man subjected himself
to material things and dulled his perception of spiritual values, "it
was fitting that God should provide man with a spiritual medicine
by means of certain corporeal signs; for if man were offered spiritual things without a veil, his mind being taken up with the material world would not be able to apply itself to them."[22] Hence
Christ chose the sacraments as ordinary means of salvation and commanded their use. Some He made more necessary than others. Thus
He commanded that absolutely everyone be baptized, that everyone
who commits mortal sin after baptism should receive penance.
While adults who do not receive confirmation, the Holy Eucharist,
and extreme unction can be saved, yet it is with difficulty. Two
sacraments are necessary for the Church: holy orders to supply the
ministers of the Church; matrimony, to supply the faithful.

In every administration of a sacrament the God-Man is the principal agent. Thus it is Christ who baptizes, Christ who consecrates,

[21] B. Leeming, *Principles of Sacramental Theology,* p. 431 (Westminster: Newman, 1956).
[22] *Sum. Theol.,* III, 61, 1.

Christ who absolves. Sacramental action is one of the chief activities of the Vine which is Christ. By her phrase *ex opere operato* the Church emphasizes the fact that the sacraments are a divine, not a human, work. While other men may labor for a man's salvation by teaching and exhorting him, their words cannot penetrate and effect changes in the core of his being. Only God can do that by converting the sinner into a new creature, the just man into a very holy person. Assuredly the penetration of a man's being is done by grace and it seems that this is more readily done by sacramental than by nonsacramental grace. For the sacraments render easier man's cooperation with grace. Therefore, the Christian life is essentially sacramental.

In addition to Christ, the chief agent, there must always be the visible minister who acts in His name. The sacramental ministry has not been entrusted to angels but to men. Thus the branches have a unique part in the activity of the Vine, for without the human minister the sacraments would not be available. The function of the minister is to unite the proper form to the proper sacramental matter thus producing the sacramental sign. To do this one must have proper authority from Christ and the Church, realize what he is doing, and intend to do what the Church does. He who performs the rite is presumed to do what the rite means; if, however, he resolves not to do what the Church does, he has not sufficient intention, and the sacramental rite does not come into being. It is not necessary for validity, however, that he know and intend *all* the purposes of the sacrament nor that he have the true faith and be in the state of grace. While any man can be minister of baptism and any Christian of matrimony, priestly consecration is required in him who consecrates the Holy Eucharist and administers penance, confirmation, extreme unction, and holy orders.

The sacraments can be administered only to the living. For the *valid* reception of a sacrament certain conditions are required of the recipient. Before one is baptized he is incapable of receiving the other sacraments. Infants and those who never have the use of reason are barred from penance, extreme unction, and matrimony; women from holy orders; those who are in good health from extreme unction; those who labor under a diriment impediment, from matrimony. Dispositions of mind and will cannot be required of an infant for the reception of the sacraments of which he is capable. Except for penance, the adult who is capable of receiving a sacrament need not have faith for its *valid* reception, but he must have a proper intention of receiving the sacrament. The rational being must be willing to receive the favor of God. The reason why faith is essential in penance alone is that sorrow for sin on the part of the penitent is a necessary part of the sacrament, and this cannot be had without faith.

The conditions for fruitful reception are: for sacraments of the dead, that sorrow for sin which theology calls attrition[23]; for sacraments of the living, the prudent judgment that one is in the state of grace; for all sacraments, that in general one does not seek a sacrament from an unworthy minister.

The Sacramentals

These are what their name indicates, namely, things which are like sacraments. The Church says they are "objects and actions which the Church, in a kind of imitation of the sacraments, is wont to use in order to obtain through her supplication certain effects which are chiefly spiritual."[24] They resemble the sacraments in that they are visible signs of some supernatural effect. For, as the sacraments contain the infallible promise of Christ that they who receive them rightly will receive the grace they symbolize, so in the sacramentals there is the prayer of the Church that they who use them with devotion will be given by God certain spiritual and temporal effects. The sacramentals consist of various blessings, consecrations, exorcisms, and blessed objects like holy water, ashes, palms, candles, etc. Of outstanding value are the blessings which withdraw persons or things from secular use and give them to the service of God, such as the veiling of a virgin, the consecration of a church or sacred vessels. Violation of this consecration involves the sin of sacrilege.

---

[23] See p. 170 below.
[24] Code of Canon Law, No. 1144.

Sacramentals differ from the sacraments in several respects. First, they were not instituted by Christ but by the Church. Only the supreme authority can say what is to be accounted a sacramental. Second, the sacramentals do not produce their effect infallibly. For they do not work *ex opere operato* as the sacraments do, but only *ex opere operantis,* that is, on account of the one performing or benefiting from the action. The efficacy of the sacramentals depends primarily on the intercession of the Church; secondarily, on the faith and love of God in the faithful who use them. Third, there is a difference of effect. Only the sacraments produce sanctifying grace. However, the one using a sacramental may receive an increase of grace or the remission of sin on account of his charity. Through a sacramental one can receive actual graces, remission of temporal punishment due to sin, protection from demons, temporal favors.

Even though the use of sacramentals is not obligatory on the faithful, they should esteem and treat with reverence whatever the Church has blessed. They should not, however, put them to a superstitious use, that is, expect from a person or blessed object an infallible efficacy which neither nature nor the will of God has given it.

The Number of the Sacraments

The third most significant statement of the Church about the sacraments is that they are seven in number, no more, no less: baptism, confirmation, Holy Eucharist, penance, extreme unction, holy orders, and matrimony. Such is the doctrine which Innocent III prescribed as of faith to the Waldensians,[25] the Council of Florence to the Armenians,[26] the Council of Trent[27] to the Reformers. True, this statement of faith is of late development, but that was due to lack of definition and classification of the Christian symbols. That the doctrine, however, is of apostolic origin is clear from the agreement of the Eastern and Western Churches. The Eastern Schismatics of the twelfth century and the Eastern heretics of the fifth and sixth centuries teach this doctrine as of faith. The sole reason for their agreement with the Church on this matter is that,

---

[25] *Den.* 424 (*TCT,* 658).
[26] *Den.* 695 (*TCT,* 663).

[27] *Den.* 844 (*TCT,* 665).

before their separation, the doctrine was taught by an undivided Church as of apostolic origin. When the Reformers denied the doctrine, they were merely being consistent with their rejection of tradition as a source of revelation and of a visible Church.

The seven sacraments correspond to the seven great supernatural needs of man. The first need is supernatural life which is supplied by baptism. Maturity is given by confirmation and nourishment by the Holy Eucharist. Since man is subject to ills, he is restored to spiritual health by penance and is freed of his defects so as to be ready for glory by extreme unction. Since he is a social being, his rulers in the kingdom of God on earth are supplied by holy orders and the social members by matrimony.[28]

Baptism

Baptism is a sacrament because it is an external rite instituted by Christ to symbolize and confer the grace of regeneration. It is the first and most important of the sacraments because it is the only means of entry into the Church and without it no other sacrament can be received.

The external rite. The matter used in this sacrament ordinarily is water blessed for this purpose on Holy Saturday. In a case of necessity natural water suffices. But no other liquid can be substituted for water. The washing with water may be by pouring or sprinkling or immersion. The words of the form, which must be said while the water flows, must express the person being baptized, the action of cleansing, and an explicit determinate naming of the Blessed Trinity. The form given in the Roman Ritual is: "I baptize thee in the name of the Father and of the Son and of the Holy Spirit."

The grace of regeneration. Baptism is the divine remedy for original sin which involves separation from God and supernatural death. Since we come into the world dead to God, we need to be reborn unto Him: for, "unless a man be born again of water and the Spirit, he cannot enter into the kingdom of God."[29] The being born

---

[28] Cf. St. Thomas, *Sum. Theol.,* III, 65, 1.
[29] Jn. 3:5.

again of water and the Spirit is effected by baptism which has two aspects corresponding to the main evils of original sin. Negatively baptism is (*a*) *a bath of purification*. The sin which makes us children of wrath must be washed away. Thus the Corinthians, who once were sinners, are reminded by St. Paul: "And such some of you were, but you have been washed, you have been justified."[30] Again He says that Christ sanctified His Church "cleansing her in the bath of water by means of the word."[31] The bath is baptism because it imparts grace which simultaneously takes away all sin, original and actual, together with all punishment due to sin, and gives the soul the divine life. The cleansing is complete; the grant of life real. The newly baptized is made a new and splendid creature.

Although baptism remits original sin, it leaves us with concupiscence, a suffering body, and corporal death, until, at the resurrection of the dead, these defects also are taken from the just. Meantime it is fitting and profitable that we endure them. By battling our concupiscences we gain a more glorious crown. Indeed the grace of baptism gives us power to overcome these assaults against which the unbaptized stand unarmed.

Positively baptism is (*b*) *our incorporation into Christ*. Sin severed the mystic bond between us and God. Baptism restores it by engrafting us into Christ and making us one with Him in His mystical body. Because of our incorporation into Christ the mysteries of Christ are mystically reproduced in us, namely, death to sin, resurrection, ascension, and sitting at the right hand of the Father. "Do you not know that all we who have been baptized into Christ Jesus have been baptized into his death? For we were buried with him by means of Baptism into death, in order that, just as Christ has risen from the dead . . . so we may also walk in newness of life. For if we have been united with him in the likeness of his death, we shall be so in the likeness of his resurrection also."[32] The baptisteries of the ancient Church symbolized this summary of the Christian life. The candidate went down into the baptismal water by one set of steps which symbolized the descent into death — death to the world, the flesh, and Satan — and he ascended from the saving waters by

---

[30] 1 Cor. 6:11.   [31] Eph. 5:26.   [32] Rom. 6:3–6.

the opposite steps which represented his arising to a new life with Christ. Having been made one with Christ, the newly baptized is freed from the ancient dominion which Satan exercised over men, and is dead to sin. Since he is also risen with Christ, he embraces a new life and seeks "the things that are above, where Christ is seated at the right hand of God."[33] Even more, our union with Christ depicts us sitting with Christ in glory at the right hand of the Father. For "God . . . brought us to life together with Christ . . . and raised us up together, and seated us together in heaven in Christ Jesus."[34]

Baptism not only makes us other Christs, it also provides the full complement of supernatural faculties necessary to live a Christlike life. For, says the Council of Trent, "when a man is justified, along with the remission of his sins, he receives through Jesus Christ in whom he is implanted these gifts: faith, hope and charity."[35] However, baptism is pre-eminently the sacrament of faith. For it gives the supernatural power of inwardly accepting the unseen mysteries of God and by it one outwardly professes himself a member of the kingdom of God on earth. By it he accepts and commits himself to God's plan of salvation and embraces the obligations of a Christian.

Baptism also imprints a sacramental character. This seal gives one a general share in the priesthood of Christ but not the power to consecrate and immolate. What is granted is union with the offerer of the Christian sacrifice, the priesthood of the laity mentioned by St. Peter: "You are a chosen race, a royal priesthood, a holy nation."[36] The baptized are admitted to the Holy Eucharist and the Christian liturgy. Only sacramental baptism gives this character and only he who has it is capable of receiving the other sacraments. Since any valid reception of the sacrament imparts the character, the sacrament cannot be repeated. The Council of Trent says the character is indelible.[37] It is of faith, then, that during mortal life the character will be a link binding the soul to Christ, even though it be in mortal sin. By sin the Christian cuts himself off from

---

[33] Col. 3:1.
[34] Eph. 2:4–7.
[35] *Den.* 800 (*TCT,* 564).

[36] 1 Pet. 2:9.
[37] *Den.* 852 (*TCT,* 673).

the full life which flows from the vine which is Christ. He becomes a dead member, and should he die in that state, his end is final reprobation. But before that catastrophe the sinner is still united to Christ and need but reopen his heart to grace to become again a living member. It is good theological opinion that for the eternal glory or shame of the soul the character remains throughout eternity.

Institution by Christ. It is of faith that Christ Himself designed baptism in water as the rite of entry into the Church. For He said to Nicodemus: "Unless a man be born again of water and the Spirit he cannot enter into the kingdom of God."[38] Again He commanded the Apostles: "Go, therefore, and make disciples of all nations, baptizing them in the name of the Father, and of the Son, and of the Holy Spirit."[39] Such also is the doctrine of Pius XII.[40] It is generally held that Christ Himself unalterably fixed "the matter and form" of this sacrament. When He did this is not certain.

It is also of faith that, by the explicit command of Christ, all men are obliged to receive sacramental baptism. This is clear from the references cited just above, from the manner in which the Apostles acted,[41] and from various declarations of the Council of Trent.[42]

Can anyone then be saved who does not receive sacramental baptism? Concerning persons who have not the use of reason and are about to die without baptism, many ingenious theories have been advanced to show how God regenerates these souls, but it is quite certain that they can receive sanctifying grace only through baptism. Concerning adults, we must remember that baptism does not make salvation more difficult but easier. Consequently that perfect conversion to God, which justified the sinner before the coming of Christ, still retains that power. The adult cannot be justified without a turning from sin to God, the motive for which may be more perfect or less perfect. If one's motive is less perfect — fear of the divine punishments — God will not justify the sinner without the

---

[38] Jn. 3:5.
[39] Mt. 28:19.
[40] Encyclical, *Mystici Corporis, AAS*, 35, p. 204.
[41] Acts 2:37–41; 8:12–16; 9:10–18.
[42] *Den.* 861, 869 (*TCT*, 691, 699).

sacrament. If, however, his motive is perfect — love of God for God's sake — God justifies him even before he receives the sacrament, as Scripture testifies in the case of Cornelius the centurion.[43] A merciful God does not withhold immediate justification from one who is perfectly disposed. For Christ has said: "He who has my commandments and keeps them, he it is who loves me. But he who loves me will be loved by my Father, and I will love him and manifest myself to him."[44] Since perfect love of God includes the will to do all that God wants for salvation, and since baptism is absolutely commanded, such love of God contains the implicit desire for baptism. Hence perfect love of God on the part of those who have not been sacramentally baptized is called *baptism of desire.*

Baptism of desire remits sin and justifies, for the Council of Trent says that justification "after the promulgation of the Gospel is impossible without the bath of regeneration or its desire."[45] However, it does not necessarily take away all punishment due to sin nor does it impart the character of baptism. When they who were justified by baptism of desire learn that sacramental baptism is necessary they are seriously obliged to accept the sacrament.

The most perfect expression of love of God is death willingly and patiently undergone for His sake. "Greater love than this no one has, that one lay down his life for his friends."[46] Whoever dies in this way for Christ is a martyr, and if he has not received sacramental baptism, he is baptized in his own blood. This is *baptism of blood,* and while it does not imprint the character nor make the martyr a member of the Church militant in case he does not die, yet it takes away sin totally and gives one a unique standing in heaven. Since the effects produced by martyrdom do not necessarily depend on perfect love in the martyr (as is true of the Holy Innocents), martyrdom may be said to operate quasi-sacramentally. It is one of the most precious gifts God can give to man.

Since baptism is so necessary, anyone can baptize in a case of necessity, even an unbeliever, provided he intends to do what the Church does. The dispositions which are necessary in adults for a

[43] Acts 10:44-48.
[44] Jn. 14:21.
[45] *Den.* 796 (*TCT,* 560).
[46] Jn. 15:13.

fruitful reception are: the intention of being baptized, repentance, and faith. Infants who are incapable of dispositions can nevertheless share the grace of baptism. Indeed from ancient times the Church has required that the children of the faithful be baptized soon after birth. When baptized children come of age, they must *not* be required under penalty of lapsing from the Church to reaffirm the baptismal promises given in their names by their sponsors,[47] for the sacrament has made them permanent members of the Church.

Confirmation

The name of this sacrament is from the Latin *confirmare*, which means to strengthen. By baptism we are born to Christ; by confirmation we are brought to mature age in Christ. Baptism imparts the grace necessary for the saving of one's own soul. Confirmation brings to perfection what was given us in baptism for our own good, and furthermore enables us to act on behalf of others like responsible adults in the Church of Christ.

That confirmation is a sacrament distinct from baptism and instituted by Christ is the teaching of the Church, confirmed by declarations of the Second Council of Lyons,[48] the Council of Florence,[49] and the Council of Trent.[50] In the Acts of the Apostles we see the Apostles administering this sacrament. "Now when the apostles in Jerusalem heard that Samaria had received the word of God, they sent to them Peter and John. On their arrival they prayed for them, that they might receive the Holy Spirit; for as yet he had not come upon any of them, but they had only been baptized in the name of the Lord Jesus. Then they laid their hands on them and they received the Holy Spirit."[51] The Council of Florence uses this text to illustrate its doctrine about confirmation. There is the sensible sign distinct from baptism — the prayer and imposition of hands by the Apostles; there is the special effect of grace — the coming of the Holy Spirit. Christ had promised to give the Holy Spirit to

---

[47] Council of Trent, *Den.* 870 (*TCT*, 700).
[48] *Den.* 465 (*TCT*, 660).
[49] *Den.* 697 (*TCT*, 707).

[50] *Den.* 871 (*TCT*, 708).
[51] Acts 8:14–18.

all believers to strengthen them against enemies. Thus He was given
to the Samaritans and to the Ephesians.[52] An external charismatic
giving would not be enough; to be effective it had to be also internal
such as the Apostles received on Pentecost. That the rite was instituted by Christ is clear from the fact that the Apostles performed
it. They did these things only because Christ so instructed them.
When He gave these instructions we do not know; probably it was
after the resurrection when "he showed himself alive . . . speaking
of the kingdom of God."[53]

There is a special connection between this sacrament and the
Holy Spirit. While the Holy Spirit is given in every grant of sanctifying grace, He is given in this sacrament in a very special way — for
strength. Just as the Spirit was given to the Apostles on Pentecost
to enable them boldly to fulfill their mission, so He is given to the
faithful to enable them to be perfect Christians. Being a perfect
Christian has a double aspect. As regards oneself, there is given in
this sacrament the *plenitude* of the gifts of the Holy Spirit. This
fullness of grace, necessary for perfect Christian living, is called
possession of the Holy Spirit. As regards others, the sacrament gives
an illumination of the mind which enables one to expound the faith
and an inspiration to the will so that one can defend the Church.
The grace of confirmation may be called the layman's mandate to
participate in Catholic Action.

Confirmation cannot be repeated because it imparts a sacramental
seal and a larger share in the priesthood of Christ. While baptism
is more necessary, confirmation confers more grace. This further
share in the priesthood of Christ, communicated by the seal of confirmation, is probably something of Christ's prophetic office, enabling
one to explain and profess the faith boldly and to combat pro-
fessedly the enemies of the faith.

In the Eastern Rites of the Catholic Church the priest usually
confers confirmation immediately after baptism. In the Latin Rite,
in keeping with the practice established by the Apostles, the bishop
alone is the ordinary minister. A priest may administer it only if

---

[52] Acts 19:5–6; Eph. 1:13.
[53] Acts 1:3.

he has special authority. The matter of the sacrament consists in the bishop laying his hand upon the head of the one to be confirmed and anointing his forehead with holy chrism. This is a mixture of olive oil and balsam, blessed by a bishop on Holy Thursday, for sacramental use. The form is: "I sign thee with the sign of the cross and I confirm thee with the chrism of salvation in the name of the Father and of the Son and of the Holy Spirit."

Confirmation is not absolutely necessary for salvation, but he who neglects the reasonable opportunity of receiving it does wrong, especially when dangers to one's faith abound. St. Thomas well says that "this sacrament should be given to those who are on the point of death that they may be seen to be perfect at the resurrection."[54] The Church now grants pastors permanent faculty to administer this sacrament to dying members of their flock.

The Holy Eucharist

The name Eucharist is most apt because it means thanksgiving. This mystery of love summarizes the blessings of creation, redemption, and sanctification, and was given us by God that we might have the appropriate gift for the acknowledgment of God's goodness to us. Indeed this sacrament comes into existence only when the Church offers its official act of thanksgiving and renders back to God the gift of His Son first given to us in the Incarnation.

The Eucharist began at the Last Supper when "our Savior, about to leave this world for the Father, instituted this sacrament wherein, as it were, He poured forth the riches of His divine love for men, making remembrance of His wonderful works, and commanding us in the consuming of it to cherish His memory and show forth His death until He come to judge the world."[55] Thus He bequeathed to us a memorial of His death which consists of His true Body and Blood to be eaten and drunk by His faithful ones. He showed us what He wanted done by changing bread and wine into His Body and Blood, which He offered to the Father, and gave to His disciples to eat and drink. Then He gave them power to do as He had done

[54] *Sum. Theol.*, III, 72, 8, ad 4.
[55] Council of Trent, *Den.* 875 (*TCT*, 720).

and commanded them and their successors in the Christian priesthood to renew the rite as a perpetual remembrance of Him.

The basic truth about the Holy Eucharist is that "after the consecration of bread and wine our Lord Jesus Christ, true God and man, is truly, really and substantially contained under the appearances of those sensible things."[56] The Eucharist is no mere symbol serving to remind us of Him and to stir up faith in Him. It is Himself. We know this, first, because He promised to give us His flesh for food and His blood for drink. In the synagogue of Capharnaum, after the multiplication of the loaves, the Jews complained when Jesus said: "I am the bread that has come down from heaven." Despite their unfavorable reaction Jesus insisted: "I am the living bread that has come down from heaven. If anyone eat of this bread, he will live forever; and the bread that I will give him is my flesh for the life of the world." Then the Jews said with passion: "How can this man give us his flesh to eat?" Since His hearers took His words in their literal sense, Jesus should have put them straight if He had been speaking metaphorically. But far from seeking to correct any misunderstanding of His meaning, Jesus continued to emphasize the need of eating Him. There is no hint of metaphor in His exhortation: "Unless you eat the flesh of the Son of Man, and drink his blood, you shall not have life in you. He who eats my flesh and drinks my blood has life everlasting. . . . For my flesh is food indeed, and my blood is drink indeed. He who eats my flesh and drinks my blood, abides in me and I in him." His disciples understood Him literally and some of them complained: "This is a hard saying. Who can listen to it?"[57] Even when some of them abandoned His company because of these words, He made no effort to hold them on the ground that they had misunderstood Him. If He did not wish His words to be taken literally, He spoke dishonestly and acted foolishly.

Second, Jesus fulfilled His promise at the Last Supper when He "took bread, and blessed and broke, and gave it to his disciples, and said, 'Take and eat; this is my body.' And taking a cup, he gave thanks and gave it to them saying, 'All of you drink this; for this

---

[56] Council of Trent, *Den.* 874 (*TCT*, 719).
[57] Jn. 6:41–62.

is my blood of the new covenant, which is being shed for many unto the remission of sins.' "[58] Jesus on the night before He canceled the Old Law and struck an everlasting agreement with men to be sealed with His blood on the cross, put into the hands of His disciples the Body which would be given in sacrifice; and in the cup, which went from hand to hand, was the Blood, which would be shed for sins. Heresy and the so-called learning of unbelievers have tried to destroy the effect of these words by saying that Jesus never spoke them or that they do not mean what they say. But in vain! He did not say this is a symbol or reminder of His Body; but this — the thing I hold in My hand — is My Body. Against every attempt to substitute private thinking for revealed fact the Church stands firm. The words mean just what they say. This is the doctrine which the Apostles taught and which the Church of all times has firmly believed. The words of Trent are still most apt: "For thus all our predecessors in the true Church of Christ, who have discoursed on this most holy sacrament, have openly professed that our Redeemer . . . said in precise and unmistakable words that He was giving [His disciples] His very body and blood. These words, recorded by the Holy Evangelists and repeated afterwards by St. Paul, have their proper obvious meaning and were so understood by the Fathers. Hence it is a shame that contentious and evil men should distort these words into spurious and fictitious figures of speech that deny the truth about the body and blood of Christ, contrary to the universal understanding of the Church."[59]

The mystery, therefore, of the Real Presence is that Jesus, body and soul, humanity and divinity, is contained under the appearances of consecrated bread and wine. Even though He is the victim of sacrifice, He exists in the sacrament, living, glorified, and immortal. He is present with all His human powers, faculties, and senses. "Nor," says the Council of Trent, "is there any contradiction between these facts, namely, that our Savior ever sits at the right hand of the Father in heaven according to a natural mode of existing, and that He is yet sacramentally present to us in many places by His substance according to a mode of existence, which we can scarcely

---

[58] Mt. 26:26–28. [59] Den. 874 (TCT, 719).

put into words, but which nevertheless by our understanding illumined by faith we can conceive to be possible to God and ought
steadfastly to believe."[60] Jesus exists wholly in every consecrated host
and wholly in each part of every host. If a host is broken, Christ is
not divided: He exists wholly in each fragment. There is division of
sensible appearances but not of the substance which is Christ.

How does Christ become sacramentally present? By the consecrating words, This is my Body, bread becomes the Body of Christ.
Since Christ is indivisible, the whole Christ becomes present under
the form of bread. By the consecrating words, This is my Blood,
wine becomes the Blood of Christ. Since the Blood of Christ does
not exist apart by Itself, the whole Christ is present under the appearance of wine. The process by which bread ceases to be bread and
becomes the Body of Christ and wine ceases to be wine and becomes
the Blood of Christ is, says the Council of Trent,[61] aptly called by
the Church Transubstantiation. The word means that one substance
passes over into and becomes another substance.

The substance of a thing is that underlying stuff by which, for
example, gold is gold, a horse a horse, a tree a tree. Substance is
different from the qualities and appearances of a thing; it is that
abiding element which remains the same and makes the thing to be
this thing despite all superficial changes. Thus it is the same man,
George Washington, who was a babe in arms, grew to manhood,
had such a career, and was wasted by his final illness. While substance is the abiding element in a thing, a substance can change
into something else. Thus uranium disintegrates into two other things.
A portion of sodium and a portion of chloride can unite to form salt.
Now when by natural process one substance changes into another
the qualities and appearances of the old substance disappear and
the new substance has new appearances. In the change of substances
in the Eucharist, however, there are no changes of qualities and
appearances. A consecrated Host looks, tastes, and smells like bread.
But it is not bread. It is the Body of Christ and It will remain the
Body of Christ as long as the appearances of bread remain. When
the consecrating words were pronounced what happened to the

---

[60] *Den.* 874 (*TCT,* 719).   [61] *Den.* 877 (*TCT,* 722).

bread? Was it annihilated? No; it was converted into the Body of Christ. What caused the change? The principal cause was God, the instrumental cause was the words of consecration. How can human words effect such a change? They have been endowed with that power by the Creator. It is no more problem for the Creator to change one thing into another, making human words His instrument, than it is for Him to make something out of nothing by the fiat of His will. An immediate conclusion of the doctrine of the Real Presence is that the sacred host and the precious blood are worthy of divine honor.

Christ instituted the Holy Eucharist that it should serve "as the spiritual food whereby they are nourished and strengthened who live by the life of Him who said: 'he who eateth me, the same shall live by me,' and as an antidote by which we are freed from daily faults and preserved from mortal sins. He desired, moreover, that it be a pledge of our future glory and everlasting happiness, and hence a symbol of that one body of which He is the Head, and to which He willed that we, as members, be united by closest bonds of faith, hope and charity so that we might all speak the same things and there be no schisms among us."[62]

The Holy Eucharist is both a sacrifice and a sacrament. The sacrifice is the Mass and without it the sacrament is impossible, for it can come into existence only through the consecration of the Mass. The Eucharist as sacrifice looks to the past and commemorates the Passion of Christ. As sacrament it looks also to the present and the future. As regards the present it is the sacrament of the Church's unity whereby the members of Christ are joined together and is called a Communion. As regards the future it foreshadows the enjoyment of God in heaven and supplies the means of getting there.

The Holy Sacrifice of the Mass

The predominant notion in sacrifice, it seems, is the giving of a gift to God. Sacrifice is a sacred sign that man is or attempts to be in harmony with God. It is the full human way of manifesting that

---

[62] Council of Trent, *Den.* 875 (*TCT*, 720).

interior submission and dedication which everyone owes God as Creator and the source of all happiness. Since sacrifice is the prayer of the entire man — of mind, heart, word, gesture — it is the supreme mode of worship. Since, moreover, man finds his fulfillment only in social life, sacrifice is a social act; the gift is from the community and the community offers it through one who is commissioned to act in its name.

In a sacrifice then these things are necessary: (1) the gift, some visible thing of value, which is a symbol of man and whose offering to God portrays man's interior dedication to God; (2) the priest who acts for the community with God and not only offers the gift but also (3) does or has done to it that which makes it sacred. While all things may be *offered* to God, only those are *sacrificial gifts* which are immolated. Immolation is the religious action which signifies that the gift has passed over to God. This can be done by destroying it in whole or in part or by blessing it. (4) The altar or place of immolation. A fifth point may be added though it is not found in all sacrifices, namely, the giving back of the gift or victim that the offerers may eat it in a sacrificial meal.

Against heretics who were content with a religion without altar, priesthood, and sacrifice, the Council of Trent exposes these points of doctrine: (1) Jesus, eternal Priest according to the order of Melchisedech, at the Last Supper established a new Pasch to celebrate His passage to the Father (2) by leaving His Church a sacrifice representative of His death on the cross. He accomplished this by (3) offering Himself to the Father under the appearances of bread and wine and (4) by making His Apostles priests who in their successors would (5) renew this sacrifice forever.[63] After these preparatory statements the Council defines the dogma that in the Mass there is a true sacrifice which consists in offering Christ to God as a victim to be consumed by us.

The Supper, the Cross, and the Mass are essentially one sacrifice. Clearly the Mass and the Supper are one so that, whatever the Supper is, that also is the Mass. According to Scripture both are sacrifices. First, the Supper saw the establishment of a new covenant between

---
[63] *Den.* 938, 939 (*TCT*, 747, 748).

God and men which, like the covenant made through Moses, was sealed with sacrificial blood. "This cup is the new covenant in my blood, which shall be shed for you."[64] Since that which the Apostles drank was the blood of sacrifice, Jesus must have offered sacrifice. Second, since Jesus was "priest according to the order of Melchisedech,"[65] He should offer sacrifice with bread and wine. The only time He could have done so was at the Supper. Third, the Mass is the memorial and continuation of the sacrificial death on the cross. St. Paul says: "For as often as you shall eat this bread and drink the cup, you proclaim the death of the Lord."[66] Finally, the Supper and the Mass provide a ritualistic meal wherein the participants partake of gifts offered in sacrifice. St. Paul says: "The cup of blessing that we bless, is it not the sharing of the blood of Christ? And the bread that we break, is it not the partaking of the body of the Lord? . . . Are not they who eat of the sacrifices partakers of the altars?" He goes on to say that no Christian may eat of the offerings made to idols for "You cannot drink the cup of the Lord and the cup of devils; you cannot be partakers of the table of the Lord and the table of devils."[67] The Council says that "table" in both instances means "altar." The Supper was the first Mass, the model of all Masses. The difference, however, between the Supper and the Mass is this: Jesus alone offered the Supper and the Body He offered was yet mortal.

The Mass and the cross are one, first, because the offerer of both is the same. "The Same Person now offers Himself through the ministry of priests who then offered Himself on the cross."[68] Although Jesus has completed the one sacrifice of redemption, His priesthood does not end; for "he, because he continues forever, has an everlasting priesthood."[69] He continues to offer Himself through the hands of His priests. Indeed He is the principal offerer of every Mass. The priest we see at the altar is only the representative of Jesus the High Priest. He acts in the name of Jesus and when he consecrates, he uses His very words, This is my Body, This is my Blood.

---

[64] Lk. 22:20.
[65] Hebr. 7:17.
[66] 1 Cor. 11:26.
[67] 1 Cor. 10:16–21.

[68] Council of Trent, *Den.* 940 (*TCT*, 749).
[69] Hebr. 7:24–25.

Second, as Jesus was the victim on the cross, He is the victim or offering in every Mass. He is the gift which the Church gives back to God in the Mass because "at the last supper . . . desirous of leaving His beloved Spouse, the Church, a visible sacrifice . . . our God and Lord offered His Body and Blood in sacrifice to God the Father under the appearances of bread and wine. Under the same symbolic figures He gave His Body and Blood to His Apostles to eat and at that time made them priests of the New Law, commanding them and their successors in the priesthood to offer the same victim."[70] Moreover, Jesus is the Victim without blemish because the Council goes on to say that in the Mass is fulfilled the prophecy of Malachy about the clean oblation: "From the rising of the sun even to the going down, my name is great among the Gentiles, and in every place there is sacrifice, and there is offered to my name a clean oblation."[71] The sacrifices of the Old Law have all been supplanted by a new Pasch, a sacrifice that is perfect and clean: perfect, because the gift offered is infinite; clean, because this sacrifice cannot be defiled by the unworthiness of him who offers it.

The Mass, however, in no way derogates from the value of the cross as the Reformers insisted. The repetition of the Mass does not mean that the cross was insufficient and, like the sacrifices of the Old Law, had to be repeated constantly. The cross was the unique and all satisfying sacrifice wherein the God-Man completely achieved his merciful objective of redemption. It will not and cannot be repeated. For Jesus "having risen from the dead, dies now no more."[72] "Jesus, having offered one sacrifice for sins, has taken his seat forever at the right hand of God . . . by one offering he has perfected forever those who are sanctified."[73]

While the Mass is essentially the same sacrifice as the cross, there are differences, chief among which is the condition of the Victim. On the cross the Victim was mortal and His blood was shed; in the Mass the glorified Victim is not physically slain. The cross is in a class by itself, for it is not a figure of sacrifice yet to be nor does it represent a sacrifice that has taken place. It is the Sacrifice of all

---

[70] Council of Trent, *Den.* 938 (*TCT*, 747).
[71] Mal. 1:11.   [72] Rom. 6:9.   [73] Hebr. 10:12, 14.

time. The Mass, however, is a representation of the cross. By the
cross we were redeemed; by the Mass the efficacy of the redemption
is applied to us.

The Mass, however, is not a mere harking back to, or empty
dramatization of, Calvary; it is itself a true sacrifice. What is the
essence of the Mass? Are the verbal offertory, the double consecration, and the communion of celebrant and the faithful essentially required? It is now certain that the essence of the Mass consists solely
in the double consecration, for Pius XII says: "The Eucharistic
Sacrifice of its very nature is the unbloody immolation of the divine
Victim which is made manifest in a mystical manner by the separation of the Sacred Species and by their oblation to the Eternal Father.
Holy Communion pertains to the integrity of the Mass and to the
partaking of the august sacrament; and while it is obligatory for the
celebrant of the Mass, it is only something earnestly recommended
to the faithful."[74]

But how does the double consecration make the Mass a true
sacrifice? When theology attempts to penetrate to the heart of divine
mysteries it meets with obscurities, as it does in this inquiry into
"The Mystery of Faith." However, Pius XII offers us this much
explanation: "The august sacrifice of the altar is no mere empty
commemoration of the passion and death of Jesus Christ but a true
and proper act of sacrifice, whereby the High Priest offers Himself
a most acceptable Victim to the Eternal Father, as He did on the
cross. . . . But the manner in which Christ is offered is different.
On the cross He completely offered Himself and all His sufferings
to God, and the immolation of the victim was brought about by His
bloody death, which He underwent of His free will. But on the altar,
by reason of the glorified state of His human nature, 'death shall
have no dominion over Him' . . . still according to the plan of Divine
Wisdom, the sacrifice of the Redeemer is shown forth in an admirable
manner by external signs which are symbols of His death. For by
the transubstantiation of bread into the Body of Christ and of wine
into His Blood, His Body and Blood are both really present: now
the Eucharistic species under which He is present symbolize the

---

[74] *Mediator Dei, ASS,* 1947, p. 563 (cf. N.C.W.C. trans. No. 112).

actual separation of His Body and Blood. Therefore the commemorative representation of His death, which actually took place on Calvary, is repeated in every sacrifice of the altar, since Christ Jesus is symbolized and shown to be in a state of victimhood through distinct signs of His death."[75] From these words one may conclude that the double consecration is a real but mystic immolation of the same victim by the same Priest.

This is clear from the following consideration. Sacraments are symbols endowed by Christ with sacred power, for what they signify they produce and contain. Since the Mass is a sacramental symbol of the death of Christ, it must contain it, not as a historical but as a sacramental reality. The consecration of the bread signifies, produces, and contains the Body of Christ. The consecration of the wine signifies, produces, and contains the Blood of Christ. Taken together both consecrations symbolize the death of Christ because, by consecrating the bread apart from the wine, we mystically represent the separation of Blood from Body which was His death on the cross. As Jesus was immolated on the cross by His physical death, so He is immolated in the Mass by His mystic or sacramental death. We distinguish the visible world of historical reality from an invisible sacramental world. The latter is Jesus producing effects of grace in the souls of men by means of sacred symbols. Both worlds are real. It is just as real that a baby is reborn to Christ by baptism as that it was first born to its natural mother. In the world of historical reality Jesus was immolated and died once. In the sacramental world He is mystically immolated every time Mass is said.

The application of the Mass to men introduces consideration of the Holy Eucharist as a communion. Communion applies to the Holy Eucharist both as a sacrifice and a sacrament. Hence communion here means more than reception of the Holy Eucharist; it is used in the wider sense of a mutual union of God with us and of us with God.

The Mass is a communion because it is the sacrament of ecclesiastical unity. Between Christ and His Church exists a most mysterious union and one of the great factors in that union is the

[75] *Ibid.*, p. 548 ss. (cf. N.C.W.C. trans., No. 70).

Mass. Much of the divine life won for us on the cross is transmitted ←
to us by the Mass. The Mass is the Church's supreme act of worship,
the official token of reverence, love, and supplication which she
tenders to the Bridegroom. Not only do Christ and the priest offer
the Mass; the Church also offers it. For as beloved Spouse she is
united to her Head as Offerer and Victim. She is an offerer, and the
Mass is her worship, her praise, her sacrifice. The words and actions
of the Mass proclaim its social character. Although some Masses are
said in private, yet every Mass is a public offering on the part of all
the members of Christ. While the people present truly participate
in the oblation, they do not do so as sacrificing priests; they exercise
merely that wider priesthood spoken of by St. Peter.[76] The Church
is also offered as a victim, for by baptism all Christians are made
sharers in His victimhood. Evidently, then, the Mass is the true
center of Christian life. Without the Mass a true Christian community is impossible.

How unity with Christ is effected we see by considering those who
benefit by the Mass. Each Mass brings a general benefit to (1) the
Church on earth and in Purgatory. All mankind indeed, except the
damned, is helped. There is a special value of impetration and satisfaction belonging to (2) that person, living or dead, to whose welfare
the Mass is directed. From ancient times he who paid the expenses
of the Mass, or, as we say now, gave a stipend for it, was allowed
to name the recipient of this value. Finally, (3) the priest who offers
the Mass and, in proportion of the closeness of their co-operation
with him, those who are present and offer it with him, receive a
unique and untransferable benefit of merit, as well as impetration
and satisfaction. The amount of benefit received by priest and participants depends upon their good dispositions. However, in (1) and
(2) the good accomplished is independent of the faith and charity
of the celebrant and congregation. In this sense the Mass, like the
sacraments, works *ex opere operato,* for the Mass is "that clean
oblation which cannot be defiled by any unworthiness or malice in
those who offer it."[77]

---

[76] Pius XII, *Mediator Dei,* §§ 81–84 (N.C.W.C. trans.).
[77] Council of Trent, *Den.* 939 (*TCT,* 748).

What else does the Mass effect? As the supreme act of religion it gives God adoration and thanksgiving, it satisfies for sin and begs blessings. Adoration and thanksgiving necessarily follow from the offering of an infinite Victim, and in this sense the Mass, like the cross, produces an infinite effect. This is God's dividend from the Mass, if God can be said to be benefited by anything. What is man's dividend? The Council of Trent says: "We obtain mercy and find grace when we need it. For, the Lord is appeased by the offering of the mass and by granting grace and the gift of repentance forgives even heinous crimes and sins. . . . Wherefore, in keeping with apostolic tradition, the mass is offered not only for the sins, punishments, satisfactions and other necessities of the living faithful but also on behalf of those who have departed in Christ but are not yet fully purified."[78]

The souls in purgatory are kept from perfect union with Christ by unpaid debts of temporal punishment. By offering Masses for the faithful departed, the faithful on earth show that they understand how efficacious is the Mass for the payment of these debts. This effect is produced by the Mass directly and immediately but not in infinite measure. For, although the Mass is capable of canceling an infinity of punishment, yet God wills that it produce only a limited effect for the Holy Souls. Otherwise, since one Mass applied to a soul would wipe out all punishment, the Church would not allow, as she does, hundreds of Masses to be said for one soul. The sins of the living are forgiven through the Mass, but it does not directly remit them as does the sacrament of penance. What the Council means is that God is placated by the Mass and grants individual graces of conversion. Through the Mass also satisfaction is applied against the debt of temporal punishment of the living. As for other temporal and spiritual blessings, besought through the Mass, we always obtain whatever Christ requests. For the intercession of the Mass is the voice of Christ crying from the cross, more powerful to be heard than the blood of Abel. Jesus is the suppliant who is always heard. The favors granted are only such as will promote our salvation but, what the circumstances are under which Christ

[78] Den. 940 (TCT, 749).

will make our petition His own, we do not know. While Christ's power of intercession is unlimited, the favors we get through the Mass are limited.

The Holy Eucharist as a Sacrament

That the Holy Eucharist is a sacrament follows from its institution by Christ and the doctrine of His Real Presence. The form which brings the sacrament into being are the words of consecration: the remote matter is wheaten bread and wine made from grapes.

It differs from the other sacraments in this: the other sacraments exercise their power to sanctify only in their use but the Eucharist is a sacrament even before it is used. It is a permanent sacrament; that is, once it comes into being Jesus is sacramentally present as long as the appearances of bread or wine remain. Luther held that Christ was present and the sacrament exercised its power to sanctify only at the moment of use and consumption. He was condemned by Trent[79] which teaches that the sacred species may be reserved on the altar for purposes of adoration and for distribution as the spiritual food of the faithful.

Therefore the Holy Eucharist is the greatest of the sacraments because It contains the Author of all grace and its sacramental effect — union with Christ in charity — is the consummation toward which the other sacraments are directed.

The supreme benefit of the Holy Eucharist arises from personal reception of the sacrament which is aptly called Holy Communion. Here the notion of communion is fully realized. A communion is not a one-sided but a mutual union. Man ever craves communion with divinity. It seems that a natural culmination of a sacrificial offering is that they who make the offering should sit down to a sacred banquet and feast upon the offering. The joyous feast testifies to divinity's willingness to receive man. The Mass is properly called the Supper of the Lord and by it we give God a gift — His Son — which testifies to our desire for union with God. Then by receiving the sacrament we get back the gift and eat the offering. This shows God's desire to be one with us. And so the circle is complete — we to Him

---

[79] *Den.* 886, 889 (*TCT*, 731, 734).

and He to us! In the commingling of the Body of Christ and the body of the recipient, the mystery of the Incarnation is brought home to the individual, producing in him potent results of sanctity.

Just as His coming to the human race gave it the life of grace, as St. John says, "grace and truth came through Jesus Christ,"[80] so by coming sacramentally to the soul He causes more grace to be there, as Jesus says, "He who eats me, he also shall live because of me."[81] Since this sacrament is the memorial of the death of Christ, it produces in the soul the same kind of unitive effects which the cross produces in the world. We may not claim, however, that the full power of the cross flows exclusively through this sacrament, for the reconciliation of souls with God is done chiefly by the sacraments of baptism and penance. This sacrament aims at intimate union with God. There is vital contact between our bodies and the Body of Christ which must in some way sanctify the flesh and tame its corruption. The main thing is that this sacrament leads to greater mystical union with Christ. "Mystical" is an unsuccessful attempt to make a full explanation of the union which exists between the Vine and its branches. This union is physical and moral — but something very mysterious. "Mystical" is used to cover our ignorance of that mysterious character, the full nature of that mysterious oneness which grace effects between us and Christ. This oneness is fostered because the Holy Eucharist (1) remits venial sins which are the chief obstacle to loving union with God; (2) gives greater facility in embracing His will, a greater control over the sources of sin, and a subduing of passion; (3) closer union with the members of Christ. Since they are part of His Mystical Body, we cannot unite ourselves more closely to Him without becoming more united to them. For "by this will all men know that you are my disciples, if you have love for one another."[82] Therefore St. Thomas calls this the sacrament of ecclesiastical unity and St. Augustine exclaims: "O Sacrament of piety! O sign of unity! O bond of charity!"[83]

For a valid reception one does not have to receive the species of both bread and wine. While consecration of bread and wine is

---

[80] Jn. 1:17.
[81] Jn. 6:58.
[82] Jn. 13:35.
[83] Tract. xxvi in Joannem VI, 13. PL 35, 1613.

necessary for the sacrifice, and while reception under both kinds was the custom of the ancient Church and is today of the Eastern Churches, the Latin Church from the thirteenth century, for reasons of practical utility and greater reverence to the sacrament, has given the sacrament to the laity only under the form of bread. To communicate validly a small portion of a consecrated host suffices, for Christ is totally present under the tiniest particle.

For the worthy reception of the sacrament faith is not enough; one must also be in the state of grace and have the intention of communicating. Whoever is conscious of mortal sin may not approach this sacrament without first going to confession; eliciting an act of perfect contrition is generally not enough. Whoever is conscious of mortal sin and receives this sacrament, receives indeed the Body and Blood of Christ, but he also "eats and drinks judgment to himself."[84]

Finally, the Holy Eucharist looks to the future perfect union of the soul with God. For "he who eats my flesh and drinks my blood has everlasting life and I will raise him up on the last day."[85] This is the promise of a happy immortality. Moreover, the union of our bodies with the Body of Christ is life eternal, as far as this can be had in the darkness of faith. It is a present outpouring of grace and a token payment toward the unending union of eternity. Since it is the food of the traveler who walks the journey thither, we call it Viaticum, the provision for the way. The Holy Eucharist is Viaticum, not only in the liturgical sense of preparation for the last few steps which bring us to death, but also in the wider sense that the whole of life is a pilgrimage and the food of pilgrims is the Body and Blood of Christ. The Holy Eucharist does for our supernatural life what food does for our natural life; that is, It sustains, gives increase, restores strength, and affords delight. As the first paschal lamb was the food of pilgrims leaving Egypt, as Elias ate the food the angel gave him and by its strength walked forty days and forty nights until he came to Horeb, the mount of God, so the Eucharist enables the Christian to walk the journey of life and arrive at his Father's house. One cannot say that the Holy Eucharist is strictly necessary

---

[84] 1 Cor. 11:29.   [85] Jn. 6:55.

for salvation but under ordinary circumstances the salvation of the adult, who is exposed to so many temptations, depends on his use of this sacrament. The perfection of Christian life or any kind of close intimacy with God is practically impossible without the graces of the Holy Eucharist.

Penance

Since the time of Tertullian penance has been known in the Church as the second plank of salvation after the shipwreck of sin. The first is baptism. Penance, then, is the sacrament whereby the sins committed after baptism are forgiven through the absolution of a properly authorized priest.

The Reformers denied that confession, as the faithful call it, has a sacramental character, that it is the outward sign of an invisible grace. In this rite, however, two things purportedly could represent a real remission of sin, namely, the turning away from sin manifest by a penitent and the imparting of forgiveness in the name of God by a priest. Granted that the sign is completed by both parties doing all that is required of them, the supreme question is, Did Christ make the rite an infallible sign of God's forgiveness?

The Church[86] has ever taught that Christ did just this on the night of the Resurrection when He said to His Apostles: "Receive the Holy Spirit; whose sins you shall forgive they are forgiven them; and whose sins you shall retain they are retained."[87] These words are not a commission to preach the Gospel but "by unanimous agreement the Fathers have ever held that, by an act so significant and by words so clear, the power of forgiving or retaining sins was granted to the Apostles and their legitimate successors for the reconciliation of the faithful who sin after Baptism."[88]

This power is part of the general authority which Christ gave the Apostles and whose primacy is in Peter and his successors. This authority to bind and to loose is limited only by the end for which the Church was instituted — the salvation of men. Hence the author-

---

[86] Council of Trent, *Den.* 894 (*TCT,* 788).
[87] Jn. 20:22.
[88] Council of Trent, *Den.* 894 (*TCT,* 788).

ity of the Church includes not only external social power to make laws, pass judgment, impose penalties, but also the power of forgiving and retaining sins in the realm of conscience. Jurisdiction by the Church over the conscience is necessary for attaining the end of the Church and the salvation of souls. However, since the Jews had said that only God could forgive sins, and since no man dreamed of exercising this power before the coming of Christ, He took pains to make the grant of it to His Church most explicit.

It is defined doctrine that the power of the keys extends to *all* the sins of the faithful. This means, first, that there are no unforgivable sins. For the sacrament exists "to reconcile the faithful to God as often as they may fall into sin after Baptism."[89] When Holy Writ says that certain sins, like the sin against the Holy Spirit, will not be forgiven, the meaning is that they cannot be forgiven so long as the sinner is impenitent and closes his heart to the entrance of grace. To say that a truly penitent person cannot have enormous sins forgiven is to contradict the infinite mercy of God and the unqualified statement of Christ: "Whose sins you shall forgive they are forgiven them." Second, all mortal sins committed after baptism must be submitted to the power of the keys. Divine law, says the Council of Trent,[90] requires as a necessary condition for forgiveness the confession in the sacrament of penance of each and all such sins — even the most secret sins of thought and desire — and all these are to be described and enumerated according to their proper moral nature. It is good and salutary to confess venial sins, but the confession of them is not necessary; they can be remitted by means other than this sacrament.

It is also defined[91] that this sacrament is administered as a kind of judicial process. The judge is the priest; the penitent is the accuser and the accused. No lay person can absolve from sin; for this function the consecration of holy orders is absolutely necessary. The judicial case is settled by the priest granting or withholding absolution — a thing, however, that cannot be a matter of arbitrary whim.

---

[89] Council of Trent, *Den.* 911 (*TCT,* 800).
[90] *Den.* 917 (*TCT,* 806).
[91] *Den.* 919 (*TCT,* 808).

Since the priest passes judgment as the representative of Christ, his judgment must accord with these norms of the Church: he is obliged to grant absolution to all who seek it and are certainly properly disposed; he must refuse it to one who certainly lacks the proper dispositions; in a doubtful case he may defer it, or grant it conditionally.

Not every priest can absolve everywhere. Since the forgiveness of sins is a judicial act, there is required, besides the power of orders, jurisdiction to administer sacramental justice. The ultimate source of this authorization is the Sovereign Pontiff and the law which he gives to the whole Church. Thus the law gives jurisdiction to all pastors in virtue of their office. Other priests get it from some legitimate superior who is usually the local bishop; he has it because he is a successor of the Apostles.

The form of the sacrament is the words of absolution: "I absolve thee from thy sins in the name of the Father and of the Son and of the Holy Spirit." The matter of the sacrament is the acts of the penitent. Ultimately these are the sins of the penitent. Proximately, however, these acts are what he must do about his sins in order to have them forgiven. Luther said the penitent's part consists in experiencing terrors of conscience and feeling trust in Christ that his sins are forgiven. The Council of Trent[92] denies this and says that the penitent must be sorry for his sins, tell them to the confessor, and make satisfaction for them. The Council does not put examination of conscience among the three necessary acts of the penitent, but it does say that we are obliged to confess each mortal sin "which we can call to mind after proper and diligent reflection."[93] It stands to reason that if we are to confess *all* serious sins we must honestly try to find out what they are. God does not demand the impossible in this respect. How exacting and detailed the scrutiny of conscience should be depends on the kind of life one leads and the frequency of one's recourse to the sacrament.

The outward sign which is the sacrament of penance must show that the sinner has renounced his sins and that God has forgiven them. The latter element, however, is completely dependent on the former: God will be reconciled with the sinner only if the sinner

[92] *Den.* 914 (*TCT,* 803).   [93] *Den.* 899 (*TCT,* 793).

gives up his sins. The prophet says: "Be converted and do penance for all your iniquities: and iniquity will not be your ruin."[94] Our Lord says: "Unless you repent you will all perish in the same manner."[95] St. Peter says: "Repent therefore and be converted, that your sins may be blotted out."[96] If the sinner seeking absolution does not renounce his sins from the heart, the sacrament cannot come into existence, for he fails to contribute an essential part to the sacramental sign.

The sinner renounces his sins by his contrition, which is sorrow of soul and detestation of his sins together with the serious resolve not to sin again. Sorrow of soul involves a change of mind and heart about past sins. What the sinner approved and chose, namely, his rejection of God and preference for the creature, he now rejects as evil. This change of heart, says Trent,[97] includes a parting from sin, the resolution to begin, and the actual beginning, of a new life, and (the emphasis is the Council's) *hatred of one's past wickedness*. While this hatred need not be accompanied by *emotions* of regret and remorse, nevertheless the presence of such feeling indicates great intensity of will against sin such as the prophet manifested: "I will recount to thee all my years in the bitterness of my soul."[98] While the practical indication of genuine sorrow is the earnest resolve to quit sin for the future, yet the force of that resolve is proportioned to the detestation of past falls. It is quite possible, however, to renounce sin here and now even though there may be fear of sinning again through human weakness.

Contrition is an exercise of the *virtue of penance* which aims at the total destruction of sin *insofar as it is offensive to God*. Therefore not every sort of sorrow suffices to win divine forgiveness. Purely natural sorrow — regret for the personal shame and hurtful consequences involved in our past misdeeds — is not enough. We must regret them because they offend *God*. That our sorrow may be truly effectual, it must proceed from a supernatural motive, extend to all mortal sins, and we must regard a serious offense against God as the first of all evils.

---

[94] Ezech. 18:30.   [96] Acts 3:19.   [98] Isa. 38:15.
[95] Lk. 13:3.   [97] *Den.* 897 (*TCT*, 791).

The motive for sorrow must spring from considerations of faith. Only a motive of this kind will lift our sorrow from the natural and personal to the divine and supernatural level. Such a motive may be the malice of an offense against God, its disorder as thwarting the divine plan, loss of heaven for the sinner and the pains of hell, love of God for God's sake. The last is the perfect motive and the sorrow which it begets is Perfect Contrition. This is based upon that childlike love of God exemplified in the Gospel by the Prodigal Son. It reconciles the sinner as soon as he elicits it, even before he receives the sacrament. However, it does not excuse him from submitting his sins to the power of the keys.

Sorrow, motivated by the foulness of sin or fear of divine punishment, is attrition. Great controversies have centered around it. The Reformers said such sorrow was hypocritical and immoral, but fear of divine punishment cannot be immoral if John the Baptist tried to stir it up: "Brood of vipers! who has shown you how to flee from the wrath to come? Bring forth therefore fruit befitting repentance."[99] Our Lord appeals to the same motive: "But rather be afraid of him who is able to destroy both soul and body in hell."[100] If, however, one is sorry solely because of hell so that he would go on sinning if there were no hell, his attitude is sinful. The Reformers also said that according to Catholic teaching one could get his sins forgiven without surrendering his attachment to sin. This is a misrepresentation. The Council of Trent[101] has defined attrition to be the gift of God; and if it be accompanied by hope of pardon and a firm resolve to quit sin, it prepares the soul for reconciliation. "And although it cannot by itself bring the penitent to justification without the sacrament of penance, yet in the sacrament of penance it disposes him to obtain the grace of God."[102] Since nothing more is required, attrition, coupled with the power of the sacrament, is sufficient for forgiveness. Thus the New Law has made easier the reconciliation of the sinner. But to have the attrition which is the gift of God, the sinner must give up sin absolutely, be sorry because it offends God, and regard it as the worst evil in the world.

[99] Mt. 3:7–8.
[100] Mt. 10:28.
[101] Den. 898 (TCT, 792).
[102] Ibid.

The second contribution of the penitent to the sacramental sign is the confession of all mortal sins according to their kind and number. "Since all mortal sins, even those of thought, make men children of wrath and enemies of God, it is necessary to ask pardon for all of them by a clear and humble confession."[103] This requirement is of divine law and its necessity follows from the judicial character of the sacrament. The priest could not decide whether sins are to be forgiven or retained unless he first knew them. "For it is clear," continues the Council, "that priests could not pass this judgment without a knowledge of the case nor could they observe justice in imposing penalties if the faithful declared their sins in general and not specifically and singly."[104] Since each sin is a case to be settled by the judge, it must be clearly presented to him: its moral nature must be sufficiently described so that he may know the precise kind of sin it is. When the same sin has been repeated the number must be told. However, the obligation to tell all sins and all circumstances which change their moral nature cannot be exacted when this is humanly impossible.

Deliberately to omit a mortal sin is itself a mortal sin because it violates the command of Christ that all mortal sins be submitted to the keys. Moreover it is a sacrilege because one attempts to bring a sacrament into being and only succeeds in frustrating it. Sins are forgiven by the infusion of grace but, if in the act of seeking grace one commits a serious sin, grace cannot be given. For grace and mortal sin cannot be in the soul at the same time. It would be foolish to imagine that the sins confessed would be forgiven even though the sin deliberately concealed remained unforgiven. Either all mortal sins are wiped out or none. Since in this case none is forgiven, the sacramental sign has been attempted in vain. To do this is sacrilege.

If one has innocently forgotten a mortal sin, the sacrament is valid, provided, of course, the other requirements have been met. The person need not hurry back to the confessional as soon as he remembers the omission, for he has received the grace of the sacrament which has taken away all mortal sins. The forgotten sin was

---

[103] Council of Trent, *Den.* 899 (*TCT*, 793).
[104] *Den.* 899 (*TCT*, 793).

remitted indirectly but there still remains the obligation of telling it the next time he confesses.

If one doubts whether he has committed a sin or whether the sin is serious or whether he has already confessed it, it seems clear from the Council of Trent[105] that he is *not obliged* to confess such matter. However, for the guidance of one's conscience and for peace of soul it is often well to reveal such doubts. For the confessor is not only a judge but also a teacher and a physician of souls.

The final act of the penitent is satisfaction. This is acceptance of penitential obligations, such as prayer, fasting, and almsgiving, imposed by the confessor for two reasons. The first is that the penitent make satisfaction for the injustice of sin, which consists in the sinner turning from God, the last end, to some creature as though it were the last end. For this God must inflict punishment: eternal punishment for turning away from Him; punishment of temporary duration for turning to the creature. When the sinner is absolved, eternal punishment is remitted. The Reformers said that the temporal punishment is also taken away in this sacrament, just as it is in baptism, but the Council of Trent[106] said that, since there is greater malice in the sins committed after baptism, God punishes these more severely. Of course if the penitent's return to God honors Him to the same extent that his sins dishonored Him, justice is even. But usually a debt of temporal punishment remains after absolution, which God strictly exacts, and which the penitent must pay either in this life or in Purgatory. Since the sacrament of penance aims at the total eradication of sin, it must offer the penitent some opportunity of paying this debt. Hence it is an integral part of the sacrament that the confessor impose penitential works, proportioned to the sins committed and the ability of the penitent to "do the penance," as the faithful call it. A second reason for imposing satisfaction is the improvement of the penitent, that is, that he may have the proper attitude toward sin, shed the vicious habits acquired by sinning, and become like Christ who satisfied for us.

The penitent has a serious obligation to fulfill "penances" imposed for serious sins. It is not necessary, however, that they be completed

---

[105] *Den.* 899 (*TCT,* 793).   [106] *Den.* 904 (*TCT,* 797).

before absolution is given or Holy Communion received. While the
sacramental penances of today are easy in comparison with the
ancient penances of the Church, yet, on account of their origin in
the sacrament, they have a peculiar *ex-opere-operato* efficacy. For
they "have their efficacy from Christ, by Him they are offered to the
Father, and through Him they are accepted by the Father."[107]

The penitent must also render justice to his fellow man; that is,
if he has been seriously unjust he must in confession express his
willingness to make reparation. Lack of willingness means that one
is not rightly disposed for absolution. If after absolution one deliberately fails to make reparation when he can, he commits a fresh sin
of injustice but this does not affect the validity of the sacrament in
which he confessed his injustice.

An *indulgence* is an outgrowth of the necessity of performing works
of satisfaction. An indulgence is not the remission of sin nor permission to commit future sin, but the taking away by the Church
of the temporal punishment due to sins already forgiven. It is an
exercise of the Church's power to loose just as her imposition of
penances is exercise of her power to bind. An indulgence is the act
of a merciful Mother making easier the entrance of her children
into eternal bliss.

The Church once had a severe system of canonical penances: for
specific grave sins confessed the confessor was directed by law and
custom to impose commensurate grave penalties. Since the staple
item in the system was fasting which might be protracted from one
to twenty years, the faithful often found these penances irksome.
Relief from difficult penance was sometimes given by an indulgence,
that is, an explicit act of the Church which permitted the penitent
to substitute some easier kind of penance. Thus if a person had
seven years of canonical penance to fulfill, he might be let off a year
of it if he helped in the building of a church or even if he was
present during the recitation of the canonical hours on some notable
occasion. If he took the cross and went on a crusade, he was freed
from all canonical penance.

Although the old penitential discipline has gone, indulgences re-

---
[107] *Ibid.*

main. The Church can still free her children from the temporal punishment which they owe to God. Thus whoever really gains a plenary indulgence is free in God's sight from all temporal punishment. Whoever gains an indulgence of seven years is freed from the same amount of debt which, under the old discipline, he would have paid the justice of God by doing seven years of canonical penance.

To gain an indulgence one must fulfill certain conditions. First, one must be in the state of grace at least by the time the final condition is fulfilled; second, one must have at least a habitual intention of gaining the indulgence; finally, one must do what the Church prescribes for the gaining of the indulgence.

Indulgences can profit both the living and the dead but the manner of application varies in either case. To the living person the Church grants an indulgence as an act of jurisdiction and the grant is infallible; that is, if one perfectly fulfills the conditions he is certain to obtain the indulgence sought. The case is different with the faithful departed because the Church no longer has jurisdiction over them. Hence the application of an indulgence to them is a supplication for relief made on their behalf by the Church. We do not know that these petitions are infallibly heard.

When an indulgence works and one is freed from punishment, God does not cancel the debt but accepts payment from one who did not owe the debt. Here is another application of the doctrine of the Communion of Saints. The Church has at her disposal an infinite treasury compiled by the superabundant satisfaction of Christ and the saints. These satisfactions are not lost but go into the treasury of the Church. To this treasury the Church has recourse when she grants an indulgence so that each remission of punishment, given by way of an indulgence, means that God accepts the satisfaction of one member of Christ, who no longer needs it for himself, and applies it against the debt of one who does need it.

Briefly, the sacrament of penance is a spiritual medicine for the cure and prevention of sin. The medicine consists in restoring to supernatural life penitents who are in mortal sin and in providing all penitents with a remedy against future sin. Hence the effects of penance are these: it restores or increases sanctifying grace; it takes away the sinner's status of guilt in the sight of God and all eternal punishment; it remits venial sins and at least part of the temporal punishment; it promises special actual graces to be given the penitent as he shall require them to overcome temptation; finally, the merits of good works, lost by sin, are restored.

Extreme Unction

Extreme unction means last anointing. It is not a mere relic of the charism of healing of the primitive Church, but the sacrament whereby a sick person is made ready for death by anointing with holy oil and the prayer of the priest. A merciful God has provided sacramental help for the chief states of life and no period of life is more important than that which precedes death. "For, although our adversary seeks and seizes throughout our entire life occasions to devour our souls in every way, yet there is no time when he more vigorously directs all the strength of his cunning to ruin us completely, and if possible to shake us from our trust in the divine mercy, than when he sees the end of our life to be approaching."[108]

The matter of the sacrament is oil blessed by the bishop. The sacrament is administered by the priest anointing the eyes, ears, nose, lips, hands, and feet and saying at the anointing of each sense: "Through this holy anointing and His most tender mercy, may the Lord pardon you whatever faults you have committed through sight, hearing, etc." Only a priest has power to administer this sacrament.

That the rite is sacramental we know from the unbroken tradition of the Church, from repeated definitions of Councils, and from the words of St. James: "Is any one among you sick? Let him bring in the presbyters of the Church, and let them pray over him, anointing him with oil in the name of the Lord. And the prayer of faith will save the sick man, and the Lord will raise him up, and if he be in sins, they shall be forgiven him."[109]

Although it is not a sacrament of the dead but of the living, it is fitting that, as it prepares for death, it should deal directly with sins. It is related to penance as baptism is to confirmation; that is, while

[108] Council of Trent, *Den.* 907 (*TCT*, 831).
[109] James 5:14–15.

penance is more necessary, extreme unction is of greater perfection, for it aims at the complete removal of sins and their consequences. Consequently if the person is in sin and unable to confess, the anointing will directly take away his sins, provided he is sorry for them. Its peculiar sacramental effect, however, is the removal of the *remains* of sin, those disorderly inclinations which are the result of past sins and worldly attachments. It takes away temporal punishment due to sin, and it is likely that if the person's dispositions are adequate, all temporal punishment is remitted so that at death the soul can immediately enter upon the beatific vision.

Sometimes the sacrament restores health to the body if this is good for the soul, as is indicated in the prayers which follow the sacramental anointing. Hence the administration of the sacrament should never be delayed until the person is at the point of death, for it strengthens the powers of the soul, imparts patience, and gives confidence in the mercy of God. This well-being of the soul can flow over into the body and effect its recovery. In any event the sacrament should be given in good time, when the person has full use of his faculties, and is competent to co-operate with the graces of the sacrament.

Only he can receive the sacrament who is in danger of death from sickness or old age. It can be received only once during the same danger of death. Should another illness arise, or another danger of death during the same illness, the sacrament can and should be received again.

Holy Orders

To understand the name *holy orders* we must grasp the notion of hierarchy, which is a system of persons in a graded order with inferiors subject to superiors. Thus in an army there is a hierarchy of command. Here we refer to the power to perform sacred functions. That such a hierarchy exists in the Church is obvious. First, there is a distinction between laymen, who can perform no sacred function, and clerics, who can. One is made a cleric by the ceremony of tonsure. Among the Latin clergy there are four minor grades: (1) *acolyte* whose function is today performed by a Mass server; (2)

exorcist whose function is the expulsion of demons but which may never be exercised without the express consent of the bishop; (3) *lector* or reader during divine service; (4) porter or doorkeeper whose function it once was to keep unqualified persons from attending divine service. There are three major grades: that of (1) *subdeacon*, the third minister at solemn Mass who reads the Epistle; (2) *deacon*, who sings the Gospel at solemn Mass and can distribute Holy Communion and administer solemn baptism; (3) *priest*. In the priestly office we distinguish between (*a*) the power of a *simple priest* which is to offer Mass and to forgive sins — it constitutes the presbyterate — and (*b*) the fullness of the priesthood possessed by the *bishop* — it constitutes the episcopate. A bishop is a priest who has sole power to administer holy orders and who can confirm in his own right.

Is this distribution of sacred functions a man-made arrangement? According to the Council of Trent it is of faith that there is a visible external priesthood with power to consecrate and forgive sins, that the laity is excluded from this power, that by divine arrangement there is a sacred hierarchy "consisting of bishops, priests, and ministers."[110] The Council insists on the unique position of the bishops as successors of the Apostles. They are the superiors of priests and have many powers which are not possessed by lesser members of the clergy. It is generally held that the four minor orders and the subdiaconate are of purely ecclesiastical origin.

Sacred orders also means (1) the *grade* one has reached in the sacred hierarchy, (2) the *sacred power* which goes with one's grade, and (3) the *rite* or ceremony by which one is initiated into a grade and given sacred power. By sacred orders we mean here these rites of initiation. Are they of divine or ecclesiastical origin? Are they merely sacramentals or are some or all of them true sacraments?

First, that there is a sacrament of orders has been defined by many Councils. The Scriptural evidence for this sacrament is clear. St. Paul said to Timothy: "I admonish thee to stir up the grace of God which is in thee by the laying on of my hands. For God has not given us the spirit of fear, but of power and of love and of

---

[110] *Den.* 966 (*TCT*, 849).

prudence,"[111] and, "Do not neglect the grace that is in thee, granted
to thee by reason of prophecy with the laying on of hands of the
presbyterate."[112] The meaning is that Timothy received sanctifying
grace and the power to exercise sacred functions through the laying
on of Paul's hands. This rite is an outward sign of inward grace and
was made a sacrament at the Last Supper when Christ, after consecrating bread and wine into His own Body and Blood, said to His
Apostles: "Do this in remembrance of me."[113] Furthermore, by
imposition of hands the Apostles appointed seven deacons, constituted presbyters in various cities, communicated the power of ordain-
ing to their disciples who (Timothy, for example) are warned not to
use this power hastily.

Second, not all ordination rites are sacraments. Tonsure is only
a sacramental and so are the rites of the four minor orders. It is of
faith that ordination to the presbyterate is a sacrament. It is certain
doctrine that ordination to the diaconate and episcopate, as distinct
from the presbyterate, are also sacraments.

There are not, however, nine sacraments. While the rites of diaconate, presbyterate, and episcopate are distinct, there is only one
sacrament of orders. For that which is signified and imparted by
the rite is only one — sacred power — and this can be found either
in its fullness or in a less perfect state.

What constitutes the matter and form of ordination to the presbyterate was once a lively question. In apostolic times the ordination
was by imposition of hands, a peculiarly apt way of showing that
sacred power comes from above and not from men. In the course
of time the Latin Church added to the imposition of hands the
presentation of the instruments. A dispute then arose as to what
constituted the essential matter of the sacrament: the imposition of
hands, the presentation of instruments, or both? By his *Sacramentum
Ordinis* Pius XII decreed that *henceforth* the presentation of instruments is not necessary for validity of ordination to the diaconate,
presbyterate, and episcopate, that the matter of the sacrament is a
single imposition of the hand or hands (in the case of the presbyterate the first silent imposition of hands), that the form is the

[111] 2 Tim. 1:6–7.   [112] 1 Tim. 4:14.   [113] Lk. 22:19.

words of the Preface which ask for, and signify, the grant of sacred power and the grace of the Holy Spirit.[114]

It is of faith that the ordinary minister of holy orders is the bishop alone. While a simple priest can be delegated to confer minor orders, he is not delegated to confer the episcopate, the presbyterate, or the diaconate. The reason is that he lacks the fullness of the priesthood which is necessary in him who confers sacramental orders.

The first effect of the sacrament is increase of sanctifying grace. Its peculiar effect is the imprinting of the sacerdotal character, a share in the official priesthood of Christ. It is of faith that this character is perpetual because "he who was once a priest cannot become a layman again."[115] This mark, whose fullness is in the bishop alone, is one in the same sense that the sacrament is one. With the mark comes the grant of sacred power and the right to receive, as occasion demands, all the actual graces necessary to fulfill the demands of the sacerdotal state.

By divine law no woman may receive this sacrament. For its *valid* reception all that is required is that one be a baptized male; if one is an adult he must have in addition the intention of receiving the sacrament.

Matrimony

Orders and matrimony regard the social needs of the Church. The former supplies the Church with rulers, teachers, and sacred ministers. The latter supplies the general membership.

Matrimony means two things: first, the natural institution, established by God for the procreation of the human race, and consisting of the spiritual-corporeal union of a man and a woman in a lifelong companionship; second, the ceremony by which two persons enter this union.

Recent sovereign pontiffs have taken great pains to explain this natural institution which God Himself originated in the earthly paradise. Genesis relates: "And God created man to his own image; to the image of God he created him; male and female he created

---

[114] *AAS*, 40 (1948), pp. 6–7.
[115] Council of Trent, *Den.* 964 (*TCT*, 847).

them. And God blessed them saying: 'Increase and multiply and fill the earth' "[116]; and " 'It is not good for man to be alone: let us make him a help like unto himself.' . . . And the Lord God built the rib which he took from Adam into a woman: and brought her to Adam. And Adam said: 'This is now bone of my bones and flesh of my flesh. . . . Wherefore a man shall leave father and mother, and shall cleave to his wife; and they shall be two in one flesh.' "[117]

This union has three natural purposes. The first is the birth and rearing of children. From this arises the dignity and sacredness of this institution because children, born by the power of God through the co-operation of spouses, are a great gift of the divine goodness. "And Christian parents must also understand that they are destined not only to propagate and preserve the human race on earth, indeed, not only to educate any kind of worshipers of the true God, but children who are to become members of the Church of Christ, to raise up fellow citizens of the saints and members of God's household."[118] The second purpose is to afford a decent remedy for the sexual concupiscence due to original sin. Since marriage can be only between one man and one woman, spouses are forbidden any venereal contact with a third party. The prohibition includes not only external acts but all willful thoughts and desires of such things according to the word of Christ: "I say to you that anyone who even looks with lust at a woman has already committed adultery with her in his heart."[119] The third purpose is the fostering of that mutual love which promotes the happiness of the spouses themselves. Christian spouses are not only to assist each other in forming well-integrated personalities but they are to strive after Christian perfection together. "By this same love it is necessary that all the other rights and duties of the married state be regulated as the words of the Apostle: 'Let the husband render to the wife her due, and likewise the wife to the husband' express not only a law of justice but of charity."[120] Among these three purposes the first is primary

---

[116] Gen. 1:27–28.   [117] Gen. 2:18–24.

[118] Pius XI, *Casti Connubii, AAS,* Vol. 22, 1930, p. 544 (trans. as *Christian Marriage,* America Press, p. 5).

[119] Mt. 5:28.

[120] *Casti Connubii, op. cit.,* p. 549 (*Christian Marriage,* p. 8).

so that the good of offspring takes precedence over the good of the spouses. This is the most important statement to be made about the nature of this institution.

The second important statement is that the only way of entering this union is by the free consent of the parties involved whereby each gives and receives the exclusive perpetual right to use one's body for the acts proper to procreation. No human power can supply for lack of consent. "This freedom, however, regards only the question whether the contracting parties really wish to enter upon matrimony or to marry this particular person; but the nature of matrimony is entirely independent of the free will of man, so that if one has contracted matrimony he is thereby subject to its divinely made laws and its essential properties."[121]

This mutual consent creates the bond of matrimony whose essential properties are unity and indissolubility. From the primary end of matrimony and from the statement that "they shall be one flesh," it follows that the bond can exist only between one man and one woman and is dissolved only by the death of one of the parties. However, on account of human weakness, abuses crept in so that a man might have several wives and divorce was publicly granted. When God chose the Hebrews for His people, they kept polygamy and divorce as their ancestors had practiced them. There is strong reason for believing that God tolerated these practices and that therefore they were not sinful. The reason for the toleration was supernatural; namely, without divine toleration of these practices the Hebrews were in danger of lapsing from the true faith.

Christ, however, canceled the divine permission and restored matrimony to its original unity and indissolubility. "And some Pharisees coming up asked him, testing him, 'Is it lawful for a man to put away his wife?' But he answered and said to them, 'What did Moses command you?' They said, 'Moses permitted us to write a notice of dismissal and to put her away.' But Jesus said to them, 'By reason of the hardness of your hearts he wrote you that commandment. But from the beginning of creation God made them male and female. "For this cause a man will leave father and mother, and

[121] *Ibid.*, p. 541 (*Christian Marriage*, p. 3).

cleave to his wife, and the two shall become one flesh." Therefore
now they are no longer two but one flesh. What therefore God has
joined together, let no man put asunder.' And in the house, his
disciples again asked him concerning this. And he said to them,
'Whosoever puts away his wife and marries another, commits adultery against her; and if the wife puts away her husband and marries
another, she commits adultery.' "[122]

Although in the parallel text of St. Matthew Christ seems to admit an exception in the case of adultery when he says: "Whoever
puts away his wife, except for immorality, and marries another commits adultery,"[123] nevertheless He makes no exception. For the immorality to which Jesus here refers meant to the Jews concubinage
or attempted marriage with a relative. In such a case one could dis-
miss his companion — they were not married — but whoever put
away his *wife* and married another always committed adultery. The
reason why one always commits adultery when he puts away
his wife and marries another is that the bond between them is
unbreakable.

Assuredly the doctrine stated in St. Mark, St. Luke, and St. Paul
and universally accepted in the Church is that no human power can
sever the bond between Christian spouses. It is equally certain that
in His discourse with the Pharisees Christ restored matrimony to its
primitive unity when He insisted that the spouses are no longer two
but one flesh.

Christ made another provision for the marriage of Christians: it
shall be a symbol of the mysterious union existing between Christ
and His Church. St. Paul says: "Let wives be subject to their husbands as to the Lord; because a husband is the head of the wife,
just as Christ is head of the Church. . . . Husbands love your wives
just as Christ also loved the Church, and delivered himself up for
her that he might sanctify her. . . . Even thus ought husbands to love
their wives as their own bodies. He who loves his own wife loves
himself. For no one ever hated his own flesh; on the contrary he
nourishes and cherishes it, as Christ also does the Church. . . . For
this reason a man shall leave his father and mother and cleave to

[122] Mk. 10:2–12.   [123] Mt. 19:9.

his wife, and the two shall become one flesh. This is a great mystery — I mean in reference to Christ and to the Church."[124]

Christian spouses are to be one and to react to each other as Christ and the Church are one and mutually react. Nothing could better show the vast expectations which the New Law entertains of men corrupted by sin. However, to accomplish so lofty a purpose Christian spouses require a permanent source of divine assistance. This is given them by the sacrament of matrimony.

Christ made His greatest contribution to the well-being of Christian matrimony by elevating the marriage ceremony of Christians to the dignity of a sacrament. When He did this we do not know but that He did it is a matter of faith. The constant and universal tradition of the Church in this regard is embodied in the declarations of the Second Council of Lateran, the Second Council of Lyons, the Council of Florence, and in the solemn definition of Trent. It is, therefore, of faith that every marriage between two baptized persons is sacramental. It is now morally certain that the baptism of one party does not make the marriage a sacrament even for that party. It is quite commonly held that the natural marriage of two unbelievers becomes sacramental upon the baptism of both parties.

The marriage ceremony is the outward expression of a real internal consent and is a contract. Consequently the ministers of this sacrament are the parties themselves who produce the sacramental sign by their exchange of consent. The matter of the sacrament — the less determined part of the sacramental sign — is the giving of consent; the form of the sacrament — the more determining part of the sign — is the acceptance of consent. The priest who assists at the ceremony is not a minister of the sacrament but an official witness of the Church.

It has been said that the contract and the sacrament are distinct, that the sacrament is something in addition to the contract, that the contract falls under the care of the State, that only the sacrament is the care of the Church. This view is wholly false. While there is a natural contract of marriage between nonbaptized persons, in the marriage of Christians the contract and the sacrament are inseparable

124 Eph. 5:22–32.

so that the contract is the sacrament and the sacrament is the contract. The only way one Christian can marry another is sacramentally.

Some early Christians had doubts about the lawfulness of entering
another marriage after the death of one's spouse. However, a marriage is not eternal; death dissolves it. Since this sacrament does not
imprint a character, it may be repeated; the surviving party is free
to marry again.

Matrimony, as a sacrament of the living, imparts an increase of
sanctifying grace. Its peculiar effect is to give the spouses "particular
gifts, dispositions, seeds of grace, by elevating and perfecting the
natural powers. By these gifts the parties are assisted not only in
understanding, but in knowing intimately, in adhering to firmly, in
willing effectively, and in successfully putting into practice, those
things which pertain to the married state, its aims and duties, giving
them in fine the right to the actual assistance of grace, whensoever
they need it for fulfilling the duties of their state."[125]

Matrimony is not a sacrament which is necessary for each individual. For the obligation of propagation lies upon the race. Hence,
except for personal or accidental reasons, no one is obliged to marry.
Indeed, if one chooses not to marry and to practice perfect chastity,
he chooses a nobler state than matrimony, as the Council of Trent
has defined.[126] Nor is it required that the celibate or virgin enter the
priesthood or religious state. For there is an honorable status of
virginity in the world and it too is a holy state, more honorable than
matrimony.

Since matrimony is the basis of the family, which is the basis of
the State, the good or evil condition of matrimony produces wide-
spread social effects. Consequently matrimony must be regulated
for the social good. In a nation of unbelievers this supervision falls
to the State. Its matrimonial laws, however, cannot be arbitrary but
must be in keeping with right reason and the law of nature. But the
State can have no power over the essentials of Christian marriage.
It may regulate "the civil effects of marriage," that is, make laws
about dowry, inheritance of property or titles, community of goods,

---

[125] *Casti Connubii, AAS,* Vol. 22, 1930, pp. 554–555.
[126] *Den.* 980 (*TCT,* 866).

social status, income of widows and the like, but it has no power whatsoever of determining what is a valid or legitimate Christian marriage. The Church alone can do this because matrimony is a sacrament and the Church alone has the care of the sacraments.

How far does the power of the Church to regulate Christian marriage extend? First, it is the duty of the Church to explain what God has decreed about matrimony. This divine law the Church cannot change; she can only expound it. Hence the Church cannot alter the purposes of matrimony, the unity and indissolubility of the bond, the need of consent, the prohibition of bigamy and of marriages between parent and child, and such like fundamental matters. Second, by divine authority the Church has certain powers over the natural bond existing between nonbaptized parties and over the sacramental bond of the baptized.

In two instances the Church can sever the natural bond. The first is that of the Pauline privilege whose terms, announced by St. Paul,[127] are these. If one party to a natural marriage is baptized and if the other party refuses to live with the Christian spouse or persists in being a constant and proximate occasion of serious sin to the baptized party, the Church may declare the baptized party free to marry a Christian. A new marriage to a Christian would dissolve the old natural bond.

The second is the Petrine privilege. It means that under certain circumstances the Roman Pontiff may dissolve a natural marriage in order to permit a convert from unbelief to marry a Christian and lead a Christian life.

A Christian marriage which has been entered upon but never consummated may be terminated by the Roman Pontiff for a sufficiently grave cause. Such a marriage is automatically dissolved if one of the parties pronounces the solemn vows of religion. When we say the Church does not grant divorces as that term is commonly understood, we mean that it has no power to terminate a Christian marriage which has been consummated. For just cause the Church may grant the parties to such a marriage a separation, that is, allow

---

[127] 1 Cor. 7:12–15.

them to live apart, but it can never declare them free to marry again until death dissolves the bond.

The Church can also declare the conditions under which alone the matrimonial contract is valid. By the law of nature the matrimonial contract requires no other external form than a free consent mutually rendered. Consent given without witnesses is a naturally valid consent and is called a clandestine marriage. The Council of Trent declared the clandestine form of marriage to be hereafter invalid for Christians and required that Christian marriages be solemnized by the presence of one's parish priest and two other witnesses.[128] Today this law binds only those who have been baptized in the Catholic Church.

Finally, the Church can declare the conditions under which certain persons cannot marry certain other persons. This is the power of establishing matrimonial impediments or legal hindrances to certain kinds of marriage. It is heretical to say that the Church cannot establish impediments or has erred in establishing them.[129] And if the Church can declare these hindrances to marriage, it can also, for sufficient reasons, dispense from them. The law of nature forbids some marriages. Over and above explaining these natural prohibitions the Church can establish other impediments for the sake of morality and the salvation of souls. If marriage is attempted contrary to some of these prescriptions, the marriage is invalid. These impediments are diriment. If marriage is attempted contrary to the other prescriptions, the marriage is valid but the parties commit a serious sin. These are the impeding impediments. Chief among the diriment impediments is marriage with a nonbaptized person; chief among the impeding impediments is marriage with a non-Catholic Christian.

---

[128] *Den.* 990 ff.
[129] *Den.* 974 (*TCT,* 860).

CHAPTER SEVEN

GOD THE FINISHER AND REWARDER

"The resurrection of the body and life everlasting. Amen."

THEOLOGY usually starts with the fact of God's revelation and the means by which revelation is safeguarded and taught — *God the Revealer*. It then unfolds the content of revelation, the first item of which is God Himself — *The Unity and Trinity of God*. Theology next proceeds to relate the external works of God, chief among which are angels and men whom God calls to share in His own life — *God the Creator and Provider*. It then tells how man cuts himself off from God and forfeits his destiny by sin, and how he is rescued from his folly by the Son of God made man — *God the Redeemer*. It then relates how sinful men are reconciled to God by the sanctifying action of the Holy Spirit — *God the Sanctifier*. He divinizes man by grace and the virtues which are brought to him by the seven sacraments — *The Sources of Grace*. Theology concludes with God crowning His work in man by apportioning rewards and punishments as they are deserved by man's free activity — *God the Finisher and Rewarder*.

The final consideration, therefore, involves the ultimate fate of man, the individual and the race. What has divine law prescribed for the conclusion of the human adventure?

A. *The Fate of Individual Man*

A man's attainment of salvation results primarily from God's grant of grace and secondarily from man's co-operation with grace. God calls him by actual grace, He sanctifies him with habitual grace, He restores it should he lose it, and He provides that he end his life in His favor. A man, however, can reject grace and therefore become the author of his ruin. "He who rejects me and does not accept my words, has one to condemn him. The word that I have spoken will condemn him on the last day."[1] Christ's doctrine is rejected by failure to believe in it or to live in accordance with it. Without a most special revelation from God no one knows in his lifetime whether he is saved or not but he discovers this immediately after death at the particular judgment. One and the same conclusion of life awaits all: "I learned that [wise man and fool] were to die both alike."[2]

Death

Our mortal career ends with death, the separation of the soul from the body. This was inflicted on the human race as a penalty of original sin. "Therefore as through one man sin entered into the world and through sin death, and thus death has passed into all men because all have sinned."[3] The penalty is universal and the obligation of dying lies on all. From certain passages of St. Paul, however, it would seem that the just who are alive at the second coming of Christ will not die. If this is true, then the universal penalty is, in their case, dispensed with.

We have only one mortal career. "It is appointed unto men to die once."[4] The soul will not return to earth in some other guise, for the great dogmatic truth about death is that it is the definitive end of a man's probation. It begins "the night when no man can work,"[5] that is, improve one's standing in the sight of God. In whatever condition of merit or demerit death finds a man, such will be his status forever. For Benedict XII[6] has defined that immediately after death the just who are free of sin go to heaven and those who die in mortal sin go to hell. These are unalterable states.

Death begins a life which will have no end. During the period between death and the general resurrection the soul will live apart from the body. Since the soul is spirit it has the power of living a life of intellect and will without help from the body. We know little about this manner of life.

---

[1] Jn. 12:48.   [3] Rom. 5:12.   [5] Jn. 9:4.
[2] Eccles. 2:14. [4] Hebr. 9:27.   [6] Den. 530–531 (TCT, 886, 887).

Experience shows how uncertain is the time of one's death. Hence the warning of Christ is addressed not only to the community but to the individual: "Watch therefore, for you know neither the day nor the hour."[7] Such is the nature of our probation that we must be ready to render an account of it at any time.

Particular Judgment

Since it is defined that immediately after death the soul receives its definitive fate, this dogma presupposes a previous judgment. The same conclusion is implicit in the parable of Lazarus and the rich man, where it is clear that right after death each man gets the unalterable reward or punishment proper to his mortal life. The bestowal of unalterable rewards and punishments comes by way of a judgment. It is certain that the God-Man is the judge, for the Father has placed all judgment in His hands. The judgment takes place immediately after death and in an instant. There is no standing before a tribunal or any presentation of a case and the weighing of evidence. The Sovereign Judge knows the case and its outcome, so His judgment consists in passing on this knowledge to the person judged. A divine light reveals to him the deliberate actions of his lifetime together with their reward and punishment, and he recognizes and acquiesces in the justice of the sentence. The soul is not then held in a somnolent state to await the general judgment. Nor is there a mere token apportionment of reward or punishment but the sentence is carried into immediate execution.

There are four possible outcomes of judgment: (1) the soul having died in the state of grace without any stain of sin is immediately rewarded with heaven; (2) the soul having died in the state of grace with unforgiven venial sins or some debt of temporal punishment is deprived of heaven until it is completely cleansed; (3) the soul having died in mortal sin is immediately condemned to hell; (4) the soul having died with the stain only of original sin is detained in some kind of Limbo. Since heaven and hell are better explained after speaking of the resurrection of the dead, we speak here only of Purgatory and Limbo.

---

[7] Mt. 25:13.

Purgatory

The teaching of the Church about purgatory centers around two dogmas: (1) there is a place or status of expiation in the after life called purgatory; (2) the souls detained there can be helped by the faithful on earth.

1. No soul with any taint of sin is fit for the presence of God. But since a just man can die with some stain of sin, he must be purified before admission into heaven. Hence there is opportunity of expiation after death. We gather from the Book of Machabees that prayers and sacrifices are helpful to the dead. The existence of purgatory has often been officially asserted by the Church: to the Waldensians (1208),[8] to the Armenians (1341),[9] to the Greeks (1439)[10]; by Benedict XII (1336)[11] and the Second Council of Lyons (1274)[12]; Luther[13] was condemned for saying that it could not be proved from Scripture, and the Council of Trent[14] incorporated it into its profession of faith.

The departed soul can be defiled by unforgiven venial sin, or by the remains of sin or the inclination to sin caused by past sinning, or by a debt of temporal punishment. The soul is quickly relieved of the first two kinds of defilement. For, according to St. Thomas,[15] immediately after its judgment the soul elicits a most fervent and enduring act of the love of God. This intense charity removes from the soul any obstacle to forgiveness, which God readily grants. The remains of sin, which are rooted in the body, disappear once soul and body are separated. The remains of sin, which are rooted in the soul, are purged by the intense charity with which the soul yearns for God. Hence what remains to be done in purgatory is full payment of the penalties due from past sins.

Since the soul has entered the night wherein no man can work, it cannot pay its debt by satisfaction. All that the soul can do to promote its release is to suffer the penalties appointed by the justice of God.

---

8 *Den.* 427.
9 *Den.* 535.
10 *Den.* 693 (*TCT*, 889).
11 *Den.* 530 (*TCT*, 886).

12 *Den.* 464 (*TCT*, 884)
13 *Den.* 777.
14 *Den.* 998 (*TCT*, 12).
15 *De Malo*, q. 7, a. 11.

The most grievous pain is separation from God. Drawn to God most vehemently, the soul finds itself shut away from its one true love by its own unworthiness. The only suffering more accute is that of the damned who know that their frustration is eternal. That the soul in purgatory suffers other pains, inflicted by God, is also true. Are these caused by fire? The Church has made no pronouncement on the matter, but from the time of St. Augustine the Latin Fathers and great theologians have taught this doctrine. Some interpret this fire as interior sufferings similar to those which the saints and mystics endure on earth. At any rate the sufferings of purgatory are very grievous; but, despite its sufferings, the soul is at peace; it knows that it is saved and is no longer capable of sinning.

2. Practically the same documents which prove the existence of purgatory also show that the sufferings of purgatory are lessened on account of the supplications to the divine clemency made by the Church Militant. A function of the Communion of Saints is the help afforded the suffering souls by the faithful on earth. They do this through works of satisfaction, especially prayers, indulgences, and the Mass. How much penalty is remitted on account of these petitions and how much each soul must suffer is known only to God.

Since all temporal punishment will be expiated by the time of the general judgment, purgatory will then cease.

Limbo

Limbo means first the place where the souls of the just were detained until the Redemption was accomplished. It is the hell to which the Apostles' Creed refers in the article "He descended into hell." And it was from this place that the Redeemer led the just of the Old Law when He ascended into heaven.

Limbo also means the answer to a vexing problem, namely, What happens to souls that die with only the stain of original sin? It is of faith that they are deprived of the vision of God. St. Augustine and others consigned them to hell fire. St. Thomas says they suffer no positive affliction; they are not grieved over their loss of the vision but enjoy a natural happiness.[16]

---

[16] De Malo, q. 5, a. 3.

A number of new theories have been proposed. One theory solves the problem by denying that anyone dies with merely the stain of original sin, for God gives the unbaptized soul at the moment of death light and grace so that it can either choose God and be saved or reject God and be lost. Another theory seeks a substitute for baptism; for example, the death of the child, conjoined to the death of Christ, is said to be martyrdom in expiation of Adam's sin. There is little to be said on behalf of such theories.

The Church leaves the question of Limbo open but the tendency of theologians is to accept the explanation of St. Thomas.

B. *The Fate of the Race*

As death marks the earthly end of the individual, so the race in its state of probation will have its last day, which is aptly called the Day of the Lord. In the Old Testament there were many Days of the Lord, occasions when God intervened in human affairs with a strong hand, sometimes to save His people but more often to punish evildoers. In the New Testament there is an especially great Day to which Christ refers and which St. Peter and St. Paul predict. This will be God's final intervention. Then the world as we know it will crash in a great cataclysm and we will have THE DAY OF THE LORD. Whether this will be a brief or prolonged period of time no man can say.

Various signs will precede the Day of the Lord. First, the Gospel must be adequately preached throughout the world. For "this gospel of the kingdom shall be preached in the whole world, for a witness to all nations; and then will come the end."[17]

The Jews will be converted to the Christian faith. Isaias and St. Paul testify that a remnant of Israel will be saved at the end. "A partial blindness only has befallen Israel, until the full number of the Gentiles should enter, and thus all Israel should be saved."[18] Some think that the Jews will be converted by Elias come back to earth but this is not certain.

There will be a great falling away from the Church. Christ has predicted that the charity of many will grow cold. St. Paul says that

---

[17] Mt. 24:14.   [18] Rom. 11:25.

"the day of the Lord will not come unless the apostasy comes first."[19] The perpetual struggle between the forces of good and evil will rise to a climax and evil will seem to prevail and win a permanent victory. The power of the Church will suffer temporary eclipse and the Anti-Christ will appear. He is not Satan but "the son of perdition, who opposes and is exalted above all that is called God, or that is worshipped, so that he sits in the temple of God and gives himself out as if he were God. . . . His coming is according to the working of Satan with all power and signs and lying wonders."[20] If it were possible he would lead astray even the elect but he will seduce with his flashy blandishments those who are on the road to destruction.

Great calamities will befall the human race. Tremendous catastrophes of nature will occur. Jesus has foretold wars, famines, plagues, earthquakes, and, for His followers, bitter persecution.

Despite the warning signs the end will catch men unawares. "As in the days before the flood, they were eating and drinking, marrying and giving in marriage, until the day when Noe entered the ark, and they did not understand until the flood came and swept them all away; even so will the coming of the Son of Man be."[21] One reason for this heedlessness is that the exact occurrence of the Day of the Lord is a divinely guarded secret. "But of that day and hour no one knows, not even the angels of heaven, but the Father only."[22] Furthermore, men will be paying little attention to heavenly signs because the faithful will be downtrodden and the unjust will feel secure. But God intends the cataclysm to strike them suddenly. "The day of the Lord is to come like a thief in the night. For when they shall say, 'Peace and security,' even then sudden destruction will come upon them, as birthpangs upon her who is with child, and they will not escape."[23]

It is futile to try to spell out the meaning of these portents of doom, for as St. Thomas warns, "it is not easy to know what these signs will be."[24] The Church has defined comparatively little about

---

[19] 2 Thess. 2:3.
[20] 2 Thess. 2:4–9.
[21] Mt. 24:37–39.
[22] Mt. 24:36.
[23] 1 Thess. 5:2–3.
[24] Supplement, q. 73, a. 1.

The Last Things, and Scripture uses the vocabulary of apocalypse to present what is now beyond the range of earthly human experience. This vocabulary cannot always be taken literally, nor can the description of events, their details, their apparent temporal sequence, be taken as representing literally what is going to happen. Will an archangel blow upon a trumpet on the Last Day? Will there be a real or metaphorical fire? St. Thomas disagrees with St. Augustine as to the sequence of events. However, it is of faith that four tremendous happenings will take place: the end of the world, the resurrection of the dead, the second coming of Christ, and the general judgment.

The End of the World

The truly significant history of the race consists of men coming into being, undergoing probation on earth, and then passing away to receive their reward or punishment. This process will stop when the number of the race, fixed by Divine Providence, is completed. For our Lord has foretold the consummation of the world and the passing away of the heavens and the earth. The end will come as an unimaginable upheaval, for He has predicted a great cosmic revolution. St. Peter says: "The day of the Lord will come as a thief; at that time the heavens will pass away with great violence, and the elements will be dissolved with heat, and the earth, and the works that are in it, will be burned up."[25] Some think the destruction will take place before the general resurrection; some after. Some, like St. Thomas, think the conflagration will be very real; some think the fire is the fire of judgment. Others think that the fire of St. Peter is merely a mode of expression, current in his day, used to convey the revelation of the world's destruction.

The world, however, will not be annihilated as the Gnostics and Origen thought. Just as surely as it will be destroyed, so it will be renewed to be the fitting abode of the just.

The Second Coming of Christ

It is a dogma of faith that Christ will come on the Last Day to

[25] 2 Pet. 3:10.

complete the kingdom of God by rewarding the just and punishing the wicked. Christ often foretold the Parousia or Second Coming. "Then will appear the sign of the Son of Man in heaven."[26] This, according to the Fathers, will be the cross of salvation, resplendent in glory. Whatever it will be, no one will fail to perceive it and to realize that the end is at hand. "As the lightning comes forth from the east and shines even to the west, so also will the coming of the Son of Man be."[27] Then that prophecy will be fulfilled which Christ made before Caiphas and which was the immediate cause of His condemnation: "Hereafter you shall see the Son of Man sitting at the right hand of the Power and coming upon the clouds of heaven."[28] His appearance on the clouds of heaven, accompanied by the angels, manifests His divine might and majesty. The wicked will mourn at His coming and perish, the just will be rescued, and the Anti-Christ will be revealed for what he is and slain.

The Resurrection of the Dead

It is a dogma of faith that on the Last Day all the dead will be reunited to their bodies and will rise again. There was a gradual revelation of this doctrine in the Old Testament. Isaias says that the slain shall rise again. Osee and Ezechiel use the resurrection of the body as a symbol of the rise of Israel from sin or exile. By the time of the Machabees it was taught as religious doctrine, but was rejected by the Sadducees. For this our Lord reproved them. This is an essential doctrine which the Apostles insisted on, which the Athenians laughed at in the Areopagus, and which no materialist can accept. It is contained in all the formularies of the faith and has often been defined.

All, both just and unjust, will rise, for Christ says: "They who have done good shall come forth unto resurrection of life; but they who have done evil unto resurrection of judgment."[29] It is also defined that all the reprobate and the elect "will arise with the same bodies which they now have."[30] Each will rise in his own proper

---

26 Mt. 24:30.
27 Mt. 24:27.
28 Mt. 26:64.

29 Jn. 5:29.
30 Fourth Lateran Council, *Den.* 429.

body. Just as there is a sufficient identity between the body which
is born and the body that is laid in the grave, so there will be a
similar identity between the latter and the body that rises.

The principal cause of our resurrection is God, the master of life
and death. The God-Man — His living and dying and rising — is the
proximate cause and instrument of salvation, for "as in Adam all
die, so in Christ all will be made to live."[31] He came to rebuild the
ruins made by sin and to give back to us the blessings lost by Adam.
His death won for us our resurrection and His rising is the model
of our own. Indeed, His resurrection is the beginning of our own
because He is the first-born of the dead, the first fruits of those who
have fallen asleep in death. The angels who accompany Christ at
His Second Coming will play a ministering role in the resurrection
of men.

The resurrection is man's triumph over death. For "the last enemy
to be destroyed will be death . . . then shall come to pass the word
that is written, 'Death is swallowed up in victory.' "[32] At the general
resurrection the circle will have come full again: man sinned and was
condemned to death; Christ unites Himself to man and conquers sin
and death for him; then man unites himself to Christ, and with Christ
conquers sin and last of all death.

Misinterpreting certain obscure passages of the Apocalyse, some
people have imagined that Christ at the Second Coming will bring
the dead to life and with the just will reign in an earthly messianic
kingdom for a thousand years. This is a dream which the Church
has constantly rejected. There will be no great interval between the
Second Coming and the execution of the sentence of the general
judgment. Today some think that the coming, resurrection, and
judgment are merely diverse aspects of one great "event."

The General Judgment

It is a dogma of faith that Christ, at His Second Coming, will judge
the human race and will reward or punish all men according to their
works. "For the Son of Man is to come with his angels in the glory
of his Father, and then he will render to everyone according to his

---
[31] 1 Cor. 15:22.   [32] 1 Cor. 15:26, 54.

conduct."[33] Our Lord has foretold: "When the Son of Man shall come in his majesty, and all the angels with him, then he will sit on the throne of his glory; and before him will be gathered all the nations, and he will separate them one from another, as the shepherd separates the sheep from the goats."[34] The account is anthropomorphic but the conclusion is most significant: "The [wicked] will go into everlasting punishment, but the just into everlasting life."[35] The doctrine of the judgment has been defined at least three times.

The focal point of the Second Coming is the rendering of judgment. It is idle to construct in advance a picture of an event so stupendous and unique. Certain questions, however, will always be asked about it. When and where will it be? The answer is a divine secret whose solution we leave to the event in which we shall be intimate participants. Who will be present? All the angels and the whole human race. Who will be judged? Certainly all men who had the use of reason and therefore were capable of moral testing. What about infants? St. Thomas says[36] they will be present not to be judged but to see the glory of the Judge. The Jesuit Suarez says[37] that children who die without grace will in a fashion be judged; that is, they will see that the status allotted them is just. What about the angels? Some say that they will already have had their judgment; others say that they too will undergo a judgment at least to the extent of being praised or blamed for the part they had in the salvation of men. What will be judged? Every human act will be reviewed for praise or blame; "all things that are done God will bring into judgment . . . whether it be good or evil."[38] Christ says: "Of every idle word men speak, they will give an account on the day of judgment."[39] Sentence will be pronounced upon all men upon the basis of their faith and works, and the salvation or condemnation of every man will be manifest. This will not be done orally, says St. Thomas, but mentally, "for if the deeds of each individual were to be related by word of mouth, this would require an inconceivable length of time."[40]

---

[33] Mt. 16:27.
[34] Mt. 25:31 ff.
[35] Mt. 25:46.
[36] Suppl. 89, 5, ad 3.

[37] *Opera omnia*, ed. Berton, V. XIX, p. 1089.
[38] Eccles. 12:14.
[39] Mt. 12:36.
[40] Suppl. 88, 2.

There are many reasons for the general judgment. First, the race as a group is judged and social justice is done by reversing all human injustice. Second, justice to the individual will be perfected. Since men will have recovered their bodies, the rewards and punishments made at each particular judgment will be completed. The just will applaud, and the unjust will recognize the rightness of every verdict. Third, the general judgment will be the ultimate triumph of the Messias when the whole universe will acknowledge Him as the center of all things. All things were created through Him and for Him. Not only is He the first-born of creation and the Head of the Church, but "it has pleased God the Father that . . . through him he should reconcile to himself all things, whether on earth or in the heavens, making peace through the blood of the cross."[41] The God-Man will be acclaimed for effecting the final purposes of creation, and in His exaltation God's dealings with men will be so manifest that all will adore the divine plan in creating man to the supernatural life, in redeeming him when he fell, and in guiding the just through the vicissitudes of life. The problem of evil will be solved when the beauty and mercy of the divine plan are unfolded and we see how marvelously all things have worked together unto good for them who love God. Finally, the general judgment will be seen as the complement of the first creation, the final ordering of the universe, the eternal arrangement made so that each being will share in creation as he deserves. Once the Messias is glorified, "then comes the end when he delivers the kingdom to God the Father. . . . And when all things are made subject to him, then the Son himself will also be made subject to him who subjected all things to him, that God may be all in all."[42] What came forth from God through His Word now returns to Him through the Redeemer. Either through love or justice all things have been restored in Christ. The temporary dislocation set up by sin in the universe has been taken away and the taint of moral disorder has been removed from creation. From end to end sweetly the will of God prevails: all things are in their proper place before Him. The mystery of divine good-

---

[41] Col. 1:20.
[42] 1 Cor. 15:24–28.

ness, first revealed in creation, is completed by the revelation of divine justice in the Judgment.

When the Judgment is over two fates remain for mankind — eternal reward and eternal punishment.

Hell

Hell, the Latin *infernus* or lower regions, means in a broad sense the state or place where those souls are detained who are separated from God after death. This includes the temporary Limbo of the just of the Old Law, the Limbo of the unbaptized, purgatory, and hell commonly so called or the place of punishment for demons and unjust men. It is a dogma of faith, defined by Benedict XII and by the Fourth Lateran Council, the Second Council of Lyons, and the Council of Florence, that those who die in the state of unrepented mortal sin are punished in the hell of the unjust.

There was a gradual revelation of this doctrine in the later books of the Old Testament. Isaias, Daniel, and the Book of Wisdom speak of eternal torments for the unjust. Our Lord says that sinners will be punished in Gehenna where the worm dies not and the fire is not extinguished. It is an everlasting fire, an unquenchable fire, a furnace of fire, everlasting pain; here will be darkness, weeping, and gnashing of teeth. St. Paul tells the Thessalonians that "the Lord Jesus will . . . inflict punishment on those who do not know God, and who do not obey the gospel of our Lord Jesus Christ. These will be punished with eternal ruin, away from the face of the Lord and the glory of his power."[43] He tells the Corinthians: "Do you not know that the unjust will not possess the kingdom of God? Do not err: neither fornicators, nor idolators, nor adulterers, nor the effeminate, nor sodomites, nor thieves, nor the covetous, nor drunkards, nor the evil-tongued, nor the greedy will possess the kingdom of God."[44]

From the words of St. Paul it is clear that loss of God is the essential pain of hell. Our Lord says the same thing: " 'I do not know where you are from. Depart from me, all you workers of iniquity.' "[45] Because God casts them off, the damned suffer the unspeakable

---

[43] 2 Thess. 1:8–9.   [44] 1 Cor. 6:9–10.   [45] Lk. 13:27.

frustration of never being able to do the one thing for which they were made — to know and love God. Having died enemies of God they harden in malice, forever unable to turn back to Him though they clearly see that only in union with Him does their happiness consist. They will forever hunger for God and forever hate Him and thus be torn apart at the very core of their being. The worm of conscience will devour them for they will realize that they could have been saved and are now lost through their own fault. Envy of the blessed will corrode them; absolute unrelieved despair will envelop them. Truly is hell the second death. It were better for the damned if they had never been.

The pain of loss is inflicted for the sinner's rejection of God. Because he turned to creatures as his last end, he will suffer other pains — called pain of sense — inflicted by some divinely appointed agency, chief among which is fire. Some have interpreted this to be a metaphorical fire and this opinion has not been formally condemned by the Church. However, the majority of the Fathers, of the medieval Schoolmen, and of modern theologians hold that the fire is material. To inquire how the fire will affect the condemned, especially when they are separated from their bodies, is not rewarding. Various conjectures are offered. Perhaps it will be somewhat different from the fire of which we have experience. Despite these difficulties the traditional sense of the Church believing has tenaciously held that the fire is real and material.

From the parable of Lazarus and the rich man and from the definition of Benedict XII it is clear that punishment is not delayed until after the general judgment, as some once thought, but begins immediately after death. Furthermore, the pains of hell are eternal, for the last judgment concludes with the definitive statement of Christ: " 'These will go into everlasting punishment, but the just into everlasting life.' "[46] Hell is as enduring as heaven. Since this is a most unpleasant truth some people try to wish it out of existence, but no argument addressed to the intellect can shake it. The prophet Daniel calls hell an eternal reproach; our Lord says it is an unquenchable fire, an everlasting fire. Isaias asks: "Which of you [sinners] can

---
[46] Mt. 25:46.

dwell with . . . everlasting burnings?"[47] The Apocalypse says: "The smoke of their torments goes up forever and ever."[48] The doctrine of the eternity of hell is deeply fixed in Catholic tradition. Although Origen (d. 205) and St. Gregory of Nyssa (d. about 394) did teach that the damned would eventually be saved, yet they were strongly assailed by their contemporaries. The doctrine is stated in the Athanasian creed and was defined by the Fourth Council of Lateran.

Eternal punishment is a strict demand of justice, for mortal sin has infinite malice. By sinning the sinner chooses a created good and rejects the infinite good. Now rejection of Him who is infinitely good is an act of infinite dishonor. Moreover, satisfaction of infinite value — the death of the Son of God — was demanded in order to atone for sin. Since punishment should fit the crime, mortal sin deserves infinite punishment, but since the creature cannot sustain a punishment infinite in intensity, nothing adequate remains except a punishment infinite in duration.

Eternal punishment is no denial of divine mercy. Every mortal sin proclaims the heresy that something other than God is man's last end. This error destroys the fundamental relation between God and man and must be intolerable to God. God can allow sin for a time in order to test man, but if God did not hate it and eventually destroy it — and all those who persist in sustaining it — He would approve a monstrous lie and be false to His own truth and sanctity. Here mercy cannot temper justice.

By choosing to sin the sinner chooses to be without God, and when he dies with his attitude unchanged God simply allows that choice to be everlasting. Since He is Lord He fixes the time when a man's probation ends. Now end of probation means that one's moral attitude becomes incapable of change so that one is forever fixed in the good or evil disposition with which he died. He then who dies in unrepented sin is incapable of any other fate than hell. What fellowship can exist between light and darkness? Since he has no sanctifying grace and is the enemy of God, he has no power to love God; he can only hate Him. His every action becomes sinful and wrong.

---

[47] Isa. 33:14.   [48] Apoc. 14:11.

The punishment of all the damned is not alike but is proportioned to the guilt of each, for "thou wilt render to every man according to his works."[49] This truth is asserted by the Second Council of Lyons and repeated by the Council of Florence.

It has been said that, while the pain of loss is everlasting, the pain of sense can be diminished. But this does not seem possible on account of the attitude of mind of the damned. For since they are confirmed in evil, they are unable to change their evil attitude and be sorry in a salutary way for even one venial sin.

Heaven

In the older writings of the Bible we sense a belief that departed souls descended into sheol, an underworld where they lived a sunless, bloodless, joyless existence. The revelation of a happy eternity as the lot of the just was quite gradual. The Psalmist hopes for liberation from this underworld. Daniel speaks of a resurrection into eternal life. The Maccabean martyrs are sustained because they are under the covenant of eternal life. The Book of Wisdom says the souls of the just are at rest in the hands of God. Our Lord is the first to stress the notion of a happy eternity, saying that the lot of the just hereafter will be like the joy of a wedding feast, that they will have everlasting life and have it in the mansions of the Father. Heaven means both the state and the place of the just who possess their eternal reward. The place is the heavenly paradise; the state, eternal happiness. Whether the two are really distinct is not here important; our interest is in eternal happiness.

We will be perfectly happy only when we have all that we ought to have without fear of losing it. It is a basic dogma of faith that God and God alone can make us perfectly happy, for He alone is our destiny. " 'I am the Alpha and the Omega, the beginning and the end,' says the Lord God."[50] Benedict XII has defined that the souls of the just are made truly happy by the vision and enjoyment of God. The Church calls possession of God in perfect happiness the beatific vision. This consists in the soul seeing God as He is in Himself and loving Him after the manner of such knowledge. Thus we

---

[49] Ps. 61:12.   [50] Apoc. 1:8.

shall imitate God's proper life of knowledge and love. Without losing our human personality we shall be absorbed in God, participate in the inner activities of Father, Son, and Holy Spirit, and share in God's own happiness. Three things characterize the beatific vision: knowledge, love, and joy.

The blessed will spend their eternity in knowing God, for our Lord says: "This is eternal life, that they may know thee, the only true God, and him whom thou hast sent, Jesus Christ."[51] This will be supernatural knowledge. The natural way for man to know God is through deductive knowledge which presents Him as He is reflected in the mirror of creation. In the beatific vision, however, we shall attain to Him as He is without any veil being interposed between Him and us. St. John says: "We know that when he appears, we shall see him just as he is."[52] Hence Benedict XII says that the blessed "see the divine essence by an intuitive and face-to-face vision, without any mediating creature serving as object of sight, but with the divine essence immediately revealing itself to them plainly, clearly and openly."[53] Just as the eye beholds its object, so the mind will see God. We shall see, not an image of Him, but His very Self. Furthermore, we shall see Him without the help of intellectual images by which we know things in the present life: God, the omnipresent, who fills all things, will completely fill our minds and give us direct contact with the very depth of His being. This knowledge will leave nothing to be desired, for St. Paul says: "We know in part and we prophesy in part; but when that which is perfect is come, that which is imperfect will be done away with. . . . We see now through a mirror in an obscure manner, but then face to face. Now I know in part, but then I shall know even as I have been known."[54]

What shall we know in the vision of God? First, the Triune God and the divine mysteries we believed on earth. How fitting that the darkness of faith be rewarded with the brightness of the vision! Second, we shall see in God directly, or receive from Him, that knowledge of persons and things, past, present, and future, which will be needful to satisfy us as individual persons, members of the

[51] Jn. 17:3.
[52] 1 Jn. 3:2.
[53] *Den.* 530 (*TCT,* 886).
[54] 1 Cor. 13:9–12.

Church, and parts of the universe. Knowledge will accord with merit, but not even the most deserving will fully comprehend God. The most penetrating knowledge on the part even of the Mother of God will be finite.

The blessed will be ravished with love of God, as St. Augustine says: "There we shall rest and we shall see; we shall see and we shall love; we shall love and we shall praise."[55] The everlasting tie between God and the soul is love, for St. Paul says that, while faith and hope will disappear in heaven, charity will never die. The image which Osee presents of God, the spouse of the soul, finds its completion in the Apocalypse where the visionary sees the elect adorned as a bride for her husband.

What is done perfectly is done joyfully. Knowing and loving God in the beatific vision will be our supreme delight, for heaven is our entry into the joy of the Lord. "I will see you again," Christ consoles us, "and your heart shall rejoice, and your joy no one shall take from you."[56] In heaven our cup is full. For the just "shall neither hunger nor thirst any more, and neither shall the sun strike them nor any heat. For the Lamb . . . will shepherd them, and will guide them to the fountains of the waters of life, and God will wipe away every tear from their eyes."[57] Heaven is the marriage supper of the Lamb.

Now we cannot understand the mysterious happiness of heaven. What will it be like? St. Paul says: "Eye has not seen nor ear heard, nor has it entered into the heart of man, what things God has prepared for those who love him."[58]

In addition to the state of grace and complete purification, the light of glory is required for the beatific vision, as the Council of Vienne affirms. This consists in an inward permanent assistance by which God floods the created intellect, enabling it to do what is proper to God alone. This special divine illumination is sometimes used to characterize the state of bliss. Thus the heavenly Jerusalem is said to have no need of the sun or the moon because the glory of God lights it up and the Lamb is its lamp.

---

[55] City of God, Bk. 22, Ch. 30, No. 5.
[56] Jn. 16:22.
[57] Apoc. 7:17.
[58] 1 Cor. 2:9.

Heaven is the reward of the good works of this life, the crown of justice laid up for all who persevere to the end. The happiness of each one will be in proportion to the merits acquired in this life. Therefore in the kingdom of God star will differ from star in glory. How a man will spend eternity depends on his wise use of time.

Whoever enjoys the beatific vision is perfect and incapable of sinning. Since he is ceaselessly absorbed in seeing and loving God, he cannot turn from Him unto sin. St. Peter says our heavenly inheritance is incorruptible and undefiled. Benedict XII says that our vision of God suffers no interruption. While eternal rest is surcease from worry and striving for the end, it is not inertia, but, on the contrary, a ceaseless action of knowing and loving God which will never fatigue or bore us.

The Fourth Lateran Council and the Second Council of Lyons teach that the happiness of heaven is everlasting. God has promised that our reward will be an unfading crown of glory, an eternal inheritance, a weight of eternal glory, life eternal. St. Paul assures us that we shall always be with the Lord.

Heaven is not delayed until after the general judgment. It is defined doctrine that as the wicked are sent to hell immediately after death, so the just are rewarded as soon after death as they are cleansed from all stain.

In addition to the beatific vision, which is our essential happiness, God gives other blessings. Thus in the mind of the blessed there will be no error and in the will no tinge of sadness. For the just will have knowledge other than the sight of God and they will have experience of, and love, persons and things other than God. However, no one will grieve over the eternal loss of someone dearly loved in life. For sentimental reasons some people find this truth hard to understand but the explanation is simple. In the beatific vision the will of the just is in perfect accord with the divine will and its love for others is subordinate to its love for God. Since God cannot love one who is damned, neither can the just. With his mind in perfect accord with God's mind the just sees the matter from God's point of view.

Chief among these additional blessings is the glory of the body.

As it played so intimate a part in our achievement of salvation, it will have its proper reward on the Last Day. St. Paul says: "But someone will say, 'How do the dead rise? Or with what kind of body do they come?' Senseless man, what thou thyself sowest is not brought to life, unless it dies. And when thou sowest, thou dost not sow the body that shall be but a bare grain, perhaps of wheat or something else. But God gives it a body even as he has willed, and to each of the seeds a body of its own. . . . So also with the resurrection of the dead. What is sown in corruption rises in incorruption; what is sown in dishonor rises in glory; what is sown in weakness rises in power; what is sown a natural body rises a spiritual body."[59]

The glorified body, therefore, will be spiritualized matter, the flawless instrument of the happy soul. It will be of perfect age and stature, with corporeal perfections commensurate with one's merits. It will have the qualities of the glorified body of Christ "who will refashion the body of our lowliness, conforming it to the body of his glory."[60] Hence in its beauty it will shine as the transfigured body of Christ on Mount Thabor. Such a body will experience neither pain nor decay nor decrease. As the risen body of Jesus was not hindered by material obstacles but came to and departed from places as He pleased, so also the glorified body will be free of material obstacles. The glory and power of the soul will overflow into the body so that it will be able to go anywhere in the universe with the utmost speed.

Man's social instincts and capacities will not be suppressed in the beatific vision but will find full scope. His happiness will not be lonely contemplation but he will enjoy the company and conversation of the Mother of God and the angels and saints. The parables rightly compare the kingdom of God to a joyous banquet of all the children of God. In the fullest sense the Communion of Saints will be realized.

Finally the just will live in most pleasant surroundings — a new earth with new heavens. On account of original sin man's dwelling place was changed from an earthly paradise to a vale of tears, "for we know that all creation groans and travails in pain until now.

[59] 1 Cor. 15:35–44.
[60] Phil. 3:21.

For creation was made subject to vanity."[61] But the punishment of man is not forever; "creation itself will be delivered from its slavery to corruption into the freedom of the glory of the sons of God."[62] With the final conquest of sin the depressed condition of nature ceases. Isaias has foretold the purification of the universe: "Behold I create new heavens and a new earth."[63] Our Lord speaks of the regeneration, that is, the new arrangement of the world. The destruction of the Last Day will purge the universe of all taint induced by sin. St. Thomas sees in this new creation a special reward for the body. He says: "The carnal eye, however, will be unable to attain to this vision of the essence [of God]. Hence, that it may be properly comforted in the beatific vision, it will see the Godhead in Its corporeal effects, wherein manifest proofs of the divine majesty will appear, especially in the flesh of Christ, and second in the bodies of the blessed, and finally in all other bodies. Hence these bodies also will need to receive a greater inflow from the divine goodness than now . . . so as to add a certain perfection of glory."[64] It is idle to conjecture about the beauty and convenience of this new world but we are sure that a renovated universe will admirably serve the pleasure of the children of God.

With the end of the world and the final restoration, the work of the Messias ceases. He will no longer exercise the power and authority He used for our redemption, for all the enemies of God will be laid low. There will no longer be need of a mediator when all the redeemed have been gathered into one and God is all in all. Then He can say to the Father: "I have accomplished the work that thou hast given me to do. And now do thou, Father, glorify me with thyself, with the glory that I had with thee before the world existed."[65] All the prophecies will be fulfilled and the Church Militant will no longer exist. As Head of the Church Triumphant He will reign in the house of Jacob forever and of His Kingdom there will be no end; and the redeemed will salute Him: "To the King of ages, who is immortal, invisible, the one only God, be honor and glory forever and ever. Amen."[66]

---

[61] Rom. 8:22, 20.　　[63] Isa. 65:17.　　[65] Jn. 17:5.
[62] Rom. 8:21.　　　　[64] Suppl. 91, 1.　　[66] 1 Tim. 1:17.

INDEX

Pope, infallible, 11; power over matrimony, 185
Possession, demonic, 59
Practice of Church, norm of Tradition, 21
Prayer, 131 ff; object of, 132
Predestination, 65 ff
Presbyterate, as sacrament, 178
Presence, real, in Eucharist, 152
Priest, 156, 157; and confession, judge in, 167; and confession, must know sins of penitent, 171; and confirmation, may administer, 150 ff; Extreme Unction, required for, 176; and marriage, witness of, 183, 186; and Mass, importance in, 161
Priesthood, of Jesus, 83; of Jesus, perpetual, 157; of laity, 146, 161
Privilege, Pauline, 185; Petrine, 185
Procession, in divinity, 40 ff; of Holy Spirit, 43 ff; mission depends on, 49
Production in divinity, 40 ff
Promise of Eucharist, 152
Prophet, Jesus, 83
Providence of God, 65 ff; over just, 126
Punishment, due sin, 172; at general judgment, 197; immediately after death, 189, 205; temporal, paid by Mass, 162; temporal, remitted by indulgences, 173; theory of substitute, 87
Purgatory, souls in, helped by indulgences, 174; souls in, helped by Mass, 162; state of expiation, 190 ff
Purification, baptism, bath of, 145
Purposes of matrimony, 180

Queenship of Mary, 98

Race, fate of, 192 ff
Ransom in Redemption, 86
Reality, mystical, of sacramental world, 160
Rebirth in justification, 114
Reception of Eucharist, 165
Reconciliation through the cross, 89
Redeemer, function of, 86; Mother of, 93; preparation for, 76
Redemption, applied through Mass,

159; for original sin, 73; nature of, 85 ff; objective and subjective, 100; by sacrifice of Jesus, 84 ff
Reformers, on attrition, denied value of, 170; on confession, 166; on forgiveness of sin, 170; on freedom under grace, 128; on justification, preparation for, 123; on Mass, deny sacrificial character of, 158; on merit, 129; on sacraments, deny they are seven, 144; on temporal punishment for sin, 172
Regeneration by baptism, 144
Relations in divinity, add nothing absolute, 48; four, 47; identified with nature, 47; subsistent, 46 ff
Religion, purpose of, 1; the true, 1
Remains of sin, 176, 190
Repentance, necessity of, 169
Reprobation, 69 ff
Reservation of Eucharist, 163
Restoration of all things in Christ, 198
Resurrection of dead, 195 ff
Resurrection of Jesus, meaning of, 91; outstanding credential, 6
Revelation, and Apostles, complete with death of, 6; contemplated, cause of dogmatic development, 15; on hell, 199; and inspiration, different from, 16; and the magistery, transmitted by, 6; primitive, 3; private and public, 2
Rewards, at general judgment, 197; immediately after death, 189, 205
Rite of Sacred Orders, 177
Rites, religious, 134
Roman Catholic Church, one true Church, 108

Sabellius, 47; denies Trinity, 38
Sacramentals, 142 ff
Sacraments, 133 ff; integrating effect of, 138 ff; number of, 143 ff; produce grace, *ex opere operato*, 135 ff; reviving effect of, 137; and salvation, ordinary means of, 140; and spiritual needs of man, 144; and symbolized effect, 136
Sacred Heart, devotion to, 82
Sacrifice, gift to God, 84, 155; of Holy Eucharist, 155 ff; of Jesus,